Development of
Therapeutic Skills

T,M

Development of Therapeutic Skills

EDITED BY

Mary Jo Trapp Bulbrook

*Director, Psychosocial Nursing, College of
Nursing, University of Utah; Director of
Training, Hospice of Salt Lake City,
Salt Lake City*

LITTLE, BROWN AND COMPANY
BOSTON

Library of Congress Catalog Card No. 80-80588
ISBN 0-316-11472-3
Printed in the United States of America
MV

Preface

As an educator and practicing mental health clinician, I am dedicated to facilitating the development of competent psychotherapists working in any area of clinical contact. Within the diversity of our professions lies a common concern with the *process* and *content* of self-development. Yet in eight years of teaching it has become apparent to me that students have as much difficulty bridging the gap between exploring their own development and guiding others to profit from self-examination as they do relating practice to theory. This book illustrates how some real people learned to use consciously discovered personal strengths in psychotherapy with others.

The literature on psychotherapy is extensive and varied. In addition, many different professions offer therapy based on a variety of theories, thus creating confusion as to how one develops skill in providing psychotherapy in different settings. I believe that no one professional group has *the* correct approach. Rather, every therapist in training—whether nurse, physician, social worker, psychologist, counselor, minister, or educator— must examine and select from the entire range of viewpoints on the theory and techniques of psychotherapy.

But one does not become a skilled psychotherapist merely by analyzing theories or accumulating clinical hours. On the contrary, an existential growth process must take place through conscious self-examination in relation to the effectiveness of the therapeutic encounter. Even in those therapies that minimize dynamic use of the self, an existential integration is still required for the therapist. *You cannot eliminate process from learning content in psychotherapy.* Those who do not achieve the integration remain merely technicians, unable to utilize their own personal resources in creative problem-solving.

This book is intended for beginning professionals interested in development of self as the therapeutic catalyst. Consequently, the book can be used profitably by nurses, physicians, counselors, social workers, psychologists, and ministers as they attempt to apply their professional expertise to help persons deal with the problems of life through the therapeutic process.

I would like to acknowledge the invaluable help of Barbara Thurmond, Stephanie Holm, and Rose Ann Janner, students, and Patricia Cain, Billie Jean Robinson, Linda Matthews, and Louise Lastelich, graduate students, all of the Texas Woman's University College of Nursing. I would especially like to extend my thanks to Mary Nell Robertson for her participation in this effort. Mary Nell is a former client and was kind enough to share her experiences as a consumer of mental health care with us. This book is really about and for people such as Mary Nell.

                                                              M.J.T.B.

Contributing Authors

Sheila Berning, M.A.
Social Worker, Department of Human Resources, Temple, Texas

William Berning, A.C.S.W.
Supervisor, Adult Mental Health Services, Central Counties Mental
Health/Mental Retardation Center, Temple, Texas

Mary Jo Trapp Bulbrook, R.N., Ed.D.
Director, Psychosocial Nursing, College of Nursing, University of Utah;
Director of Training, Hospice of Salt Lake City, Salt Lake City, Utah

Benjamin Goodwin, M.D.
Psychiatrist, Dallas, Texas

Judy Keith, Ph.D.
Professor, Department of Psychology, Tarrant County Junior College,
Hurst, Texas

Virginia Satir, M.S.
Psychotherapist, Menlo Park, California; Co-founder, Mental Health
Research Institute, Palo Alto, California

Contents

Preface v
Contributing Authors vii

1. **Becoming a Psychosocial Nurse** *1*
   MARY JO TRAPP BULBROOK

2. **Communication and Contact** *15*
   VIRGINIA SATIR

3. **Becoming a Psychiatrist** *21*
   BENJAMIN GOODWIN

4. **Becoming a Husband and Wife Social Worker Team** *37*
   WILLIAM BERNING AND SHEILA BERNING

5. **Becoming a Nurse Therapist** *43*
   MARY JO TRAPP BULBROOK

6. **Becoming a Therapy Consumer** *51*
   MARY JO TRAPP BULBROOK

7. **Comprehensive BASIC Assessment System and Tool** *65*
   MARY JO TRAPP BULBROOK

8. **Content and Process of Types of Therapy** *77*
   MARY JO TRAPP BULBROOK AND JUDY KEITH

9. **From Theory into Practice: Undergraduate Students** *149*
   MARY JO TRAPP BULBROOK

10. **From Theory into Practice: Graduate Students** *181*
    MARY JO TRAPP BULBROOK

11. **Formal Preparation of Traditional Psychiatric Team Members** *247*
    MARY JO TRAPP BULBROOK

Appendix 255
Index 269

Development of
Therapeutic Skills

1 Becoming a Psychosocial Nurse

MARY JO TRAPP BULBROOK

BECOMING A THERAPIST

Early childhood memories are difficult to recall and emerge very slowly. I remember being five years old, standing in the large lot behind our white frame house — I was happy, singing to myself, and very observant of nature, the sky, and trees. I experienced oneness with nature, but not alienation from people. My sister, three and a half years older, was with her friends while I was off by myself: part of the world, yet in control of my own life space.

Mom was at home busy with the routine of housekeeping. Dad was at the gas station in front of our home, maintaining his traditional role as breadwinner, minding the station from 7 A.M. to 6 P.M., six days a week, and 8 to 10 A.M. on Sunday.

Spotty, my "Heinz 57" puppy, who was an important life companion for 10 years, was ever at my side, offering licks and tail wags to soothe a little girl's hurts and pains. From him and my other pets, and from being an astute observer of nature, I developed a keen ability to relate genuinely and spontaneously to strangers, friends, and family.

I remember fun times of playing "dress-up," one of my sister Carolyn's and my favorite pastimes. Dad would take his girls from room to room pretending we were out on the town. Fun times were simple. Money for "extras" was scarce. Many sacrifices were made to provide proper food, shelter, education, and health care. And love was there. We didn't directly ask for love, but expressions of love were given freely.

Dad is a great philosopher and has many favorite sayings. Both he and Mom recognized the responsibility of parenting, but they oftentimes felt unprepared for the tremendous task of caring for two children. However, as they will state today, "We did the best job we could, given what we are and what we had." This philosophy, which I adopted, permeates my life, and I in turn pass it on to my own children and my students.

When I was about seven years old, I had to decide whether or not to cross the busy street and buy some candy at the neighborhood store. I saw the cars zoom by and heard Dad's command, "Don't cross the street or you will get a spanking." I weighed the alternatives and decided a spanking lasted for only a few minutes and I did really want some candy. I decided to accept the consequences of my behavior and cross the street. The cars screeched to a stop and Dad came to deliver the consequences. This event typified a pattern in my young life that still holds true. I hear authority, evaluate for myself the implications of my behavior, make my own decisions, and accept the consequences.

Some of the values that I absorbed from these early experiences with my parents and that influenced my early life were: (1) work hard; (2) take care of yourself and others; (3) follow the teachings of your religion; (4) do what the Church and parents tell you to do; (5) obtain a good education; (6) acquire pleasing social values; (7) be critical; (8) appreciate that families are important; and (9) be good and honest.

Religion was one of the most important early influences in my life. But at that time in my life I did not question the values taught by the Church. I learned about sin and guilt and was taught to listen to and respect others. I still incorporate the Christian value to do good for others, and follow the teachings of the Catholic Church.

Grammar school and high school were really dormant periods for me. There was more self-imposed aloneness, good achievement in school, constant boredom in the summer, and a longing to be and do something. Expressions of creativity were limited to dress and hair. Singing, clowning, and drama filled the void of monotonous sameness. Reading and concentration were difficult, but the source of the problem was not identified until college, and then quite accidentally. I discovered a genetic problem that had left me neurologically imbalanced, which was at times reflected in my problems with reading and concentration. However, years of study and self-discipline have compensated for the difficulty.

The above problem hindered significantly my accomplishments and success in school. At times I would be an "A" student, but then would come up with "Cs." Only when my creativity was rewarded would I achieve an "A." The right side of my brain, which controls creativity, had not been affected. To this day I do not know why. The fact that my creativity was pleasantly rewarded led me as a therapist, teacher, and mother to encourage the development of creativity in others. I believe creativity is a unique and wonderful gift.

At this particular point in my life, life happened to me. I was made unhappy or happy by what was done to me. Many times I did not feel "OK" and was very sensitive to criticism and lack of approval. I began to observe the discrepancies between what significant others said and did, and what they expected of me. An intolerance of inconsistency and ambiguity developed. Negativism predominated and loneliness was deeply felt. I gained relief by turning to nature, music, and animals.

My dating schedule was normal. At times I became very disenchanted with the frivolous "Let's have fun today and to hell with tomorrow" attitude. But at times I did evaluate relationships according to the superficial guidelines in vogue. Frequently I checked with my friends as to how they interpreted religious teaching on boy/girl relationships. The terms and descriptions used to provide guidance seemed vague, and there appeared to be much talking around the problem. The groundwork was laid for my later attention to what was practiced as opposed to what was said. Frustration arose from all these "double" messages. Student nurses in the all-girl private college I attended had busy work and study schedules. I remember those days primarily as ones of preparation for a career. Again life happened to me — not I to life.

Significant change came toward the end of my junior year when I began psychiatric nursing. I was not prepared for what happened to me — my life's foundation began to shake. I experienced extreme confusion over who I was, what nursing was, and where I fitted into the picture. I even contemplated leaving the whole field of nursing. I wanted to fulfill my obligations as recipient of a National Institute of Mental Health grant but felt that nursing must not be for me. I sought advice from my family, friends, teachers, the director of the nursing program, and the president of the college. All gave me conflicting advice, resulting in intense confusion and physical stress.

I decided to ignore the pain and maintain my course of study in psychiatric nursing until I had a better sense of direction. I immediately experienced extreme relief when the psychiatric rotation was over, and the next day I had my answer — pediatric nursing. The children captured my head and heart, and I felt I had found my area of interest.

Upon graduation with a bachelor's degree in nursing in 1966, I worked at Cincinnati Children's Hospital. I had decided I had enough nursing education but still wanted to go to school, which

I enjoyed immensely. I decided to combine my two interests and began studying Montessori education with a teacher who was a student of Maria Montessori. I now had additional knowledge of preadolescent growth and development based on a keen awareness and observation of the emerging personality of the child.

The year from September, 1966 to September, 1967 was busy. I completed my master's degree in Montessori education, worked fulltime at Children's Hospital, got married, and moved to Texas at age 23. Until that time I had spent most of my life in Ohio with my parents. When I kissed my parents good-bye and jumped into the car, I became overwhelmed with the impact of my decision. The bird had finally jumped out of the nest. I felt I was in the air alone, my nest gone.

The following year constituted a period of reeducation. I sorted out the parental and school-taught values and began to find out who I was. Luckily, I married a man who encouraged my personal development at this time, which included continuing education, working on a doctorate, working full-time, and developing close, intimate friendships. My old pattern of aloneness was being undermined. I worked as an instructor in nursing, teaching fundamentals, pediatrics, and obstetrics. New fields of nursing and knowledge intrigued me.

In 1968, through the encouragement of a friend, I went back to school. I had become bored with work and wanted something more. Then I met Dr. D. He expanded my thinking to theory development and a whole new world of process relationships/ energy exchanges. I now knew I had to free my intellect: Ideas were the lost piece in the puzzle necessary to put Mary Jo together.

For three years I cautiously tested a renewed interest in psychiatric nursing, despite memories of extreme pain in nursing school. Luckily, I had a colleague who shared my interest and I informally learned psychiatric nursing from her. We discussed in detail concepts in psychiatric theory and practice, and I tested my ideas for clarity.

I did not realize until later, after experiences with both undergraduate and graduate psychiatric nursing students, that anyone studying psychiatric content must automatically investigate their knowledge of their own life. In other words, *one must first determine one's own psychological growth and development before determining it in others.*

Having now gained enough confidence in myself, I started graduate nursing, with clinical psychiatric/mental health nursing as my doctoral theme. Again, getting through the content was painful. It didn't immobilize me this time, however, and I could learn and achieve. I embarked on a painful three-year struggle to learn those strengths and weaknesses that enhanced or hindered me as a person, therapist, and teacher.

It was during this period that I became aware that I had an unusual talent with people. Patients and staff responded very favorably to me, although at times the staff seemed uncomfortable. A psychologist once told me that I was so direct and open that I sometimes frightened them.

My first parenting experience in 1971 coincided with this formal academic interest. Although it was a great experience, it took me two years to fully integrate motherhood into my life. I had performed all the roles of a mother, but it wasn't until in my second year that I knew I had accepted this identification.

This new, independent Mary Jo as a mother was unfamiliar to me and those who knew me. My parents, parents-in-law, and other family and friends criticized and wondered. They frequently forced me to compare my values with theirs: "You should stay at home; be a housewife; take care of kids; your place is in the home; women don't need to use their brain; working should not be so important; your role is second to your husband's."

The process of clarifying my beliefs about myself and living an integrated life was challenging and stressful, but I was overjoyed at my new me and sad that many of those from my past couldn't or wouldn't accept this new person.

The new me now saw a need to clarify my new beliefs. I pursued who I was and what I wanted to be, and accomplished many things. And I now had the courage to never look back.

My first baby was doing great. He was and is a happy, intelligent child. As a result, my parents accepted that I really could handle motherhood/wifehood/personhood and a career all at one time, and the pressure to conform ceased. When my second son arrived, there was no need to restate my position.

I compared my life style with what I read, mainly to see where I fit. Important relationships developed among colleagues in teaching and clinical practice, and with my students.

Then one day Virginia Satir walked into my life and I added a new and important piece to the mosaic that was Mary Jo. I liked everything she said and did as I experienced her therapy with others, as an outsider first, then in training with her. From there I became involved in Gestalt therapy and discovered what was important, to me, as therapy.

PROFESSIONAL FACTORS IN BECOMING A THERAPIST

In my personal work experience I found I had a varying capacity
for effectiveness, depending on whom I worked under. This
puzzled me. I knew I didn't change that much and couldn't
understand why I was more effective at some times than at
others. This prompted an investigation into the use of power
and authority and the effect of such use on the individual in an
institution. Research brought out its effect on work, and high-
lighted the importance of analyzing communication and power
in agencies. The next phase was learning how persons with different philosophies come together, work, and produce results effectively. Realization of this "unity in difference," led me to think
about the physician-nurse relationship.

PHYSICIAN-NURSE COLLEAGUESHIP: EARNED AND LEARNED

Collaborative practices with different disciplines contributing to patient
care and treatment are being established in more explicit and formalized
ways than previously . . . Changes on the part of the nurse from the past
maintenance of a role predominantly dependent upon and subordinate to
the physician to the present self-directed and colleague-sharing role have
constituted a tremendous step in liberating the nurse to her full capabilities . . . Developing ways to achieve truly collaborative professional practices remains a problem and issue for study and research [1, pp. 10–11].

For me, existentialism provides the guidance to liberate the nurse
to her full capabilities.

Existentialism's first move is to make every man aware of what he is and
to make the full responsibility of his existence rest on him . . . [2, p. 20]
Existentialism is concerned principally with freeing man from his isolation and his anonymity, freeing his mind from the confusions that prevent
him from seeing his situations and his powers . . . [3, p. 277] .

In the spring of 1976 two experiences I had made me become
aware that if nurse-educators are to prepare nurses to function
as colleagues of physicians and other professionals, attention
should be given to the process that enhances the development of
colleagueship. My position is as follows: Genuine colleagueship
is earned and learned, not imposed by authority. You can be a
colleague in name but not necessarily one in behavior or respect.
    The first experience occurred during one of my job interviews.
The position emphasized the teaming-up of physicians and
nurse-educators to prepare residents and registered nurses for

community mental health psychiatry. For this emerging field the university focused on core curricula common to doctors and nurses. The program was built on the assumptions that to function as a true team, colleagues must respect the contribution of each professional involved, and that this is achieved through successful communication. In addition, if we expect people to practice as colleagues they must first learn to study as colleagues and have appropriate role models.

The psychiatrist-director, one of the nurse-educators participating in the program, and I met to discuss the job offer. I shared with the psychiatrist my personal beliefs about psychiatry, psychiatric mental health nursing, research, and education. At no time did I try to say what I thought he wanted to hear. I had made up my mind that if we were to be a successful team from the beginning, there would have to be clear and direct communication between us before I accepted the job. I listened to his position on the same topics and had clarified for me what I misunderstood or what had not been clear. I left the interview with the comfortable feeling that we both had a clear understanding and accurate knowledge of each other's philosophy.

I was taken aback, but pleasantly so, when the nurse who witnessed the interaction exclaimed, "He really liked you and treated you like a colleague!" The nurse and I started to analyze the interaction to see what had actually taken place. Did my having a doctorate set the pace? It may have, but I believe that what occurred had more to do with earned respect. We explored each other's belief system about what works in psychiatry, and did not attack one another. We were equals trying to understand each other. The degree opened the door and produced a willingness to listen, but the "paper credentials" are soon forgotten if substance doesn't follow.

If we as nurses want to be treated as colleagues, we must know what we are talking about and not depend only on credentials. For some whose knowledge base was obtained elsewhere, all the credential offers the individual is confidence in her own worth as a contributor to the health team. As professionals we must look to humanness in establishing a baseline for earned respect.

The next experience came two days later. For the past eight months I had worked in what was a new setting for me: the Veterans' Administration Hospital, with undergraduate nursing students. I was very frustrated in the beginning at not being an equal on the health team and not able to use my clinical specialization in psychiatry. The students and I were the "visitors," the "guests" in the clinical agency. (To digress briefly: I'm not sure that educators in a clinical setting don't set themselves up to be outsiders and not colleagues. A colleague on a health team must have knowledge and successfully communicate it to others. Perhaps what they are unconsciously saying to the agency is "Well, here I am, with all this wonderful expertise. Now you must accept me and fit me into the system the way I want to be fitted into the system." This attitude should be searched for and examined if found.)

For two months I tried to set up a group therapy session based on my treatment beliefs in order to provide a role model for the students. The students were seeing only the medical model group experiences, and I wanted them to experience *reality-oriented Christian Gestalt existential therapy* (*ROCGET*, pronounced "rocket"). Despite all my efforts, I was not successful. Finally I said to myself, "Dammit, you are doing something wrong. Regroup, and use your head to figure out how to accomplish your goal!" I decided that perhaps I hadn't earned the respect from my medical colleagues that would allow them to give me the opportunity to utilize my skills. I stopped playing the game "Gee, look what I can do. Why don't you let me do it?" I decided to see if what I did was what they needed and could accept. The question became: How do two philosophical positions meet to accomplish the task of therapy? Perhaps my lack of success originally stemmed from not utilizing my knowledge as a ROCGET therapist from the beginning. When your knowledge and behavior are not integrated you have not maximized your contribution.

In the group the psychiatrist behaved like a humanist even though in group therapy he lectured on Freudian concepts of mother-child relationships, the Oedipus complex, castration worries, and so on. Over a period of several months the psychiatrist and I informally created a strong relationship based on a mutual caring, for both patients and students. Our informal dialogues centered around each other's beliefs about people, treatment, the medical model versus existential models, and education. We began to really understand and listen to each other.

Once this communication pattern was established, we moved into the next phase of the relationship. The two of us participated in group therapy for four months with the nursing students and patients. The psychiatrist took the lead for the group, using the medical Freudian model. The students began to question him after they participated in the group, trying to understand and make sense of the lecture material he was giving during group sessions.

At this point it occurred to the psychiatrist that if my students didn't understand his lecture with its psychoanalytic content, what good was it doing the patients? One day he came to me and asked what could be done to improve group interaction. I felt that the time had now come for me to demonstrate my belief system. Our relationship was firm, and it would not be threatening to him to take professional advice from a nurse. I very candidly said, "The patients who are getting well in your group do so because of your humanness — what you are, not what you say. If you would stop lecturing them and let this quality come through, I believe you would see what I mean."

He responded favorably to this directness. Next I had to help him free himself from his "doctorness" and allow the humanness to emerge and take the lead. I accomplished this by being a role model for him. I began to conduct the group on the basis of my ROCGET therapy. My humanness joined his humanness and things began to happen. All at once the patients who met for half-hours began staying one-and-a-half hours and had to be told to leave. Many patients were talking, and the group moved exceptionally fast. Although the psychiatrist participated, I could tell that essentially he was watching my techniques.

Several weeks later I gave him a copy of *Why Am I Afraid to Tell You Who I Am* by John Powell. The next group session after he had read it, he immediately began to conduct the group as a humanist, using the style described in the book. It was as if it had all suddenly clicked for him.

The students couldn't get over how he had changed. Soon our particular treatment style — person-to-person therapy (PTP therapy) — emerged. We had reached genuine colleagueship. I was more skilled with psychotic patients and could also introduce femaleness to the interaction. We were truly a PTP therapy team — male and female — for the patients to relate to. At times we would disagree with each other. Sometimes I would team up with the patients to give them strength to negotiate with the psychiatrist.

As time went on we grew and refined our PTP therapy model. And there was a beauty in our professional relationship from which I experienced tremendous personal satisfaction. The therapy model was born from our contact, a unique way to advance science. Now a scientific base for the PTP therapy model must be developed.

I was also interested in investigating further the colleagueship we had achieved. Two independent and strong-willed individuals, each espousing a very different therapy model, met, achieved colleagueship, and created a third model. How did this come about? I believe it was because (1) each of us really knew the content of our own model, and (2) we worked at opening a line of true and effective communication between us as individuals concerning what we believed — each talked and each *listened.* Ideas and information from Satir, Ginot, Sullivan, Rogers, Buber, Perls, Leininger, Vann, Glasser, Sartre, Marcel, Berne, McKuen, Berning, Smith, Denver, Selman, Dunham, Whaley, and Powell provided the background from which I formed my ROCGET and PTP therapies. The most important tool in forming a colleagueship is to know who you are and not to be afraid to say it, and to state in a way that can be heard that what you believe works.

We must begin to investigate and develop theories on how to develop colleagueship, and conduct research to validate our thinking. We will then have a knowledgeable base of theory to transmit to our students, regardless of their professional careers. Colleagueship can happen by chance, but in an educated society, surely we can do better than leave it to chance.

PHILOSOPHY OF THERAPY AND TEACHING

Before someone can develop theory, several things need to happen. First the student must have a firm foundation in the field, including in-depth knowledge of the scholarly works of the prominent contributors to the field (content). Then slowly, and usually without awareness, the student weeds out the data irrelevant to herself or himself (process). One then begins to find one's self in the position of needing to document who one is and how one will practice (both content and process).

The next step is supervised clinical experience, from which the student emerges as a practitioner with the beginnings of a particular theory of one's own. Those theories that fit the person's unique personality will work most effectively. As new concepts and techniques are incorporated into practice, the student will be awkward, but gradually an individual style will emerge.

In the educational process the instructor serves as a role model and facilitator. The more creative and articulate student will then gradually synthesize his or her thinking and formalize the process of "therapist-becoming."

Everyone has a philosophy, whether or not it can be identified or articulated. Just because a scholarly person may take the time to articulate his or her philosophy, it does not follow that it is therefore more useful. Our philosophy does not suddenly appear in a pure form, but rather it develops and changes through the gaining of knowledge and experience and gradually becomes a belief system to guide our lives, both professionally and personally. It permeates everything about us. It affects the role or profession we choose, the way we perform personally and professionally, how we interrelate man, society, and our work or profession, how we treat people and expect them to treat us, and even how we dress and act.

My particular philosophy has essentially a reality-base orientation. I look at data and examine consequences before I act. Implications for the here and now are examined. A "let's only live for the moment" attitude is avoided, although I do believe in legitimate spontaneous contact; the Child* ego state (feelings) is not in control of my professional life. When my Child ego state is activated, it is done through the direction of my Adult ego state (thinking).

I believe a person comes to therapy or education to get help in meeting their basic needs, which are mainly to feel loved and worthwhile. As a therapist and educator I concentrate primarily on the present, which includes treatment for a patient and education for a student.

Short-term goals are essential and extremely helpful, for both patients and students. The positive energy they give helps people cope with life. I try to guide my students or clients through a reality relationship with genuine caring. This true caring is a reflection of the Christian humanism that developed from strong early religious and parental influence. It is a personal commitment to help others, not for self-enhancement, but because of the Christian belief in the interdependence of mankind.

I emphatically dissociate my values from those of the patient or student. I will let them know who I am and what I believe, but their beliefs are theirs and are to be respected. My goal is to get the patient or student to make an honest and in-depth examination of who one is, what one wants to be, and how to get there. The person must assume full responsibility for himself or herself and for the consequences of his or her behavior. If at any time I find that my philosophy interferes with the learning or the therapy, I point this out to the person and recommend a separation.

*The terms *Child ego state* and *Adult ego state* are Transactional Analysis Therapy terms. A fuller discussion of them is found in the section Transactional Analysis in Chapter 8.

In this world there exists a dynamic interrelation between people, and clarification of both the built-in responsibilities of individuals and institutions and the consequences of either violating established rules or indulging in inappropriate behaviors is necessary. Therefore when someone chooses to "step on me," e.g., by stealing or killing, and so on, it will be clear how that person will be treated. Such concepts are essential for the smooth functioning of society.

Another facet of my philosophy is my belief that each person uses ego to structure his world (from Gestalt theory). Man is dynamic and made up of an interrelation of parts, the whole of which is greater than the sum. The self continually identifies its needs and structures the environment to satisfy the needs. A person in conflict rejects parts of himself by removing them from awareness, thus causing divisions in the personality. The goal of therapy or education, therefore, is to aid in personal awareness and to enable the personality to integrate knowledge that affects a person's life. The process of education or therapy is to guide people toward assuming responsibility for self, to aid them in becoming whole through an awareness of what they are and are not doing for self. A teacher or therapist cannot and should not try to decide another person's destiny. What we can do is awaken, guide, and free an individual to create his own destiny.

The belief that a person has intrinsic worth and dignity is another facet of my philosphy. A person is in a constant state of transition, emergence, and actualization. A personal sense of an identity of being comes from self-awareness, the capability of selecting what one will respond to and how one will respond. A person is thus continuously expressing his behavioral possibilities. There is a unity of person and environment, both of which are personally and subjectively defined. The world around us is not only the biological and physical world, but also a constructed social world.

The Existentialist in me radiates the philosophy I live by. I believe each person has in himself or herself the freedom to make new decisions that allow self-transcendence. My goal is to know myself and know my world, which knowledge, I believe, is necessary before entering the world of the patient or student.

I consider myself very existential as manifested by the change, unity, and originality that has taken place throughout my professional career of clinical work, teaching, research, and writing, and my personal life as a woman, wife, mother, and homemaker. Those aspects of me are integrated — they are not assumed roles.

I fit the "individualist" existential personality type, seeking intimacy and closeness in relationships. My theological beliefs are yet another facet of my philosophy. To me God, or an Energy Force (whatever suits your religious beliefs), is the Prime Mover and Designer of the world, keeping it in balance and order.

I am convinced of ultimates in which all matter and form can be reduced to basic energy levels. The subject of energy levels and systems and their relation to human communication has become a whole new field. New discoveries in the field of energy systems analysis will restructure our knowledge and experience, and I for one am looking forward to this with excitement. It may even be that, through science, we will be able to identify the "supernatural" phenomena magicians in the past used! Two excellent books on this subject are *A New Age of Healing* by Brenda Johnson and *The Structure of Magic,* Volumes I and II, by Richard Bandler and John Grinder.

MY PRESENT AND FUTURE

Threaded through the last five years has been my therapist-becoming. I sorted out bits and pieces of information and began to determine what I felt was useful in therapist-making. This information is included later in this book. I have chosen a work situation that fits my assessment of who I am and what I can do, and I know how to use those tools the job expects and wants. Only when a person integrates all these bits of pieces of himself can he maximize his potential and minimize his weaknesses.

I plan to use a person-to-person approach as my framework for life. It is one that will grow as I grow from contact with you. And isn't that what life is — a changing and a growing, an interaction with the world around us?

REFERENCES

1. Leininger, M. Winds of Change. In Leininger, M. (Ed.) *Contemporary Issues in Mental Health Nursing.* Boston: Little, Brown and Co., 1973.
2. Sartre, J-P. *Existentialism and Human Emotions.* New York: Wisdom Library, 1957.
3. Dupuis, A., and Nordberg, R. *Philosophy and Education.* Milwaukee: Bruce Publishing Company, 1964.

SELECTED READINGS

Bandler, R., and Grinder, J. *The Structure of Magic,* Vols. I and II. Palo Alto, Calif.: Science & Behavior Books, 1975, 1976.

Johnson, B. *A New Age of Healing.* Sussex, England: Polygon Promotional Group of Companies, 1975.

Maslow, A. H. *Motivation and Personality.* New York: Harper & Brothers, 1954.

Menninger, K. *The Vital Balance.* New York: Viking Press, 1963.

Powell, J. *Why Am I Afraid to Tell You Who I Am.* Niles, Ill.: Argus Communications, 1969.

Rogers, C. *Freedom To Learn.* Columbus, Ohio: Charles Merrill Publishers, 1969.

Satir, V. *Peoplemaking.* Palo Alto, Calif.: Science and Behavior Books, 1972.

Satir, V., Stackowiak, J., and Taschman, H. *Helping Families to Change.* New York: Jason Aronson, 1975.

Skinner, B.F. *Beyond Freedom and Dignity.* New York: Alfred A. Knopf, 1971.

2 Communication and Contact

VIRGINIA SATIR

The task of becoming a therapist is to create a therapeutic relationship involving a sacredness — a human sacredness. I believe that therapy brings together one human being in a place crying for help and another human being saying "I'll help you." But there is a tremendous responsibility in agreeing to be a partner with someone who wants to make some change.

A long time ago my goals as a therapist were to alleviate pain and change behavior. Although I am still interested in helping people to avoid unnecessary pain and to behave in a way that fits better what they want to do, I now focus on helping the individual to become more of a whole person and with options at his or her disposal. I call this "creative coping."

When I was a child, it seemed to me that whatever was needed would happen. Though I could not have put it into words, I had the feeling that anything in life is subject to change, and that a human being could change because he or she has the power to change. When I say this now some people think of me as a upper middle or middle-class person who has had no troubles in life. How far from the truth! Actually, I was born on a farm, the oldest of five children. Since neither of my parents had an education beyond the fourth grade, my background, from a social achievement point of view, was very limited. However, the spiritual life of the family, which was largely nurtured by my mother, was of a continually opening, evolving kind. One small example was that I didn't live with a punishing God. My parents, particularly my mother, grew all the time, putting before me a model of life of being open to life itself.

Becoming a therapist was in one sense an accident. My first personal ambition was to become a teacher. From the time that I was five years old one of the things I wanted to do when I grew up was to be a "children's detective on parents." There were lots of things that my parents and other adults did that I didn't understand and sometimes thought were unfair. To become a teacher was to become a detective on parents. Teaching was something that would be a route to understanding both parents and children. I happen to be someone who loves learning and reading; I even taught myself to read when I was three years old. Learning for me is an exciting thing, and I wanted to make it exciting for everybody else. This also I could do through teaching. I paid absolutely no attention, even in this period, to intelligence tests. I just believed that the human spirit and the human person could evolve and grow.

When I was in college I was asked to write a paper on crippled children. I said, "I can't write a paper like that. I *can* write a paper on 'children with crippling conditions'." Even then I considered the human being a sacred thing, a miracle. To me, adjectives used to describe a person really only described a certain condition of a person. A person would stand there and different kinds of conditions were like a shining light around him or her.

Another thing I learned along the way was that people had limited and rather odd ideas about certain things. They would tend to make generalizations on very little information. And I didn't want to be this type of person — I wanted my generalizations to be based on a lot of experience.

I had much book learning, but when it came to relating to people, I wanted to be clear. Consequently I had to develop my own experience and then check with the books, rather than have the books determine what my experience was. When there was a conflict between the book and my experience, I accepted my experience — I always went with my *intuition.*

Accepting experience in most cases, rather than abstract generalization, is germane to the teaching of therapists, too. For instance, you have read somewhere that all black people are this, all women are that, all six-year-olds are this way, and so on. Now you carry a yardstick of beliefs about these people with you. Then you meet someone who is six years old or black or a woman, and you compare them with that yardstick, the yardstick made up by someone else. You can very easily find that the people you are measuring fall short. By believing the yardstick instead of developing your own ideas about these people, you are not learning very much. And in order to make the experience fit the yardstick, you have to distort in some way.

Therefore one of the things I do in training is to challenge everyone's belief system. Where do your beliefs come from?

What are they based on? Then I try to build into my group as much heterogeneity as possible. I like to have old and young people and different racial groups and different sex groups — in other words, as much difference as I can. This is because I have found that a great number of people seem to feel safer surrounded by sameness, but I believe that we grow on the basis of our differences. Thus it is also essential that people have here-and-now experience in different areas.

After being in teaching for a while I decided that I was not going to be one of those people who was an expert on only one kind of experience. So I planned literally to teach different grades, both elementary and high school, for six years; and then I purposely had many different kinds of settings. I taught children in poor families. I taught rich children. I taught progressive education. I did everything I knew how to give myself a base of experience. Each night I would go home with one of the children, to come to know who they were and to become acquainted with their families. Seeing the child in the context of his or her family and home environment helped me to not minimize discipline problems. As I began to know the families better, I also began to lose the ideas that intelligence was only a factor having to do with whether or not people learned and that intelligence more or less determined behavior. I saw many situations in the family that were painful or anger-producing. I began to see that the effects of these situations could determine a child or adult's behavior as much as intelligence or learned behavior. As a result of these observations, I realized that I needed to learn more about people than just their intelligence or lack of it. I enrolled in a course of social work to meet this need.

At the University of Chicago I discovered the whole world of the emotional life, which was at that time encased by one word, *psychiatry.* I learned about those parts of ourselves that gave us trouble and pain, but intuitively I knew that there had to be more to people than just their troubled parts. I don't know when it was that I stopped working with the troubled parts and started to work with those that were healthy. I found it interesting that if I worked with the healthy parts, the troubled parts disappeared.

As I was doing this, I often found that I was able to help people become happier, healthier, and better able to cope, but was unable to do as much for myself. From there I knew I wanted to help the therapists I was training to also become healthy people. Anybody could learn techniques, but to have a therapist come to be a whole human being was to me very important.

One of the things I tried to teach was that I could not give my students my particular experience. What I could do was to try to help them become as whole as possible while gaining their own experience. They then would be able to take for themselves the steps that would enable them to be what I call good leaders of the change process: a process between two or more human beings journeying together to make something better. The journeys as a psychotherapist I take now are not only with one human being, but also with a family, as a family therapist.

I have also tried to get across my belief that the process of becoming a therapist involves always being available for new things, always growing and changing, never saying "This is it, I am now a therapist."

One element of life that I feel is very important is the element of excitement — to be excited about what you are doing, to feel that it matters not only to you but to those around you. To me excitement is aliveness. One characteristic of many people with problems, I think, is that they are not excited: they are not excited about life; they are not excited about things that are happening to them. And along with this lack of excitement there is somehow a terrible lack of a sense of humor. What I try to do is help these people become excited about themselves and their lives. To be able to do this, I need to be excited about my own life. Being genuinely excited means that I have to have hope and be willing to take risks. I never heard about these things in my growing-up and during preparation for becoming a therapist. In fact, if I heard anything about it, it was *not* to have a sense of humor or *not* to be excited, but rather make it "professional," whatever "professional" meant. But now I was thinking along the lines of: How can these people make use of their strengths; evolve themselves; be tuned in to their own excitement and potential; utilize their options and freedoms?

I believe that people are never fools. They make use of the best they have, and I think this is just as true of professionals. People cannot be condemned for not being smart before they have learned something. A person must be constantly sifting and sorting out his ideas and feelings in the light of new information. This continues the excitement and keeps the person constantly growing, even though knowledge learned tomorrow may invalidate what one "knows" today. To many this means constant uncertainty, and they feel this is bad. They feel that they must find the right way and stick to it rigidly when something new comes along. But if these people knew and accepted that change is normal rather than abnormal, this sifting and sorting process

would be more acceptable. Every two or three years I personally go through a process of discovering, removing those ideas
and feelings that don't fit with what I am at that point in time.
The more choices I have and the more things I know, the more
opportunities there are to be what I call up-to-date and relevant.
Every new situation is a new creation in terms of interaction.

The training I give reflects where I am and what I try to do.
I make room for each student/client's pictures and beliefs. Each
person learns in a different way and at a different pace. Each
person is also a new source of learning for me. This is why what
I'm teaching is a dynamic changing process, one that constantly
goes on inside of each of us, between us, between us and the
world outside of us. Thus very few people that I have taught
will be rigid. You must be relevant with what fits. For instance,
if someone is hungry and the most important thing they need
is food, then getting that person the right food is the most
important thing in the world *at that moment.*

Another concept, that of what help is, is very clear to me
at this point. When I was young in my profession, helping
meant giving someone something, helping him or her avoid pain,
doing for that person. Well, I nearly died on that one. Now I
realize that help is sharing myself as fully as I can; it is making
contracts with people about what we want to do that is honest,
about seeing that the other person has all the resources that they
need that they may not be aware of; but it is not insulting people
by taking away their opportunity for creative struggle. For example, it is not easy sometimes to sit back and watch a person cry.
Many people can't stand other people to cry, but I have learned
that crying is not always a signal to do something for the person
crying. We have to learn that crying has different meanings at
different times. My real help is to use myself to help that person
get in touch with himself/herself. It provides a context of trust
so that individuals can take risks when they are around me.
When they go away, they go away with new views about how to
deal with and stay in touch with themselves.

The psychiatric field today is split. One side says that all you
have to do is get people over their symptoms and they will then
live a better life, and there may be something to that. The other
side, which I probably represent, believes that therapy is an
opportunity for people to take active steps in their own growth,
to become fuller people. I have even noticed that some people
have felt that it was lucky for them to have some kind of a symptom, because they could then make some new possibilities for
themselves. If we use the negative things that happen to us as

opportunities to hear or see something in our actions, thoughts, or lives that may be hurting us, the whole process becomes more helpful than harmful.

Therapists who have learned how to be whole, who have felt that clients were worthy of love, of struggle, of growth, of a high feeling of their own worth, and who then have discovered an ability to be creative in whatever situation they find themselves, these are the people who have learned the techniques they need and who never get boxed into any one "method." My beliefs about myself, my beliefs about people, my beliefs about how change takes place are all part of what I've found works for therapists. I could never say that any one method I have heard of is *the* method. What works is helping people grow, whatever way is used. I use all the little things I have ever learned as resources for myself to learn more about the human being. When I come across a new kind of therapy, I read about it, look at it, look at what it has to say that might be useful to me.

Resources for learning and therapy come from many places. Probably some therapists many years ago didn't see music, body movement, exercises for healthy memory, physical exercise and nutrition, guided imagery, maybe even house-building or cooking, as resources. Therapists today, on the other hand, welcome these resources and try to use them where they will benefit the client or patient most.

For some time now many therapists have held certain fixed beliefs, for example, that people are bad and limited. This kind of thinking stems from the idea that all relationships form some kind of hierarchy, that is, that there is someone on the top and someone on the bottom and that there has to be a formula to determine who is acceptable. This concept of hierarchical structure is not acceptable to me. In the healthiest relationships, there is mutuality.

Before I end, a word about my students: if they have gotten what I tried to give them, they will be able to be creative in what they are doing. They will be able to teach me something because they will be running what I have given them through their own unique experiences, adding to it their own, opening up, and giving it back with new dimensions. And we will both be richer for our differentness. This is how professional training can grow and be very exciting for both trainer and trainee.

3 Becoming a Psychiatrist

BENJAMIN GOODWIN

My therapeutic skill has developed out of my background in general medicine, psychiatric ward work, psychiatric administration, and private practice. My patients are a composite group; I now work with individuals, couples, families, and groups. I blend my psychoanalytic background with Gestalt and family therapy. I therefore have a variety of ways of working with people according to their needs and my energy level. As I think of you who are reading about becoming therapists, I ask myself some of the questions you may be asking those of us who are therapists now, questions about our families, our work, our play, or questions about our philosophies and religions, about different ways of living, and more pragmatic questions about training and technique.

An earnest student must also ask other questions early in his or her training, since once he or she has begun a specific graduate program, it becomes increasingly difficult to change to another discipline. What form of training do I want? (This may be the most difficult answer for you to find.) How much time, energy, effort, and money do I want to put into my learning? What skills do I already have and how can I enhance them? How much power do I want? How much pleasure do I want? How broad shall my practice be, and how dependable? And still more questions: Which feelings and behavior can I tolerate? How competent do I want my teachers and supervisors to be? Will my profession help me to develop and use my inner excitement and creativity? Will it contribute to my own growth? Will I refer my patients to my colleagues? Will I feel a continuity of my own integrity? How unique to my profession will I be? My goal in writing this chapter is to present those factors that were important in my own development as a psychiatrist, to show how the answers I found to some of these questions aided my growth and development in the field, and to share with you some of my ideas about therapy and growth.

I grew up in close contact with three neighborhood families, two of which were close to my parents, giving me frequent opportunities for comparison. This contact allowed me to see how each family structure differed from the others, to note how each had a different way of dealing with feelings and behavior. I became sensitive to the difference of lifestyle in each home and to what behavior would be permitted when the parents were home and when they were away. As a child I learned who was to be included and excluded in the games we played. I learned the risks of intimacy. I observed different methods of punishment and teaching. Early I became aware of space, of walls and doors. I learned to be attentive to what I wanted, where I was, and whom I was with. I learned who would interrupt our games and who would enhance them. I contrast one of my most pleasant memories, that of being chosen first when we were choosing sides to play baseball, with the many times of being chosen either last or not at all. I recall the importance of this decision-making process in play, in the expense of time and energy in "one potato, two potato," or in throwing someone a bat, alternating hands up the bat, and then throwing the bat over my shoulder to show that I had won the right to choose.

I finished high school early and attended college during the war years. During my high school and college years, I conformed to the authority system of my family and of their conservative church. During my premed training I found the available information in biology, chemistry, and physics very stimulating and rewarding. The skills developed to observe my world became sharper. I was fascinated with the possibility of knowing about and identifying every living organism around me. Although I felt considerably limited in what I would let myself experience, I felt a great freedom and challenge to learn what I could within those limits.

During my years at Southwestern Medical School, I worked as a private duty nurse and in the summer as a ward nurse on the Isolation Ward during a polio epidemic. My experience as a nurse was different from my experience as a medical student. I learned to work on both parts of the chart at the same time, that is, writing nurses' notes as well as doctors' orders and progress notes. This balance caused a softness as I developed more "low authority skills," those skills associated with greater and closer contact with the patient and his family.

While nursing, I learned the difficulty of carrying out orders that doctors and medical students had written. I learned that it was not even possible to fill many of these orders. I learned how many patients and families come to feel neglected as the hospital routine appeared to take over.

On the other hand, as a medical student I learned to accept my power more carefully, to be responsible to others with power. I learned the medical models of scientific thinking, validation, and openness. I appreciated the case conferences, the open give-and-take between students and learned and creative teachers. I watched the early use of sulfas and penicillin and the early development of many medical subspecialties. I dealt directly with the core of the life process, with birth and death as well as with fractures and sunburn. I delivered babies in homes. I did an epidemiologic case study to locate a typhoid carrier. I experienced responsibility, competition, and support.

After graduation from medical school in 1949, I had a rotating internship and maintained a basic interest in general medicine. I still saw psychiatry in a negative way, as something dealing with psychosis and the administering of shock therapy. During the internship I joined the Navy and asked for an overseas assignment. I was assigned to work in the Navy hospital on Guam and to teach in a medical school for nationals from the Trust Territory. The medical work load was heavy during the early days of the Korean war but lessened considerably as we became overstaffed a year later.

My arrival on Guam confronted me with the major cultural differences between my society and those of the nationals of the various Pacific island groups who were attending school on Guam. I was frequently told by students, "You really don't understand our people, our way of life." Often this comment would precede a detailed criticism of some of my presumptions about their personal values in contrast to their own information. I had the feeling that I was on the edge of their more intimate lifestyles just as they were on the edge of the American way of life. I felt they were protecting me, as if the actual information about their lifestyle would be morally offensive to me. I did, in fact, have considerable difficulty accepting these major differences in lifestyle without feeling judgmental. When I was not being so moral, I developed a great appreciation for their skills, for their different way of life.

At the end of my Navy tour I returned to Dallas to enter general practice. During a year of this practice my primary interest changed from general to psychosomatic medicine. The psychodynamic element in those patients with psychosomatic illnesses was new and of great interest to me. I sought out and applied for a training program in psychiatry at the University of Colorado. As I was deciding to leave general practice and to enter the psychiatric residency, an earlier application to Civil Service to work in the Pacific islands had been approved, and an opening became available on Yap, Western Caroline Islands, Trust Territory. I accepted it.

Yap is an undeveloped island known for grass skirts and stone money. Although the people had no written language, they maintained, without much outside influence, their strong heritage through stories, dance, and "family secrets" covering more than 800 years. Again I observed individuals and families in a culture very different from mine with growing awe and respect. As I accepted the differences between our ways of life, my standards of morality became less rigid.

I experienced also the intense pleasure and extreme exasperation of Civil Service medicine in such a remote area. I had an 85-bed general hospital and made field trips to a selected few of the hundreds of outer islands around Yap. Sometimes I visited islands where there would be a population of only one to three hundred people whose major contact with the outside world was these infrequent field trips. On the trips I had to function alone, out of my "black bag," without the support of the hospital. I truly practiced primitive medicine with limited time as well as limited facilities. To bring a patient to Yap would entail bringing his family also. They would all have to remain on the island for two to four years until the next field trip. This experience gave me greater respect for my medical team as well as respect for my own independence.

Yap had a 20 percent incidence of active tuberculosis and a 5 percent incidence of leprosy among its population of 3,500. During my year on the island, various anthropologists and medical epidemiologists visited to research illnesses that were endemic to the area. It had been generally accepted that the Yapese had a low level of resistance to leprosy, since there was nearly 100 percent mortality in those in whom the disease was acute. Up to my time there, these patients were sent to a distant leprosarium. I obtained permission to build a leprosarium on Yap, where those more seriously ill could remain closer to their own lifestyle and where their food taboos would continue to be respected.

This direct confrontation with a culture so foreign to my own caused me to reexamine my beliefs and to look inside myself for a deeper human value. I became so preoccupied with my medical activities and with my fascination for the native culture during my year on Yap that I did little preparation for my entry into psychiatry in Denver.

Back at the University of Colorado, I found that the program was in a state of transition. The emphasis was shifting from mental health programs and psychiatric education to psychoanalytic training. The teaching staff represented both positions. Our group of residents was mixed also, with such a variety of national backgrounds and medical experience that my years of island experience and general practice did not make me unique. I enjoyed the intellectual confrontations and stimuli and the return to the discipline of an organized training program with close supervision, case presentations, and theoretical discussions.

During my first year I worked with in-patients. I recall the discomfort of my first hour of being supervised. After presenting my first patient, I was asked for my diagnosis and dynamic formulation. At that point I did not even know what diagnosis was available. I became fascinated with the value of psychodynamic observation in addition to the familiar medical history, physical findings, and laboratory studies. I learned how the patient's own personal development, family, and environment had become interrelated in such a way as to produce symptoms, illnesses, and strengths. I found that psychoanalytic theory presented a clear concept of personality formulation and psychopathology. From this theory I learned another language to describe many of my varied personal experiences. The total experience was like looking at an x-ray film for the first time.

My second year included six months of neurology and six months of consultation in psychosomatic medicine. I was again on the familiar ground of medical care and again working closely with physicians in the familiar fields of medicine, surgery, and obstetrics. A necessary part of my training was the task of integrating one discipline with another. I recognized the relative indifference of most of my medical colleagues to the significant contributions of psychiatry and psychoanalysis. Slowly I began to develop bridges across this gulf between medicine and psychiatry.

Around this time I became interested in Zen Buddhism when I volunteered to review D. T. Suzuki's book *Zen and Psychoanalysis.* To me the book opened the door to a treasure chest of related views, and I continued my reading with the works of Alan Watts and others. I moved then to reading about yoga and the use of awareness, breathing, and meditation. I found a great need to integrate the exciting concepts of Zen with my blend of island experiences, medical studies of body function, and psychiatric studies of mental mechanisms.

My conservative religious background, too, was being challenged and questioned as I was exposed to new information and new viewpoints. I was somewhat relieved when one of the other residents who was more outspokenly conservative than I took strong stands in controversies. I was able to listen to and observe a position that otherwise *I* might have taken. I was growing, reaching, trying, and experimenting.

I was also especially fascinated by the beauty, warmth, and caring of Dr. Rene Spitz, which was so evident in his films, his family, and his warm interviews. The open, frank dealing with sexuality and other feelings exemplified by Dr. Spitz created another gulf with my conservative background. My choices began to be clarified. I could avoid some of this new information in order to hold on to my former tradition, or I could drop my conservative church and the friends related to it, or I could try a difficult form of assimilation. I chose to do a little bit of all three.

I developed a warmer and closer relationship with selected staff members working with me in my residency. I had a special fondness for those analysts who worked closely with children and families, and I appreciated their encouragement to pursue my own way. At the time of my early confusion I was not aware that I was laying down a pattern that would be basic for me throughout much of the remainder of my life and one that I would observe in my patients later — how to be different without being alienating. In therapy this was a basic process. At the time, however, I felt overloaded. I wanted analysis for myself but could see no way to make this possible financially. I knew of no form of either group therapy or short-term crisis intervention that was available to me on my limited resident's salary.

In an effort to slow down my pace of change, I chose to spend two years at a remote Veterans' Administration hospital in Sheridan, Wyoming. I also wanted a chance to work as a ward psychiatrist. In this chronic-care hospital, staff people had been working together for long periods of time. The aides had an average seniority of 15 to 20 years, and the nurses 5 to 10 years. Only the doctors changed every few years. Because of this relatively rapid change, doctors were perhaps the most irrelevant to the hospital climate.

Now I had the time and the opportunity to reappraise myself. I worked with psychiatrists who had been trained in a non-analytic setting. I felt awkward as I watched the high dosages of drugs and electroshock used on various patients. Such experiences made me want to identify and define good therapy more exactly. Slowly I developed a different form of ward management, one that integrated my experience of previous years with my newly found analytic approach.

Once, partway through an orientation course I was giving for new aides and nurses I felt that the usual psychiatric language had been sufficiently communicated; I wanted to use the remaining time for discussion from the class. We developed the dynamic attitude that the essence of the hospital was that people, both patients and staff, were living together in a unique setting. Good therapy occurred when people were living (working) together in a clear, caring, and nourishing way. The new aides and nurses might have had less experience in working in a psychiatric service, but they had experienced years of living and most of them had children. Attention began to shift from psychiatric language to a discussion of the various age levels of our children and a discussion of our family truths. We subsequently developed a language of behavior and limits related to our lives as individuals. A new relevancy seemed to be emerging. I was confident that the elements of our discussions could be synthesized in a meaningful way and result in a dynamic ward.

I took the information gained from the class of new aides and nurses to my maximum security ward. I began to listen to the aides and nurses talk about their personal ideas about caring for children — that is, how dependency needs could be met — and then how they would change our ward if they could. Because of the nature of hospital security some of the ward patients had not actually left the building for a period of up to ten years, although most were transferred from that ward to other wards within a period of one to two years. I began to spend more and more time on my ward, talking with orderlies, nurses, and patients, simply observing and participating in ward activities. My presence in a nonauthoritarian way brought major changes.

As I became familiar with the way in which the ward was managed, I also became increasingly aware of how little information could be obtained from the usual form of nursing report. As an example, I would be on the ward in the evening and observe a critical experience first-hand; the next morning during the usual competent routine report, I would find distortion in the reporting of the incident. Unfortunately such distortion and dilution were inevitable when compared with observations made at the time of the actual incident.

Our ward conferences continued in an "institutional" way but we began to share concerns and more personal information. We developed for each patient a color-coded system of privilege or status that reflected our concern for their behavior, a system that perhaps corresponds to children in a family. Green status represented our lowest level of concern, or our greatest level of confidence, similar to our feelings for teenagers. Blue status indicated a middle level of concern, characteristic of our feelings for children of elementary school age. The red status was reserved for those of high concern to us, comparable to our concern for toddlers. Concern to us meant the potential of these patients to do harm to themselves, and their security in terms of the doors and windows.

The system seemed very logical and simple as we first formulated it, but it became much more complex as we began to apply it to patients and tried to make status more relevant. The procedures of the ward became much more personal. Staff members from all services contributed explicit information about how they would express concern for these age levels in their own families. We learned, too, about each of the "family rules" of the various staff members. We learned that some of the rules had developed from experience while others were ideals and had not yet been really used. We were then able to determine a variety of ways to express our concern for the patients.

The problems came, however, when we began to focus upon our concern about the patients' behavior. It first appeared that individual staff members had "favorites" among the patients. The decision was then made not to attempt to be purely scientific and objective, but to start with the dynamic premise that we were, in fact, living together as an "extended family." Our goal was to be concerned first with the real comfort and concern level of each staff person, whether we were consistent or not. As this change evolved, we found many inconsistencies in the application of our rules, as happens in our own families. After much discussion about our rules of life and the expectations of the people around us, we were able to concentrate more directly on the situation in the ward.

We found that few of us were comfortable giving electroshock treatments and large doses of medicine. Further discussion revealed that our greatest source of discomfort was the process of isolating and physically restraining patients. What we were doing, however, appeared to be reasonable from the standpoint of tradition. A typical expression of this feeling was "It's just a part of my job that I don't like."

We first concentrated on those patients of our ward with red status. Since we now thought of our patients as toddlers, we needed a confined area in which we could more easily retain verbal and visual contact. Therefore we put a small circle of chairs in the day room near the nurses' station in which both television and reading materials were available. This area became our "red area," our substitute for seclusion, restraint, shock, and heavy medication. The "red" patient was expected to remain in this area. When it was necessary to leave it either for exercise, meals, bathroom use, or bed, he or she would be taken to these activities in a manner that was familiar to all of us. When he or she left this area in defiance, there was great anxiety and concern among both staff and other patients. This caring with clear limits became our new therapeutic tool.

We agreed that any aide or nurse could decrease a patient's status from green to blue or blue to red without a doctor's order. The aide or nurse was then required to describe the incident that had caused concern about the patient. A raise in status, however, required staff action. As we became more dynamic, specific difficulties developed. Some of the personnel, both nurses and aides, were simply unable to change from an institutional ward style with its fixed roles. Some found the process interesting and intriguing, but were openly unable or unwilling to share their own personal rules; they felt that asking for this information and using it was an intrusion into their personal lives. Because of the discomfort, the few people who found themselves in this situation usually requested transfer. In one or two cases it was necessary that transfer be granted.

In our ward conferences we discussed the obvious dilemma of dealing with feelings that people have for each other that are not usually talked about in the average ward. We were all aware, at one level or another, for example, that the staff tolerated the occasional beating of patients by either staff or other patients. There were stories, too, of various forms of sexual involvement and/or acts of tenderness and affection that were difficult for us to cope with. Discussing these difficult-to-describe feelings and generalities produced tremendous anxiety, especially among those personnel who were already uncomfortable with our process. The others of us could only talk about the subject in a general way.

As we were undergoing this process, the institutional part of ward routine continued. Patients were still worked up medically and psychologically by the social workers, psychologists, and psychiatrists. Progress notes and doctors' orders were written. The ward was frequently managed by more traditional or institutional personnel when they were on call or as they rotated through the ward. The process of status-concern and "living together," then, was an addition to our usual method of function rather than a substitution.

As we moved back and forth from institutional to dynamic modes, there were many humorous incidents. On one occasion I entered the ward to find a red card up but after much inquiry could not find that anyone had changed a patient to red status. I was about to change the card when a nurse arrived who had been working with a small group of patients. I inquired whether she knew the red patient and she said no. When I called her attention to the red card, she replied, "Oh, that's for me. I'm really strung out today and I want everyone's attention." Our laughter was mixed. We were all caring, needy people, all becoming increasingly able to communicate our own concerns and feelings.

After a time the hospital management granted permission to provide a similar program on an open ward, one that was primarily blue-green in contrast to the maximum security ward. For the major part of their experience, the personnel had been working with an open ward and patients with short-term rather than chronic problems. The basic system accommodated itself and again the same process of developing a language unique to the personnel was used, rather than carrying over a predetermined policy from the other ward. The process of getting staff participation was still important but took a shorter time for us to develop. We found surprisingly few changes in the basic dynamic process. It remained difficult, however, for personnel to eat with patients. And the patients, accustomed to greater freedom, were more sensitive to the limits on their time and the problems of sleeping near the nursing station.

Our ward conferences also changed. Although the importance of the ward doctor remained, the nature and the use of my own power changed. The group generally felt that the change was one of softening. The "heaviness" of our conference and the base of power was changed in such a way that many times certain staff members, including myself, would be late or absent from a conference and the meeting would continue without a sense of someone important being missing. This change in the function of power was very profound and yet most difficult to describe.

We found it necessary to retain the role of charge nurse in order to maintain liaison between various hospital nursing functions with reports, committees, and schedules. We developed a separate role of therapy nurse, who became responsible for the specific therapeutic activities. In order to do this, we changed hours to enable the therapy nurse to be present for the noon and evening meals, when the patients returned to the ward from their work assignments, at the time the day staff reported to the evening staff, and when the red patients were put to bed.

The therapy nurse's function, as well as the change in function of all the personnel, became the pivotal point for the effectiveness of dynamic ward management. As the process developed, we found that all ward personnel attained a much higher level of importance and that there was a change in power structures and in male-female roles. It was as if we had added to the patriarchal system present in the regular institutional functioning a more matriarchal system in which all people, men and women, patients and staff, were accepted as important and different. In the latter kind of system function is more directly related to feelings and needs, as in our own family lives.

Even during these developments in my hospital experience, I still felt that I needed personal therapy in order to clarify my own confusions and my own change of power identification both for myself and for others. I needed help to clarify my religious and philosophical dilemmas. I resented the time and cost limits of analysis, but there were few briefer methods yet developed that could provide me useful short-term therapy.

I returned to Denver for my last year of residency, in which out-patient therapy and child psychiatry was stressed. The year was one of gentle integration. I found that I had matured in resolving some of my earlier conflicts. I had more security as a therapist, and I saw more clearly my desire to concentrate on administration and teaching. My desire for my own analysis was still strong.

I considered further training in an analytic institute and felt that although this would help me work better with individuals, it did not seem to help with some of my other wants. I considered private practice in either Denver or Dallas. I finally accepted the position of Chief of Psychiatry at the Veterans' Administration (VA) hospital in Dallas and a teaching position at Southwestern Medical School. In my new position I worked closely with all services to establish the concepts of dynamic ward management that I had used at the Sheridan VA hospital. The new program worked very well. The heavy influence of congruent concern and status again eliminated the need for isolation, seclusion, heavy medication, and electroshock treatment.

I enjoyed administrative work and teaching and felt that I was meeting a greater number of my needs. I took my psychiatric boards the same week in which we opened the new ward. The examinations were more comprehensive than I expected. I was examined by an analyst, which was a familiar experience, and I was presented a chronically ill patient, which was also familiar. At times, when there would be three or four examiners at a time, I was frightened that I was failing. Apparently, however, my blending of analytic training with psychiatric administration and the care of chronically ill patients was an asset since I passed the boards. The boards are an important tribal ritual of initiation. The trial is a shared experience; the notice of passing is solitary, quietly coming later, in the mail.

Later I decided to become the medical school's liaison consultant to the Terrell State Hospital in the establishment of a combined residency program. I developed further the concept of dynamic ward management, this time using residents instead of nurses and aides. The method was used in eleven different wards. I also entered part-time private practice at this time.

This was an exciting and full period for me. In my practice I was able to meet different personal needs. I worked more intensively with individuals. I began my analysis. I met the need of working with families by associating with a psychologist and a social worker who worked individually with the other members of a patient's family. I feel that intense therapy is enhanced by the support of primary people. Living with a person in therapy is not easy and family therapy helps.

I came to view therapy as having three aspects: intrapsychic, transference, and clarification of interpersonal relationships. In the first process, *intrapsychic,* the therapist learns about the patient, and, in sharing this knowledge with the patient, the therapist helps the patient to see himself or herself more clearly and more as a whole person. Repressed behavior, memories, and feelings are brought to the patient's awareness. Each new experience is integrated and related to what is already known, resulting in a greater ease of flow of awareness or association. As greater self-awareness is developed, the patient develops feelings about sharing this new self with another person. The nature of these new feelings is such that they are transferred from important people in the past to the therapist, and this is the development of the second aspect of therapy, *transference.* In the resolution of transference the patient comes to recognize himself or herself as a being separate from the therapist and to see the therapist also as a whole and separate person. With the support of this therapeutic alliance, the patient is now ready for the third aspect of therapy, the clarification of one's own interpersonal relationships and the recognition of one's transference to and from others. This third aspect is also called *working-through*.

Each patient has a personal set of priorities as does each therapist or each therapeutic modality. Often a patient's priorities may not fit his therapist's. One or the other must yield, and it is usually the patient. Any model of therapy is only partial unless it at some time deals with all of these three aspects.

It is important that learning to be a therapist not be a substitute for personal therapy or personal growth. I see personal therapy as an essential part of becoming a therapist, although becoming a therapist is certainly not the valid end-point of therapy. Furthermore, it is important that the intensity of personal therapy not become a substitute for excitement in our personal lives. Our patients need not be substitutes for our families and friends. On the other hand, in some way our families and friends must accommodate the risks and emotional demands of our learning and of our experiencing therapy.

The goals of personal therapy are to resolve the fear of confusion, of past-present-future, of truths and experience, of unconscious and conscious; the fear of certain feelings, intensities, situations; and to share first with the therapist the new skills that have developed and then to integrate the new, more whole self with one's family, friends, work, and community.

These changes, which are usually major, can pose threats to previous relationships. They can result in divorce, changes in modes of parenting, change of friends, or change of religion. Risks can often be avoided, however, by avoiding or interrupting meaningful personal therapy, which can be done by learning "about" therapy (without experiencing it and the risks), developing academic techniques, and becoming qualified or certified.

As my own analysis evolved, I came to value my dream life, to share with the therapist the array of intense feelings within me as an important part of my working-through, the third phase of therapy.

Joining a travel club enabled me to take frequent weekend trips during which there were opportunities to form friendships with people removed from the pressures of my own work, family, and local situation. Almost every skill or mood or attitude was available. I felt subsequently that people around me could find more clearly my anxiety levels, my need for stimulation, pleasure, and security. These needs were not fixed in strength, but rather included a range of intensity according to my energy level or according to the strength of the relationship involved at any given time. I appreciated the close friends who were willing to give me straight, level messages about themselves or voice their opinions of me and my behavior. I found this closeness to be another important part of my analysis.

In 1968 I continued my interest in Zen Buddhism by attending services in the San Francisco Zen Center and by being a guest at the Zen Monastary at Tasajara, near Monterrey, California. At the latter I came to experience first-hand the actual practice of Zen Buddhism and meditation. There were also opportunities for discussion with the Zen Master Shunryu Suzuki Roshi, as well as with other Zen students.

From Tasajara I was able to go to Esalen Institute where I naively signed up for an encounter workship with William Shutz. My contact with the Roshi had been an intensely profound and peaceful one. In contrast, at Esalen I felt totally disjointed, confused, disoriented, anxious, excited, alarmed, frightened, bored, judgmental, and impressed. I could not believe the intensity of moods that were created within me. I was involved in fantasy trips both as a participant and as an observer that were totally new experiences for me in my personal and professional life. I met Fritz Perls in the dining room and was aware of the esteem that others had for him and for Virginia Satir, but at the time I knew nothing of their importance. I returned reeling from that trip of 1968 and feeling that I had done very relevant things and had made good use of earlier therapy and knowledge of myself. I saw an opportunity to learn even more about myself in these methods of encounter.

I then began to work with Edward Maupin on body awareness and with Fritz Perls in Gestalt therapy. I was excited with Perls's blend of analysis, Zen, and psychodrama. I made arrangements to take part in, with my wife and our six children, a two-week workshop with Virginia Satir. This became a high point in my life during which I could integrate my own interests and those of my family. I became aware of the value of a workshop, which included the feeling of unlimited time with the therapist and the combination of work and play. Intense psychotherapy is the polar opposite of the workshop, but each has its unique value. To me, the ideal would be to have both if both had competent therapists. I was excited over the workshop model and anticipated its coming to Dallas.

Upon my return to Dallas from the workshop I contacted friends and colleagues to help organize HARA, a nonprofit community educational organization that sponsors experiential and didactic seminars in the behavioral sciences. It is a human growth center where skilled leaders like Virginia Satir are available for teaching, for providing therapy, or for conducting work-shops. This is an example of how personal experience, in this case mine, can be integrated into the community. The presence of important Gestalt therapists here led myself and others to form the Gestalt Institute of Dallas. Both organizations have brought to Dallas outstanding therapists such as Virginia Satir. HARA has also been a means of bringing to the area various educators and religious leaders such as the late Alan Watts and Lama Govinda and has provided opportunities for training in Aikido, Yoga, and T'ai Chi. Both in workshops and in organiza-tional work, HARA has continued to urge joint spouse participa-tion and has frequent programs for families, couples, and children while remaining open to single people. The variety of programming offers to me and to the community an opportu-nity to experience a wide variety of psychological, religious, and physical programs that are unique and innovative.

The many encounter groups have also put me in contact with people who have had prolonged therapy in modalities that I have not experienced, and with other people who have com-pleted formal analysis. The variety of programs in HARA has given my own patients opportunities to experience different therapists and programs presided over by skilled leaders.

I have come to see myself as a more open therapist, particu-larly with patients going through the later stage of therapy, the working-through process. I also find that their participation in encounter-type groups can add considerable reinforcement to individual therapy. For those patients who already have meaning-ful contact with a number of friends and family members, how-ever, there does not seem to be any comparable need.

My work in Rolfing, Alexander technique and Aikido has given me a more dynamic use of meditation, better concepts of energy flow, and a new quality of energy in myself as I work with various patients. I am less fatigued than before and no longer have my previously frequent backaches and neckaches. I have come to care more about the tensions of my body and the means of releasing them. I now have more energy available to focus on either the individual or the family dynamics with which I am working.

I wish to say again how important my personal background is to me and how important it is for me to "own" it as mine and not to presume it to be even of slight relevance to others. In reexaming early memories, I can more clearly see what I missed and can take more deliberate steps to make my present life more whole, to choose the use of my vacation time, to choose people for close friendships, to choose colleagues to enjoy. I can make better use of future workshops and therapies. I can keep attuned to my own authority system, my family, my politics, my church. I can maintain nourishing and relevant input from each of these as well as recognition and appreciation. I continue to use my dreams as a keystone of my life, as my basic source of energy, and as an awareness of direction. I have great joy and excitement in my fantasies, and I am learning to use them in a more creative way.

I am again aware of how important training is. Knowing the literature of the discipline and having supervised experience is important, as is having good and clear role-modeling, all of which I was fortunate to have. I know the value of knowledge of psychodynamics, psychopathology, and psychotherapeutic technique. I value my personal analysis and my marital and family therapy, as well as my Gestalt and psychodrama work. I value my conservatism and my risk-taking. I long for a greater knowledge of the life in and around me.

All these things I value for myself. In terms of training and personal growth I recommend them for other growing therapists. I trust that we as therapists will continue the open medical model of making our learning available freely to each other. I appreciate the willingness of our patients to trust us in areas in which trust is dangerous and to grow with us. I hope that we will indeed support the healing process and do as little harm as possible to ourselves, to each other and to our patients.

4 Becoming a Husband and Wife Social Worker Team

WILLIAM BERNING AND SHEILA BERNING

Before we go into any detail about how, emotionally and educationally, we as individuals and as a couple arrived at our present position as a therapy team, we would like to present the philosophy of therapy we have developed over the years. These concepts are a distillation of different experiences in our lives; they also stem from what we have done with ourselves and for others in holding a marital commitment to each other and allowing each other to grow emotionally.

The goal of therapy, as we view it, is to achieve some measure of authenticity or realness. All of us wear social masks. These hide our true inner feelings. In our day-to-day transactions with each other, we attempt to project to others how we wish to be perceived. However, this image may be in direct conflict with the way in which we truly see or feel about ourselves. Thus we may many times feel as though we are living a lie. We seem to be behaving and acting outwardly in a manner not congruent with how we feel inwardly.

An example of this might be an individual who has essentially a poor picture of himself as a person. For whatever reason, that individual perceives himself to be inadequate, stupid, and bumbling. In an effort to control these feelings — and not wishing anyone to know of these feelings — that individual attempts to compensate for these feelings by projecting an image of a calm, collected, well-controlled person. A person can many times project this outward image successfully to others, and no one else is aware of the deep inner, crawling feelings of inadequacy and insecurity. This dual state creates conflict in the person and he may feel "phoney" or even unreal. His inability to accept and deal with these feelings leads to a lack of genuineness on his part and produces senses of guilt, tension, and anxiety. But in reality it is not important how well we deceive others, for that can be done easily. What truly matters is an awareness that we are only deceiving ourselves.

The central difficulty with this way of thinking, however, is that our perception of ourselves is not always accurate. We may be seeing ourselves in a distorted mirror, a mirror distorted by time, by interaction with people in our lives who didn't know how to reward us for our strengths, and by a philosophy of life that dictates that we should constantly humble ourselves and never think ourselves worthy of praise or consideration.

Our philosophy of therapy is to work to help a person: (1) to reveal to another person his masks, to uncover his true identity; (2) to realize he is important as a person; and (3) to aid him to accept any bad feelings he may have about himself and to work through those feelings. Therapy therefore becomes a process between individuals through which the goal of true genuineness and authenticity is achieved, a process which culminates in an inner feeling of comfort and acceptance of himself as the kind of individual he really is. We think this can be achieved only in an intimate, caring, warm, and accepting therapeutic relationship. We believe that this relationship is not unlike the marital relationship, wherein one also strives for intimacy, closeness, and a sharing of genuine feelings.

We began working as a team primarily with married couples about five years ago. We have since concentrated our area of work on marital therapy, premarital therapy, and some marital enrichment workshops. More recently we have been actively involved in the Marriage Encounter movement, a Christian-oriented weekend communication experience for couples who basically have a good marriage, but one that simply lacks the zest and enthusiasm it originally had. Marriage Encounter had a healthy impact on our own relationship and has helped us form some of the therapeutic concepts we adhere to today.

Individually we had somewhat different educational experiences. While we both share a similar theoretical orientation to personality theory, our internships in graduate school were considerably different. I was exposed early in my internship to a family and marriage clinic, while Sheila's internship and interest was in the field of juvenile delinquency and probation work.

Our first becoming co-therapists in a married couples group five years ago was accidental. The therapist with whom I had been regularly working left the psychiatric setting of the group for another position. Sheila agreed to fill in until I could recruit another therapist partner. Our initial interaction was rough, like two pieces of sandpaper being rubbed together. We became competitive in therapy. It was a surprise to suddenly realize the impact this open interaction with each other was having on the couples in our group. They found our ability to show anger, competitiveness, and, later, tender feelings in front of the group a comfortable model to relate to. Our honest interaction with each other allowed other couples to show each other feelings that had been buried for years.

As a result of these realizations our confidence about a husband and wife working cooperatively with married couples increased to the point that we began giving marriage enrichment workshops through church groups, local professional organizations, and on our own initiative. We gradually moved from this area into premarriage workshops, with which we have had considerably positive community support. Overall, we think we have developed a style of operating and interacting with each other within married couples groups that has, interestingly enough, carried over into our own marriage. Our involvement in the Marriage Encounter movement has enabled us to solidify some relationship concepts more clearly and functionally.

Our view of emotional dysfunction is based on our experience of working with two people to strengthen an intimate relationship and on our educational background. We believe that an individual with emotional difficulties has a poor self-image and utilizes various false social masks so that his feelings about himself will not be perceived by others. The thinking behind this idea is that "if a person sees me as I truly see myself, they will not like me and I will feel a failure and a social reject." Our efforts in therapy then are to build self-esteem in individuals, capitalizing on and reinforcing their strengths. We try to help couples realize the positive impact they have on each other, which in turn boosts their own positive images and strengthens the relationship.

We view marital difficulties as essentially the projection on one spouse of the feelings of the other spouse arising from his or her poor self-image. The lower the image one has of himself, the more likely he is to find fault, criticize, or attack the other person. As each person acknowledges himself as a contributor in intimate or other relationships, he will relax and give more of himself to each human interaction he encounters.

We believe that emotional growth occurs as a result of a meaningful engagement between two individuals, one of whom is a *C*aring, *U*nderstanding, and *E*mpathetic person dedicated to helping the other person resolve the stress he feels. The first letters of each of these three traits make up what we call the

CUE to active psychotherapy. *C, caring,* means caring in a genuine and warm way about the individual with whom the therapist is involved at the moment, and at the same time caring about his uniqueness as an individual. The warmth and caring must be strong enough for the client to feel it emotionally and thus realize that the therapist truly cares about his well-being. It must also convey to the person under stress that the therapist views him as a worthwhile person and views his life circumstances in a nonjudgmental manner. The therapist conveys the uniqueness of the person's personality, points out to him his unique strengths and goodness, and helps him see how his poor self-image is making him nonproductive.

The *U* again is *understanding.* It means attempting to understand the client's view of his life circumstances at that particular point in time. Understanding involves reflecting back to the person in stress the perception the therapist has of where the client is and the client's understanding of himself at that period of his life. If the therapist cannot bring about understanding through active listening and personal feedback to the individual in distress, there will be little or no chance for an effective relationship to develop.

The last and most important tool in effective psychotherapy, *E,* is *empathy.* Empathy, the ability to put yourself in the shoes of someone else, is probably the most effective psychotherapeutic tool a therapist possesses, without which he, as a therapist, is impotent. Although the therapist must be empathetic with his client, he must keep the client's feelings from immobilizing both himself and the client, not letting them go on to grow from the revelation, knowledge, and awareness of the feelings. With empathy one can understand at a gut level the pain another person is experiencing as nearly as one can from one's own frame of reference. When empathy is practiced with a person under stress, be it a friend, client, or relative (e.g., one's spouse), the feeling is conveyed that the therapist is really attempting to get into what they are feeling, striving to identify with those feelings as best he can. In our estimation empathy is the real *CUE* and the clue to effective therapy.

We did not arrive at *CUE* overnight. It took many years of struggle to develop these three traits in our individual lives. Fifteen years of marriage and considerable contact with people in pain — both friends and clients — enforced our gradual realization that the above traits are important in the resolution of profound emotional dysfunction in a distressed individual.

We have concluded that the use of *CUE* in the therapist-client relationship is not very different from its use in the marriage relationship, and we have found that it is as effective in one as it is in the other. For a marriage to be effective, one must *care* about the other person's needs, security, and personal concerns. Each must strive to *understand* the feelings of the other person, and each must be capable of *empathizing* or taking on the feelings of the other person as best he can. This leads to a bonding relationship and a sense of commitment toward the other individual in both kinds of relationship, which in turn leads to the ability of each marital partner or the client to have enough confidence to solve his difficulties.

Our emotional growth as individuals has been due to our giving to each other, in a totally accepting way, "growing room." We have allowed each other to explore relationships outside of our own, to delve into other people's ideas, without either of us feeling threatened. This growth, and our improved self-images, stems from our realization that we have had a strong impact on the positive growth of another human being. We recognize that the basis of high self-esteem is the awareness of the personal contribution one has to offer others and the subsequent positive impact that that has on others. This awareness in turn leads to a feeling of self-worth and gives the reassurance that one is indeed a worthwhile person. This recognition leads from there to a healthy, positive feeling about oneself, which can contribute to positive feelings to others. We now view our therapeutic role as that of a mirror to the individual(s) in distress. We reflect back the basic goodness an individual has to offer others, something he may not be aware he has because of his own inner feelings of inadequacy and his preoccupation with thoughts of his own poor self-image. Once we are able to uncover and deal effectively with the negative self-image and help the individual realize he has a great deal of love and caring to offer other people, we see growth in that person. He grows by becoming more positive toward himself and by beginning to reach out to others in a more caring and empathetic way.

In essence, then, our active therapy involves helping people learn how to *love.* Love, in our conceptual understanding, encompasses all aspects of the *CUE* to effective therapy previously discussed. But we also like to view love as defined by Harry Stack Sullivan in his book *Conceptions of Modern Psychiatry:* "When the satisfaction, security and development of another person become as significant to you as your own satisfaction, security and development, love exists" [1] . Love means the ability to readily forego one's own convenience, invest one's own time, and even to risk one's own security to promote the security and development of the other person. Unless one is able to adequately love the person in distress, personal and emotional growth will not occur.

An effective therapist must be open to developing his ability to care, understand, and empathize with another human being. He must be aware of *his* masks, which hide his own inner bad self-image, and be willing to expose his inner feelings in an intimate relationship with others. In short, the therapist must be vulnerable and capable of risking his feelings with those for whom he cares. He must be willing to become more self-aware, to explore his innermost feelings, and to develop relationships in which he can share these inner processes.

REFERENCE

1. Sullivan, H. S. *Conceptions of Modern Psychiatry.* New York: Norton, 1953.

5 Becoming a Nurse Therapist

MARY JO TRAPP BULBROOK

In this chapter we have comments of graduate students on their becoming psychosocial nurse therapists and a condensation of comments of undergraduate students on becoming psychosocial nurses. They discuss how they feel about their work, their growth struggles through school and clinical work, and how they have handled problems and growth experiences. Their suggestions as to what faculty should or should not do to help students develop as therapists could be useful to teachers or therapist makers and could provide guidelines to validating the teacher/ student growth process.

GRADUATE STUDENT NARRATIVES ON BECOMING A NURSE THERAPIST

STUDENT A

My growth struggle to become a therapist began when I entered that portion of graduate school devoted to clinical work. Learning the various theories, principles, concepts, and techniques; seeing and feeling from the clients' frames of reference; identifying problems; setting goals — all these aspects of my education to this point had to be assimilated before I could successfully apply them in the clinical area.

Establishing a relationship with a client was not difficult for me. The clients understood that I was there to help them with their problems. As they began learning new ways of solving their problems, I encouraged them, expressed pride in them, and rejoiced with them in their growth; I also experienced their setbacks and sorrows. Each growth change in a client helped me to become more self-confident as a therapist. The positive reinforcement that I received from the staff at the Mental Health Center also increased my confidence. Not having had previous experience as a therapist, I was motivated to read more and study harder, and I enjoyed every minute of it.

Faculty members noticed my personal growth as well as my growth in the clinical area. They worked with me to develop the essentials needed for expertise. Different teachers with expertise in the field who were willing to share their personal experiences provided valuable interaction and a sharing of knowledge. Interaction in the classroom setting provided not only shared experiences with other students but also a clashing of personal philosophies and values. We found, however, that we could have violent arguments yet still remain friends. Teachers carefully observed the process of these interactions while we were all caught up in the content, the source, in my own case, of much difficulty.

I found my greatest difficulty to be learning to become process-oriented rather than content-oriented. I had to consciously think of asking for the feelings that the client was trying to convey and had to clarify communications between us. Sometimes I was wrong; I would ask the client to correct me if I did not identify the feelings correctly. Many times the client would deny angry feelings, and we would work together through gut reactions, hurt feelings, and being upset, finally reaching the point where feelings were acknowledged, recognized, and accepted. Progress was then made toward learning to deal with the feelings. The universality of the problems of different clients was a revelation to me. I learned that many clients have strong parental injunctions that they still take for granted and carefully obey. I also learned that when this was the case, short-term therapy was not enough to handle these problems. The problem at hand took priority, although it was difficult for me not to deal with the problems that were really the basis for the presenting problem. The client was content to live with these underlying problems, not realizing that they *were* problems. Maybe I was expecting to accomplish too much too soon.

Throughout my learning experience my greatest success was in building relationships with my clients so that they felt comfortable with me. Whether in group therapy, crisis intervention, or individual therapy, even when I didn't say the "right" words, clients knew that I cared about them and was doing my best to help them. They knew that I was learning and that in helping them I was increasing my knowledge; they felt that they were contributing to my knowledge — and they did. Termination was always difficult for both myself and my client, but each enabled me to experience a real feeling of accomplishment and pride in the changes that I saw in both of us.

I believe that the most important contribution that faculty can make toward helping students is to encourage them to be themselves and to emphasize their positive qualities, and through constructive criticism to assist them in becoming better therapists. Giving immediate feedback and always being available for conferences when improvement is needed — these things make the student feel that the teacher is taking an interest in her as a person.

I do not believe that the classroom should be the setting for a therapy session unless both teacher and student agree. Faculty should not hesitate to contact the clinical area for reports on a student's progress. If classes are well planned, interesting, and informative, all students can share their experiences and all can learn. Group process offers an excellent opportunity for students to share their feelings in an atmosphere of confidentiality and warmth. Being a participant-observer in such an experience was most helpful to me. It contributed greatly to helping me personally and professionally.

I believe that every student has the potential for being a success. Sometimes it only takes someone else to point them in the right direction. That is why we have teachers — to help us to find ourselves, to appreciate our efforts, not to expect too much perfection, to allow us to be ourselves so that we can become therapists and then do the same for our clients.

STUDENT B
In becoming a therapist I had to cope first with my own growth struggle in graduate school in general.

I had five years' experience in working with psychiatric clients in an in-patient setting. Because there was no close and continuous patient observation, I found it was difficult to make as accurate an assessment and nursing diagnosis in an out-patient unit with less patient contact, as I had done in graduate school. This factor strengthens my belief in the extreme advantage the nurse in the hospital setting has and the importance that the multidisciplinary approach has in assisting the client.

All during graduate school I found it necessary to continually reassess and reaffirm my values. This was stressful but rewarding.

During this time also I was validating my philosophy in the clinical area. This was exceptionally valuable in that I was able to evaluate if the academic philosophy of therapy was applicable to a real situation with real clients. As a therapist this was very sobering to me since I was made acutely aware of my professional and human responsibility to the client.

Another major growth struggle involved actual client contact. My aim was to be therapeutically objective while extending my experience but at the same time be involved in therapy with a client. This was valuable experience, but difficult, for there were many processes happening concurrently. An example is that though I was not sure that I had carried some of my patients long enough in individual therapy, there was no choice but to terminate their therapy. In many cases there was unfortunately no other available therapist to carry on individual therapy.

The third and last major area of growth struggle was a personal and sometimes painful one. It involved dealing with conflicts of finances, career objectives, and what was or was not offered in the graduate school I attended. Compromises made in these areas to meet overall objectives continually presented many problems.

There are certain things I believe faculty can do to help students. Faculty should:

1. Help students select courses most helpful to each student's goals.
2. Give support and information, allowing students to progress at their own pace, within reason.
3. Encourage independent ideas.
4. Advocate that the university employ a consultant for students without charge to the student or at student rates. This consultant should otherwise be independent of the university. The student could of course choose a consultant from outside if he wished.
5. Accept that all students have different and varied reasons for whatever goals they have in relation to graduate school.

There also are two things I feel faculty should not do in regard to students: They should not:

1. Insist upon students following any one philosophy of therapy, unless this is made clear in the school bulletin and stated as school policy.
2. Insist that a student see a professional therapist unless this too is specified as school policy and is made available.

STUDENT C
My personal growth struggle to become a therapist was so intertwined with my growth and maturation as a person that it is difficult to separate the two. My background clinically was as a

medical surgical nurse and as a school nurse. I knew that I needed to improve my communication skills, and psychiatric mental health nursing was the way I chose to do this. Dealing with feelings was a completely new experience for me even though I truly thought I always had. How wrong I was. The theories we were exposed to helped greatly in developing my own stated philosophy of being a therapist. Each time I was assigned to report on my philosophy I found that it and I had grown and matured as I understood more. And I am sure it will continue to change the more I teach, experience, and read.

My greatest struggle has been to read widely enough to objectively choose, from among many theorists, my own framework within which to work. Once I got a good foundation, I was in good shape to do constructive therapy. As I grew as a person and gained more self-confidence, I began to be able to see the client as an individual and relate to him in a helping way. My awareness is so great now of how much more I need to learn that it is often overwhelming. My desire is to learn more and grow in depth and understanding to the point where I can truly feel I am continually dealing with the client on an emotional level.

There are some things I feel that faculty can do to help students over and above the imparting of information. First and foremost, faculty need to be caring human beings, not teaching machines. They need to learn the value of self-disclosure with students and get to know them as individuals, not just students. Faculty can and should state the objectives of their courses in specific behavioral statements. Structured requirements should be written so that the student will understand fully what is expected. An instructor who is having trouble communicating with students should be made aware of this and should make every effort to remedy the situation. Faculty should give mid-semester evaluations so the student can know her difficulties and deficiencies and have time to improve. In some courses, particularly beginning clinical courses, more structure is needed. Student-taught seminars are also most helpful.

On the other hand, I feel that there are many things faculty should not do for or to students. I saw some really traumatic things happen to some of my classmates. Some of the pressures from faculty were for the student's own good and professional growth and were taken as such. Some instructors in their zeal as therapists, however, decided that particular students who resisted personal therapy within a class situation still were in need of therapy. I personally saw one instructor insist that a brilliant student go to a psychiatrist of the instructor's (not the student's) choice before she could pass the course. As it turned out, it was the instructor, not the student, who needed the therapy.

It is unfair to the student for faculty members to decide that a particular student would have trouble in one class just because she had trouble in another. Faculty should also be aware that there can be conflicts between a student and one teacher that might not be present between the same student and another instructor. Instructors should not discuss their dislike of a student so as to bias the observations and supervision of that student made by another teacher. Instructors should try to be fair to each and every student, judging on merit, not heresay from a biased professional. This may be difficult to do, as instructors naturally discuss their students among themselves, but I do feel that this is completely fair to the student.

Instructors should counsel students to the best of their ability but not give therapy unless the student specifically asks for it.

REVIEW OF COMMENTS OF UNDERGRADUATE STUDENTS ON BECOMING A PSYCHOSOCIAL NURSE

A group of undergraduate junior nursing students gaining their psychiatric nursing clinical experience evaluated their educational experience as follows.

Negative comments concerned feelings of faculty aloofness and a lack of role-modeling. They in particular disliked a teacher lecturing on material out of her field. The students were perceptive and were aware that the teacher lacked depth and integrated knowledge. This left them very angry and feeling that they had been short-changed, initiating a process destructive to the educational goal.

The students emphasized the lack of cohesion between objectives, responsibilities, teaching methods, and evaluation. They complained that testing became a ritual of the student trying to find out what the teacher wanted rather than a proof that the student knew the theory behind practice.

When there was conflict between students and faculty, the students felt that they had no voice in protecting or defending themselves during evaluation of their educational experiences, or in providing actual input to the curriculum. Meetings established to meet criteria of accrediting agencies were in fact only meaningless rituals.

Evaluation was not seen as a growth-promoting experience necessary to provide guidance to the learner or as a method of ensuring high standards in the profession. It seemed rather to be task-oriented, geared at *eliminating* students.

Students were very explicit about the positive qualities teachers should have. They indicated that they wanted faculty to possess and exhibit the following: helpfulness, openness, sensitivity, flexibility, and fairness, and the ability to stimulate thinking, provide encouragement, be interested in the subject, and be well organized.

When students go through their psychiatric rotation, they always look at themselves. They become very introspective and frequently are preoccupied with the mental health or illness of themselves and that of their own family and friends. This — I call it "going through psych" — has occurred with *every* student I have taught. For some this process takes longer or is more pain- ful or traumatic. Usually after they are through it, they can then get back to the educational goal. Until education adjusts to this phenomenon, however, we will be overlooking an important learning block. Students, too, should know ahead of time what they are in for, and evaluation of the educational objectives must not be confused with the therapy process. I personally feel that psychiatry must develop a growth-promoting evaluation tool that would include professional data, content, and process, while at the same time accounting for use of self as a therapeutic agent.

Students want to think for themselves and increase their sense of responsibility for their own professional and personal growth. They expect honesty and desire mutual trust. They want the opportunity to ask questions without being penalized. If they cannot be self-directed, they expect a teacher to provide the stimulus for accepting responsibility. They look for and expect role models in clinical *and* professional practice. Their attitudes concerning effective, competent nurses involved in the community and their profession are formed from their view of the instructors.

One very important point to be gleaned from this is that *students can easily pick out teachers who don't practice what they preach!* They look to see if the teacher knows current prac- tice, and is active in the nursing organization and community. They frequently ask me in exasperation, "Why do they expect us to do what they don't do?" Where is the credibility factor? What are we *really* teaching? Behavior speaks louder than words.

Each school needs to really listen to its students and decide for itself where it fits in the above comments. Some schools are not as effective as they could be because they don't listen! In this day of accountability to consumers, teachers will soon be forced to do what they should have already done as professionals.

6 Becoming a Therapy Consumer

MARY JO TRAPP BULBROOK

This chapter offers a unique view of psychotherapy — that of the client. I believe that we, as professionals, must listen carefully to those who utilize our services; we must make sure we are indeed providing that which we claim to provide.

PAIN TRANSFORMED: NEW JOY = NEW LIFE
BEVERLY W. COON

We've come a long way, Baby! . . . since Clifford Beers, author of *A Mind That Found Itself,* dedicated his life to the improvement of institutional care for the insane after his stay as a patient in several mental institutions.

We've come a long way, Baby! . . . in my own community when mentally ill persons were often detained in our local jails and treated as criminals until the establishment of a psychiatric unit in a major hospital. It now handles crisis situations and a person can be hospitalized for short-term care and evaluation.

We're come a long way, Baby! . . . since the days we used to "warehouse" the mentally ill, committing them to institutions for often the remainder of their lives. We now know that better treatment can be effected by treating the patient in the community; first, if possible, with out-patient care and then, if necessary, hospitalization near home and family and friends for as short a time as possible. This is the community mental health concept.

Yes, we've come a long way, Baby! But we've still got a long way to go, for the word *therapy* is still very threatening to many people. It seems to indicate that there's something *Wrong* with me. This feeling is difficult for me to acknowledge and for other people to accept.

I am a consumer. I am many faces, but whatever my face you can be sure there is some pain registered there, unless I have learned to wear my mask well. Please look behind my mask. Help me break down my walls and help me share my pain with you.

When I first make contact with you I'm scared, for in most instances this is a first experience for me and I do not know what will happen. If my first contact with you is by phone, it helps if the voice at the other end of the line seems to have some understanding of my problem and some empathy with my pain, for I am hurting. In many instances it is a new kind of pain, and I do not know what to do about it or how to deal with it. It would also be very helpful if I could get some hint of what will happen to me when I first come to you. I feel very much alone and isolated. It hasn't helped me much for well-meaning persons to tell me that I shouldn't feel this way. I already know *that!* But the fact is, I *do* and *I'm scared!*

Since you are of many disciplines and I am aware that there is more than one way to treat a person who is hurting, I am not as concerned about the particular treatment modality you sub-scribe to as I am about the way you handle me as a hurting human being. Sometimes you may employ several modalities. I may not know where one stops and the other begins, but I will be keenly aware when you touch my pain.

It is not easy for me to ask for help, for I have been "pro-grammed" to believe that I ought to be able to take care of my own problems. When things are going well, who needs you? But now they are not; I feel pain and I don't know why. My coming to you will mean that I must reveal my darkest secrets, my inner-most self, and I'm not sure that I am ready.

I have heard many rumors about asking for help, some of which could indeed prove true. I may lose my job if I get mental health help. I may not be able to get a driver's license in the event I am treated by a psychiatrist — at least they asked me if I had been treated when last I renewed my current license. The stigma may follow me the rest of my days, so even in my despair I must make a decision: is it worth the price? For I am still risk-ing that you may not help me.

I've also heard rumors about some of you. Some of your fees are very high. When there's only a chance that you can help me, is it worth the monetary sacrifices that my family and I will be required to make to pay the bill? I've read that some of your disciplines have the highest rate of suicide in the nation. I've been told, more particularly by skeptics and gossips, that many of you have had individual and family problems of your own. Why then should I trust you with mine? I have also heard that you may try to keep me dependent upon you for the rest of my life. After weighing all this, I must then convince myself that you the therapist and I the consumer need to trust each other. And so I begin my therapy.

It has helped me greatly that in our first personal contact you have shown me warmth and tenderness and have made me aware that you care about me, regardless of my sex, race, age, or any other factor that might make us different from each other. I still have the basic human needs, one of which is to be accepted as I am.

I am mindful of the fact that you may try to change me, and I'm scared. For the old patterns, although often very destructive, have in many instances become comfortable, or at least I have been able to tolerate the discomfort until now. But now, aware of the fact that you may be asking me to enter into an unknown world, to become a different person, my level of uncertainty rises even higher.

Who am I? I am a middle-aged woman whose husband died prematurely and left me with two teenage children to raise alone. I am faced with many decisions. Do I let my "good mother tapes" keep me from making a life for myself?

I am a male facing retirement. Can I ever readjust from a hectic schedule to one with much leisure time?

I am a teenage girl. I now find myself pregnant. I cannot tell my family. What do I do? Where do I turn?

I am terminally ill with cancer and I want to talk about it to somebody. My family members do not seem to understand how important this is to me. I wish they wouldn't treat my impending death in such a hush-hush way.

I am a woman whose 30-year marriage seems to be disintegrating. I do not wish to burden my family or friends with my problem. To whom do I turn? I feel like such a failure.

I am a young mother who must stay at home with several small children. I do not have the money for babysitters, nor are any available through family members. I feel trapped. I know that if I don't get some relief soon, I will do something terrible to one of my babies. I feel so ashamed and scared.

I am the father of a handicapped child. I feel so helpless. I also feel guilty. What have I done that my child should suffer so?

I am 8 years old. My mom and dad don't love me as much as they do my 12-year-old sister, so I do bad things. At least when I do, I get their attention.

I am 79 years old. I live alone and I am very lonely. I wish my children and grandchildren would come around more often, but they are too busy. I feel so useless. I wish I could die.

I don't know what's the matter with me, but I feel like a spring that is ready to fly apart. Please help me make some sense out of what's happening.

I have been crying on the inside for a long time. Now I am crying on the outside. I can't seem to stop.

I begin to pour out my heart to you, the therapist, and my mask slips just a little. Thus is marked the beginning of the journey you and I will take in search of myself!

I begin to learn many things, the most important of which is the fact that *I* am responsible for what I am feeling and how I respond to that feeling. I also now see that my personal growth process must necessarily include *unlearning* and *relearning.* One of my problems, you see, is that I have seen you the therapist as only that, a therapist, a professional to see only in crisis situations. I had never before viewed you and your fellow "people helpers" as professionals to help me *prevent* crisis situations. I now know that had I contacted one of you a long time ago to help me find a direction and to help me learn ways to reach my potential more fully, I would have prevented many problems I have made for myself in the past. At least I am very thankful that now I am learning skills to prevent my everyday concerns from mushrooming into crisis situations in the future.

I have learned in therapy that I have *options.* This has become a new word in my conscious vocabulary, for I was never offered any options as a growing child in my family. I therefore never learned how to receive options for myself nor how to give them to others. I am learning that now, and I am happier with myself as a result.

I am developing the courage to be imperfect. Many of us are all too eager to assess fault and place blame — on someone else! We all need to be able to assume responsibility for our errors. I therefore need fewer scapegoats than I used to. Hopefully, when I really grow up emotionally I won't need any at all!

I am learning that there are no right or wrong options, even though factual questions may have right or wrong answers. I am learning that I am free to make my own judgments, to have an opinion different from someone else's, and to feel OK about it. I am getting a new lease on life in learning to trust in myself, no matter what others might think or say.

It is a liberating experience to realize that I am free to be . . . me! I am relearning that I do not have to respond in *any* way, if

I so choose. I do not have to become defensive nor do I have to bite back. I am still trying to learn to let others have their say, their feelings, their inadequacies, their hang-ups, without trying to change them or redo them. Often this is a very difficult task because I feel so good after changing myself that I sometimes "crusade" too strongly for others to change; and I have found that that can alienate them. Some people, in their apathy, seem to enjoy misery. I must make myself understand that this is their right, their choice!

I can now affirm more sincerely that *I have value.* A saying I read recently — "God don't make no junk" — is more meaning-ful, and believable. I am learning to give to others and to receive for myself unconditional love. The kind of love that says "I love you for *being*" is so much greater than the conditional love mes-sage "I love you for *doing.*"

I am learning *healthy selfishness.* Most of us are taught from childhood that to think of ourselves first is wrong and sinful. As a result, we feel great guilt when we feel we *must* put self above others for whatever reason, even one of survival. But we must take for ourselves a creed that will allow us the freedom to be honest, to like or dislike, to cry, frown, laugh, and still know that we are not bad, that we are merely living our humanity. Robert Louis Stevenson wrote over 100 years ago, "To be what we are, and to become what we are capable of becoming, is the only end of life."

I am learning to listen. To be able to voice *feelings* to some-one is a privilege few know how to take. Even fewer know how to really listen and to hear. Because of these lacks, too many of us are filled with pain that gradually becomes hate, distrust, dis-gust, disillusionment toward someone whom we once loved very much, someone who doesn't understand the need to listen. In such a situation, if one is to survive emotionally, one looks at the options, chooses the one appearing the most constructive for oneself, and proceeds to live. A safe sounding board is helpful at these times.

I am learning to use my anger in a constructive way. I now know that it's acceptable for me to lose my temper, to show anger and displeasure. I've known for a long time that because showing anger was unacceptable to some of my loved ones, I was beginning to hate, to turn away, to feel rejected, to know great pain. When at last I was able to make myself heard, much of my pain disappeared. Now I know "I'm not bad just 'cause I get mad!"

I am learning and accepting the fact that I can't be all things to all people. Even though I don't know everything, I'm still OK. I can't have, and don't have to have, the solution for every problem brought to me by someone else. But I *can* say, "I'm sorry you are hurting; I'll give you my loving support while *you* decide which solution feels right for you."

I am learning the value of fun, although the fun may result from different activities than it once did. I am insisting upon being allowed to play, to be a child at times, to have fun. I can always return to my adult world when the situation calls for it and be refreshed for having been silly or childlike for awhile. When I was down on myself all the time, I was unable to demand this for myself.

I am learning to live, which is quite a different experience from existing. When feelings are joyful each day is welcome, for something wonderful is bound to happen, even if it is only that at the day's end you realize that you made it through whatever came. But even more than that, when you feel good, you want to *do* something. You don't want the day to just hurry up and end so you can go to sleep and forget about hurting until you wake up next morning. You realize that life is to live . . . not just to flounder painfully through.

I am learning that feelings are "catching." When feelings are good, the condition is like a communicable disease. (Unfortunately painful feelings are contagious, too, and many who are hurting want everyone else to hurt too.) It has given me great pleasure to recognize some spillover, however tiny, of my joy in the past few years. I hadn't always realized how little it takes to make some people smile, how infectious my own good feelings could be at times. My joy in myself has made me much more capable of being a friend, of loving — in all the different ways one loves.

Let me now try to explain some of my personal joy and share more concisely what it's like to feel good:

I know that if I want to be loved, I must allow it. I must disclose myself. It's great to feel good enough to be able to do this.

Feeling good means I'm free to be me. I no longer have to think up ways to avoid letting other people know the real me!

Feeling good means I've the courage to confront reality even when it's painful.

Feeling good means I live my life, that I don't sleepwalk through it — as someone said, "Living life — not letting life live me."

I can and do touch people often. This is important to me. I like to touch and I like to be touched. I have yet to be aware of anyone whom I've touched being offended. This feels good.

I know that getting rid of anger allows loving feelings to freely flow toward people closest to me. This feels good.

I can know myself now, and I must never again be a stranger to myself. I now know that I'm the best friend I have. It feels good to be convinced that I am quite an addition to my list of friends!

I am very aware now that it is difficult for someone else to injure me if I don't first place the weapon in his hand.

Good feelings about myself have given me what might be called "emotional surefootedness" in matters that in the past would have decimated me.

Feeling good means so many things, so many people, are treasurable to me. And I am learning to treasure *me*.

Feeling good means that there no longer is a hollowness, an emptiness in the center of my being. My life at any given time can be as full as I choose to make it. I've found that the choice is mine.

Joyful feelings make me know that "there is no relationship between external and internal success." Sidney Harris wrote that in one of his columns and I say a loud "Amen."

Good feelings take away the feeling of isolation, make possible tranquility in human relationships. I'm able to make genuine contact with another mind and spirit. *I'm aware. I can share.* I'm no longer lonely, often.

Second-guessing and chastisement of myself is almost a thing of the past. Little time is spent these days whipping myself. And this feels good.

I don't have to be a martyr for anyone for any reason. This feels good also.

I know I'm not perfect. I'm glad I don't want to be. I don't have to appear so to anyone. This feels good.

Feeling good means I no longer depend on others to define myself. No external validation gives me the feeling of self-worth that my own inner security gives me.

I am grateful to you, the therapist, for this new insight and awareness. Thank you for giving me *new life!*

MENTAL ILLNESS: A PRISON
MARY NELL ROBERTSON

[I am particularly pleased about the following contribution. Mary has a unique source of information: first-hand experience.

She has been involved with psychiatric services since she was 14 years old. She is now 31 years old and had been in and out of hospitals for years. At one point she totally lost contact with reality, and it appeared that she would spend the rest of her life in an institution.

In 1973 my graduate students and I came in contact with Mary. She participated in our group therapy while in the hospital and then as an out-patient. As of 1976 she called me and said she is well. And I know she is right. We both know she will have hard times — a fact of life — but she now feels she is important to herself and others.

"Mary, you've come a long way." This book is dedicated to you and those like you. Thank you for sharing yourself with us and others who are now studying to be therapists. We will listen so others can be helped. Forgive us for not listening sooner when your voice was weak. Ed.]

People behind bars are not the only people locked in prison. Most of us are locked up in prisons of our own making. Fear is a prison. We can be paralyzed by fear. Fear can keep us locked in our shells; it keeps us from doing the things necessary to pierce our shells and become a living part of the world around us. The maximum security cell in the prison of fear is the state in which we are immobilized by the fear of making a decision. People can really be afraid of making the simplest decisions.

Another form of fear is the "passion for self-distrust." This lack of faith in ourselves keeps us locked securely in our cells. How can we have faith in ourselves? Our judgment has been proved wrong repeatedly. Even when it told us to be confident, we made a mistake and ended up locked-in again. This fear of making mistakes keeps us in a prison of the status quo. We're afraid to venture out and try new things, afraid to make decisions. We might get hurt that way. Failure to risk something can keep us in a rut and in a state in which we don't mind our padded cell, the one padded with security and routine, the one in which our basic needs are met. You see, finding the key to getting out of one prison enables us to get out of the next one. We have to do it step-by-step and be satisfied with small gains.

Fears are myriad and strange (these are just a few) but they are nonetheless *very real* to the person experiencing them.

Prejudice is another prison, but the key to this one is in someone else's hand. Prejudice is felt by people who are nervous, by mental patients, by epileptics, and by those who are handicapped. These people have to lie, in some instances, in order to get a job to put food on their table and clothes on their back.

The tragic part is that these people ask only for a chance to have a job and lead a normal life. In many cases they have the ability to be useful, productive citizens. Instead they remain locked in their prison because society is too prejudiced to allow them a chance to develop into the persons God intended them to be. Society has a firm grip on the key to this prison, keeping the people in prison and supporting them with their tax dollars, not making an effort to help them help themselves. *It's easier to give money than it is to give of yourself.*

A shell is another type of prison. Buffeted about and knocked back every time we attempt to advance, we retreat into our shell and spin fantasies. As time passes this shell can become many layers thick. We become like turtles — afraid to stick our necks out unless we can quickly retreat.

Solitary confinement is one of the most miserable kinds of prisons. We're afraid of other people and don't even like or trust ourselves. And solitude with someone you dislike — yourself — can be very tiresome. This self-disgust really makes us miserable. Since we are alone we dwell on our problems and get even more depressed. Unable or unwilling to accept ourselves, we are pre-vented from accepting others. This in turn reinforces our soli-tude and makes us rely totally on our own resources, even though we don't even believe in ourselves. It becomes a vicious cycle.

Loneliness is another type of prison. We fence ourselves in behind our walls. We feel sorry for ourselves and yet we're too afraid to break down the walls and try to associate with people. Fear keeps us locked in. Even when we venture out into a crowd, the shell we can't get out of makes us feel even lonelier. Loneli-ness can cause depression, another type of prison we lock our-selves into. We dwell on our problems and then wonder why we are depressed. Not going anywhere only makes it worse. Depres-sions can be manufactured by our self-destructive behavior.

Anxiety is still another one of our fears. Because we don't trust ourselves, we are even more fearful of the future.

There are many types of prisons, but just as we lock ourselves in prison, we also have the keys to the prison within ourselves if we only have the courage to use them.

The Keys to Our Prisons
The key to the door leading out of the prison of fear is simply facing the fear and doing the thing we are afraid to do. That is really hard, but it works every time! The paralyzing grip of the decision-making fear can be broken by making one simple

decision at a time and praising ourselves each time we make a decision. When we praise ourselves we feel secure, and when we feel secure we perform in a sure and confident manner.

The key that unlocks the prison cell of the passion for self-distrust is believing in yourself. You *are* an important person. Give yourself praise every time you do something positive. Even if you try and fail, praise yourself for the effort you put forth and for having the guts to give it another try. Having spontaneity and the courage to make mistakes also will help you break out of this prison. Have faith in yourself. You are never hopeless. I know this from personal experience. In order to get well, I had to believe in myself at a time when I had lost contact with reality. I finally did believe in myself and got well. Try new things. Be spontaneous. Security is strictly dullsville! Become a living part of the world around you and be willing to take risks. It's worth it.

Prejudice can be overcome when we realize that it doesn't matter what other people think as long as *we* believe in ourselves. People will give you a chance if you are willing to give yourself a chance. Make your own luck. Take charge of your future in a confident manner. You *can* make your life what you want it to be. I know. I'm doing it. We can't prevent prejudice or the impact it has on our lives, but we can change our attitudes toward it. You can't control the other person, but you *can* control yourself.

The way to break through our shells is to attack them, one layer at a time. We would like to retain our shells so we can retreat from reality if we feel it's becoming too much for us. This can be conquered by facing reality and coping with it successfully. Each time we do this we become stronger and more capable of independent action. We have to have the courage to make mistakes and to trust our basic functions in spite of the fact that it seems as if we've been knocked back every time we've tried to get going! Confidence gets stronger each time we believe in ourselves and face reality. It's not that bad really. In fact, you get a really good feeling from facing reality and coping with it. Accepting responsibility for your actions combats the tendency to retreat and spin fantasies. Turtles who retreat and never stick their necks out miss a lot of the good things of life. So stick your neck out, even if only an inch at a time, and learn to enjoy living.

Learning to be your own best friend certainly helps make solitary confinement more bearable! In turn liking and accepting yourself will enable you to accept others. It works every time.

Think of others, get involved, stop dwelling on your own problems, and solitary confinement will become a thing of the past. When you like and accept yourself, being alone at times can even be fun.

Loneliness can be conquered by mixing with and listening to other people. Venture out and do new things. Cultivate outside interests, and you'll meet people you have something in common with. Accept yourself! Relate to people even if you have to force yourself to. It gets easier each time you do it. Maybe the other person is just as lonely as you are and wants to be your friend. Reach out to other people. Stop enforcing the strength of loneliness by playing the game of "poor me." Count your many blessings instead.

Counting our blessings also helps banish depression. Think about others and do something for them. Get out and do things. Thinking and acting positively are two keys that are guaranteed to unlock the cell of depression. Anxiety can be counteracted by trusting. Trust is the key to the prison of anxiety because anxiety feeds on fear, and trust is just the opposite of fear. Trust the future, live in the present, and start each day by believing in yourself and trusting and believing that it will be a good day for you; then make it a good day by thinking and acting positively.

We really can let ourselves out of prison if we will use our keys and escape into the mainstream of life once more.

How Therapists Helped Me

I was really helped when I was accepted and liked in spite of everything, even when I goofed. The most helpful thing anyone ever did was first to look at me and see that I could be a winner and then help me to become that. Therapists have been patient with me and let me progress at my own pace unless I really needed to be prodded out of the rut I was in.

When there were really a lot of obstacles to be overcome, my therapist took the attitude "It's no hill for a stepper." So I took my first faltering steps and started climbing, one at a time, the hills I had to get over to get well. The first time I ever tried to stand on my own two feet, I fell flat on my face. My therapist made sure no one came charging to my rescue. I rescued myself, learned how to cope with adversity in a positive way, and turned a lemon into a lemonade.

Therapists let me make mistakes and learn from them. I was allowed to use my own judgment, even though the therapists were wise enough to know it was bad. The only way I know for nervous people to learn to trust their judgment is by trial and error. They have to work at exercising and developing their own judgment, because previously everyone made decisions for them. The therapists let me use them for reality testing, and I finally learned to trust my judgment.

I was given the chance to make major decisions when I was a patient. This helped me learn to make decisions and to take responsibility for myself.

Therapy helped me to realize that I really am no different from other people. I had been treated differently since I was 14, and I actually believe I *was* different until a therapist made me realize I wasn't. This helped me to like myself in spite of everything and to accept myself because I was accepted and liked by therapists.

In some way or another I even learned to be patient and be satisfied with small gains. It really is hard to give yourself time to unravel the mess you've made of your life. The encouraging thing is that it doesn't take nearly as long to get well as it did to get sick. It's a lot harder, though.

Therapists helped me to face reality and to recognize a delusion of grandeur whenever it popped up. These were second nature to me after living in a fantasy world most of my life. The hardest thing the therapists taught me was to accept the fact that I can function best on a "fork and spoon" level, not on the grandiose level I imagined I could. They helped me to be patient and master one level before I tried another one. Even though I don't have very many actual limitations, it's hard to take things one step at a time, and accepting my limitations hasn't been easy.

Therapists taught me that one of the most positive ways to cope with the prejudice and stigma attached to having had a nervous breakdown and being epileptic is to perform well on the job. It works, too. I was shown how to turn my liabilities into assets. For example, it doesn't take any more determination to be persevering than it does to be stubborn. It's all a matter of channeling your energies in a positive direction.

Therapists taught me to believe in myself. They gave me opportunities to do positive things that reinforced my belief in myself. The therapist who helped me weather many a crisis had a great attitude. She never said "Well, you did it again." She just helped me learn as much as I could from a mistake. How to use mistakes wisely is a very important lesson for therapists to teach people. Winners learn from mistakes; losers repeat them. She was also still my friend in spite of my mistakes, even if her efforts boomeranged and hurt her also.

She taught that you never really fail until you quit trying.

This was important to me. I was forced by circumstances to cram 13 years of growing-up skills into 4. I failed many times, but I still kept going. Persistence and perseverance are two of the most valuable things I learned.

Therapists taught me, *not* guilt or blame, but to help myself and take responsibility for my actions. They taught me Recovery. Recovery is a system of self-help psychotherapy developed by Dr. Abraham Low. It was the only survival kit I could use even when I wasn't in contact with reality. Recovery helped me to live, and not as a vegetable in a state hospital for the rest of my life, which is what one doctor said might happen.

Therapists taught me that it is possible to "climb every mountain" if you really want to and try hard enough. If you are unable to climb a mountain to the top, you can enjoy getting up to the highest levels you are capable of reaching. Mountains have to be climbed one step at a time. What you learned in order to reach one level on your climb can help you reach the next level.

I also learned from a therapist that being a person *totally* committed to getting well isn't anything to be scared of. It can be handled, even if it is scary at times.

The most valuable thing I learned from a therapist is this: I don't need therapy anymore except in a crisis, and I can even handle some of them on my own. I know I can because my therapist was in the hospital during my latest crisis.

I'll always be grateful to therapists. At a time when I was really a hopeless case, a therapist cared enough to give me individual attention. Every time I would do something negative or be a "little rebel," she counteracted this by having me use Recovery in a positive way. A therapist cared enough and believed in me enough to fight for me until I cared enough to save myself by helping myself get well.

There is one thing, though, that therapists do in a hospital or even sometimes in a mental health clinic that seems wrong to me. A lot of staff members or therapists accept and trust you *only* when you begin to behave in a normal manner. I don't understand why they expect a psychotic person to behave in a normal way, like an Adult*. It seems to me they should realize that the definition of psychosis is the obliteration of the Adult and dominance of a mixed-up Parent and Child.

The reason for both my negative attitude and my little rebel being so active was that my Adult was really underdeveloped. It

*These words — *Adult, Critical Parent, Parent, Child* — when capitalized in this manner, are terms used in the type of therapy known as Transactional Analysis (TA). More details about this type of therapy will be found in the TA section of Chapter 8.

wasn't strong enough to take control away from the Critical Parent or my little rebel. There were very few therapists wise enough to give me an opportunity to develop and strengthen my Adult. When I was given the chance to do this, it grew and my behavior improved. When my Adult got back into the picture and gained some strength, I learned to try to control my behavior, even if I couldn't always do it. I hope that someday therapists will realize that it is better to give a person a chance to use his Adult, allow it to grow back to its normal size, than it is to impose good behavior by keeping that person doped up with medicines.

I know from the experience I had during my first two months at the state hospital that you can't always do what your Adult wants to when it's so weak. I didn't want to have a negative attitude or to rebel. I wanted to cooperate from the very beginning, but it was two months before I could use my Adult to control my behavior. I had been strengthening it over this time by using Recovery.

I've really been helped more than hurt by therapists. Guess what? Some of them are even human and *act* like it too. The way one student therapist helped me most was to care about me in a genuine manner. He was honest. The only tricks he ever used were ones he knew would help me. He never treated me like a guinea pig. He was the first student therapist I had ever met who was genuine. He treated the people he worked with like nervous people, instead of nervous patients.

7 Comprehensive BASIC Assessment System and Tool

MARY JO TRAPP BULBROOK

The Comprehensive BASIC Assessment System is composed of an integration of bits and pieces of information developed by the author from a variety of sources, including reading material and data based on experience. BASIC* is an acronym made up of the first letters of the words *biological, affective, social, intellectual,* and *communicative,* symbolizing the dynamic, interactional, and reactive states within an individual. The foundation of the system is Weed's Problem-Oriented System [1], which has four parts: data base, problem list, plans, and progress notes. Many excellent texts on the Weed system are listed in the Selected Readings for those who would like to go deeper into the subject. This format is used in the case studies reported in chapters 9 and 10.

Applying the system to psychiatry has been a slow process since our profession has difficulty in being scientific about psychosocial problems. Some new books on the subject, however, are specifically applicable to psychiatry.

In the Problem-Oriented Medical Records system (POMR), the defined data base is specific and includes history, physical examination, x-ray data, and laboratory information. A problem list is then determined (each problem is given a number by which it is identified throughout the record), which can include medical, social, demographic, and psychological problems. A plan is developed including diagnostic, therapeutic, and educational elements. Progress notes are determined for each problem and include narrative notes, found in the case studies in chapters

---

*BASIC = biological: referring to living matter in all its forms; affective: pertaining to emotions or feelings; social: pertaining to human society or the interdependence of society to meet people's needs; intellectual: that aspect of a person involving mental faculties; communicative: referring to an interchange of thoughts. For more details on the BASIC system, see Chapter 13.

9 and 10 under the acronym SOAP (S: subjective data —
patient's comments or complaints; O: objective data — actual,
measurable clinical findings and observations; A: assessment or
conclusions; and P: plan of immediate or future actions and any
departure therefrom) and flow sheets (clinic data record kept by
the hour, by the day, or by clinic visit).

The POMR system is an excellent tool for auditing and teaching. It can correct deficiencies in student or practicing clinicians,
which in turn leads to good patient care. From this POMR base
was developed the extensive Comprehensive BASIC Assessment
System Tool, the components of which will be given below. The
more complete the data base, the more thorough is patient-
centered care.

Different professionals show varying expertise in collecting
parts of the system. At times there is an overlapping of roles in
who is qualified to collect what data and how. It doesn't matter
who does what (notice that the work is not divided by labels —
nurse, physician, social worker, and so on); what does matter is
that all information is correct and examined — it is hoped by the
person who elicits the information. Data, however, are divided
by competency-based behavior. One person takes her piece of
patient-centered data and puts it with another person's data.
They then *jointly with the patient* determine, evaluate, and
implement a course of action. This new approach of joint
responsibility is based on the interrelationships between workers,
providers, and consumers.

The components of the Comprehensive BASIC Assessment
System styled after Weed's Problem-Oriented Medical Record
are: (1) a comprehensive BASIC data base, (2) a complete problem list, (3) an asset list, (4) an initial plan for each problem,
(5) progress notes, (6) nursing orders and (7) a discharge summary.

COMPREHENSIVE BASIC ASSESSMENT SYSTEM TOOL
  I. Data Base
    A. Individual profile: name, birthdate, race, marital status,
       number and age(s) of children
    B. Individual status on the health-illness continuum
      1. Present need or problem (chief complaint): concise
         statement of the reason a patient seeks medical
         attention
      2. History of this need or problem
      3. Nature of the referral
      4. Previous experience with the problem

      5. Expectations from the patient

C. *Biological* component

      1. Medical history

         Pediatric and adult illnesses

         Immunizations

         Allergies

         Habits

         Current medications

         Past hospitalizations

         Trauma

         Transfusions

      2. Family medical history (Use pedigree when possible. Key: MGF, maternal grandfather; MGM, maternal grandmother; PGM, paternal grandmother; PGF, paternal grandfather; F, father; M, mother, S, sibling.)

      3. Review of systems and physical examination (see text for specific details)

D. *Affective* data

      1. Appearance: calm, anxious, depressed, friendly, involved, enthusiastic, aggressive, hostile, dependent

      2. Emotional state: stability, lability, range of emotions, depression, withdrawal, autism, expressiveness, body image, confidence, self-esteem, self-control, anger, fear, phobias, compulsion

      3. Self-description

         a) Outstanding characteristics

         b) Sources of worry, doubt

         c) Difficulties to overcome

         d) What he or she would do if free of symptoms

         e) Description of persons most like and most unlike him or her

         f) Patient ideal

         g) Most important learning points in life

         h) Illustration of success and failures

         i) Main resources of help in time of need

E. *Social* data

      1. Family of orientation

         a) Names — who is named after whom

         b) Dates of important events

         c) Number of children in family of origin and their relationships with these

         d) Current locations and occupations of family members

         e) Occupations in family system

  2. Extended family (same data as 1. above)
  3. Birth and development
  4. Early recollections (child history)
   a) Parent/child interaction
   b) Peer relationship
   c) School (likes, dislikes)
   d) Fun things (hobbies, talents, interests, aspirations)
   e) Three wishes
   f) Maddest, saddest, happiest times
   g) Fears, worries, scary things
   h) Nightmares, daydreams
   i) How child saw self
  5. Education and training
  6. Work record: business and/or financial status
  7. Recreation and interests
  8. How family sees problem
  9. Courtship (where, when, how)
  10. Marriage (when, where, attitudes of family members)
  11. Major events since marriage (moves, illness, change of jobs)
  12. Major events between leaving home and marriage
  13. Significant relationships
  14. Crisis periods (what kind, how dealt with)
  15. Family rules
  16. Religious beliefs
 F. *Intellectual* data
  1. Vocabulary
  2. Range of information
  3. Memory
  4. Judgment
  5. Thought process: speed, coherence, abstract thinking, flexibility, suggestibility
  6. Thought content
   a) Central themes
   b) Abnormalities of content
    (1) Delusions
     (a) Type: persecutory, grandiose, somatic
     (b) Intensity: mild, moderate, severe
    (2) Obsessive ideas
    (3) Phobias
    (4) Idea of reference
    (5) Autistic thinking
    (6) Ambivalence
  7. Insight

G. *Communicative* aspects
1. Misperceptions of role and meaning
2. Illusions
3. Hallucinations
   a) Sensory modality: auditory, visual, olfactory, tactile
   b) Intensity
   c) Content
4. Attention
   a) General direction
   b) Fixation
5. Clarity of consciousness
   a) Depersonalization
   b) Orientation: time, location, place, person
H. Drug/alcohol supplement
1. Age started drinking/using drugs
2. Drinking/drug pattern
3. Kind of alcohol/drug
4. Reason seen by client for use of drugs or drinking
5. Where alcohol is drunk or drugs used
6. How much is consumed daily
7. Relationship of alcohol/drugs to physical condition
8. How client views drinking/use of drugs
9. If client considers himself or herself addicted

Suicide lethality scale

	Low	*Medium*	*High*
1. Stress	Normal ups and downs	Moderate reaction to stress	Intense reaction to stress
2. Communication	Directly tells what he or she is going to do	Interpersonalized suicide goal to cause guilt or force changes in others	Very indirect and nonverbal; internalized suicide goal
3. Support Persons	Available	Available but individual not willing to use them	Resources not available
4. Life Pattern	Stable personality	Acute suicidal behavior, but personality stable	Suicidal with unstable personality
5. Plans	No plan	Bizarre plans, moderately lethal attempt made	Specific plans made and date decided on; method available and very lethal

    I. Nursing history of specific BASIC needs
        1. Comfort: pain or no pain
        2. Rest/sleep
        3. Personal hygiene
        4. Safety
        5. Vision
        6. Hearing
        7. Nutrition
        8. Elimination
        9. Oxygen
        10. Medications
        11. Allergies
   II. Complete Problem List
        A. Classification of problem(s)
            1. Diagnosis
            2. Physical findings
            3. Symptoms
            4. Abnormal laboratory findings
            5. Social problems
            6. Demographic problems
            7. Psychiatric problems
        B. Status of problem(s)
            1. Active
            2. Inactive (resolved)
  III. Asset List — all positive resources and traits of
       client
   IV. Initial Plan
        A. Collate additional data
            1. Treatment
            2. Patient education
        B. Initial short-term and interim plans made for each of
           client's problems
        C. Kinds of plans
        D. Problem-oriented method uses only the information
           necessary for future analysis and management of the
           problems
    V. Progress Notes
        A. Pertain to all plans for each problem
        B. Components
            1. Narrative notes (SOAP)
                S: subjective symptomatic data — patient's com-
                   ments or complaints
                O: objective data — actual measurable clinical
                   findings and observations

A: assessment (or conclusions) — evaluation of
problem based on analyzed S and O data
P: plan — plan of immediate or future actions and
any departure therefrom
2. Flow sheets — clinic data record: by hour, by day,
or by clinic visit
VI. Nursing orders — used to implement Initial Plan for each
of the client's problems
VII. Discharge Summary — summary of situation at time of
client's discharge.

PHYSICAL EXAMINATION
General Principles
The examiner should have respect for the patient and provide
for his privacy. He should determine the patient's comfort level
and stop if the patient becomes tired. He should be gentle and
empathetic but acknowledge and apologize for any discomfort
caused. He should consider the patient's anxiety and fears, watch
his facial expressions, and listen to his comments. Conversation
should be limited, but everything that is being done should be
explained. And, to prevent carelessness through haste, adequate
time for the examination should be allowed.

Techniques of Examination
A specific order of progression through an examination is usually
followed. The specific steps are: inspection, palpation, percussion, sounds, and auscultation.

INSPECTION
Inspection is the most difficult technique to learn. Observation
must be deliberate and planned. It requires concentration and is
dependent on the knowledge of the observer.

PALPATION
Palpation means to feel, to touch. The tips of the fingers are
most sensitive for touch. The dorsa of the hands or fingers is
most sensitive to temperature. The palmar aspects of metacarpal
joints are most sensitive to vibrations. A grasp with the fingers
will reveal most accurately a sense of position and consistency.

PERCUSSION
With percussion the surface of the body is struck to emit sounds
that vary in quality, according to the density of the underlying

tissue. Types of percussion are: direct (body surface is struck directly with one or more fingers) and indirect (middle finger is laid on body lightly and is then struck by other middle finger). Wrist action determines accuracy. Feeling for vibrations is as important as listening.

SOUNDS
There are normal sounds over various body organs or parts and these should be noted. Resonance is heard over the upper anterior lung field; tympany over the stomach bubble; dullness over the liver; and a flat sound over muscle.

AUSCULTATION
Auscultation is the act of listening to obtain physical sounds with the stethoscope. Earpieces of the stethoscope should adapt comfortably to ear canals. Sounds from the lungs and heart have a frequency range between 60 and 3000 cycles per second. The stethoscope's bell transmits all sounds, but especially the low-pitched sounds. Its diaphragm excludes many of the low-pitched sounds and focuses on the high-pitched ones. The bell should touch the chest wall lightly. The diaphragm should be held tightly against skin.

Equipment
The following equipment should be on hand: (1) blank assessment tool (data base) and pen; (2) thermometer, sphygmomanometer, stethoscope, and scale; (3) pen light and tongue blade; (4) ophthalmoscope and otoscope; (5) reflex hammer and pin.

Actual Examination
The first step is to take the medical history, eliciting symptoms caused by lesion or problem, the chronology of appearance, change, or disappearance of lesion or problem, and what conditions promote relief or worsen the situation. The last step of the actual physical examination is the careful checking of the following: skin, lymph nodes, head, eyes, ears, nose, mouth and throat, neck, breasts, chest and back, heart, abdomen, genitourinary and rectal tracts, joints of extremities, and neurosensorium.

REFERENCE
1. Weed, L. L. *Medical Records, Medical Education, and Patient Care.* Chicago: Year Book Medical Publishers, 1971.

SELECTED READINGS

Abdellah, F., Martin, A., Beland, I., and Matheney, R. *New Directions in Patient-Centered Nursing.* New York: Macmillan, 1973.

Arieti, S. (Ed.). *American Handbook of Psychiatry.* New York: Basic Books, 1969.

Becknell, E., and Smith, D. M. *System of Nursing Practice: A Clinical Nursing Assessment Tool.* Philadelphia: Davis, 1975.

Benjamin, A. *The Helping Interview.* Boston: Houghton Mifflin, 1969.

Bermask, L. S. Interviewing: A key to the therapeutic communication in nursing practice. *Nursing Clinics of North America* 9:206–214, 1966.

Bernstein, L., and Dana, R. H. *Interviewing and the Health Profession.* New York: Appleton-Century-Crofts, 1970.

Bjorn, C., and Cross, H. D. *The Problem-Oriented Private Practice of Medicine.* Chicago: Modern Hospital Press, 1970.

Bloom, J. T., Bressler, J., Kenny, M., Molbo, P. M., and Pardee, G. P. Problem oriented charting. *American Journal of Nursing* 71:2144–2148, 1971.

Bonkowsky, M. L. Adapting the POMR to community child health care. *Nursing Outlook* 20:515–518, 1972.

Brill, N. *Working with people. In the Helping Process.* Philadelphia: J. B. Lippincott, 1973.

DeGowin, E. L., and DeGowin, R. L. *Bedside Diagnostic Examination.* New York: Macmillan Co., 1969.

Dinsdale, S. M., and Massman, P. L. Problem-Oriented Medical Record in Rehabilitation. *Archives of Physical Medicine* 51:448–492, 1970.

Easton, R. E. *Problem-Oriented Medical Report Concepts.* New York: Appleton-Century-Crofts, 1974.

Eckelberry, G. K. *Administration of Comprehensive Nursing Care.* New York: Appleton-Century-Crofts, 1971.

Enelson, A., and Swisher, S. *Interviewing and Patient Care.* New York: Oxford University Press, 1972.

Evraiff, W. *Helping Counselors Grow Professionally.* Englewood Cliffs, N.J.: Prentice-Hall, 1965.

Fast, J. *Body Language.* New York: Evans and Co., 1970.

Field, F. W. Communication Between Community Nurse and Physician. *Nursing Outlook,* 19:722–725, 1971.

Garrett, A. *Interviewing: Its Principles and Methods.* New York: Family Service Association of America, 1972.

Grant, R. Application of Weed system to psychiatric records. *Psychiatry in Medicine* 3:119–129, 1972.

Hardiman, M. A. Interviewing or social chit-chat? *American Journal of Nursing* 67:2088–2090, 1967.

Hurst, J. W. The art and science of presenting a patient's problems. *Archives of Internal Medicine* 128:463–465, 1971.

Hurst, J. W. How to Implement the Weed System. *Archives of Internal Medicine* 128:456–462, 1971.

Hurst, J. W., and Walker, H. K. (Eds.). *The Problem-Oriented System.* New York: Mecom, 1972.

Joel, R. A proposal for base line data collection of psychiatric care. *Perspective in Psychiatric Care* 11:48, 1973.

Judge, R. D. Medical History and Physical Examination. In R. D. Judge and G. D. Zuidema (Eds.), *Physical Diagnosis: A Physiologic Approach to the Clinical Examination.* Boston: Little, Brown, 1963.

Kahn, R. *The Dynamics of Interviewing.* New York: John Wiley, 1957.

King, J. The Initial Interview. *Perspectives in Psychiatric Care* 9:247–248, 1971.

Lewis, G. *Nurse Patient Communication.* Dubuque, Iowa: W. C. Brown Co., 1969.

Lewis, L. *Planning Patient Care.* Dubuque, Iowa: W. C. Brown Co., 1970;

Little, D. E., and Carnevali, D. L. *Nursing Care Planning.* Philadelphia: J. B. Lippincott, 1970.

MacBryde, C. M. (Ed.). *Signs and Symptoms.* Philadelphia: J. B. Lippincott, 1964.

MacKinnon, R., and Michels, R. *The Psychiatric Interview in Clinical Practice.* Philadelphia: W. B. Saunders, 1971.

Manthey, M. A guide for interviewing. *American Journal of Nursing* 68:68–75, 1968.

Marriner, A. *The Nursing Process: A Scientific Approach to Nursing Care.* St. Louis: C. V. Mosby, 1975.

Morgan, L., Jr., and Engel, G. L. *The Clinical Approach to the Patient.* Philadelphia: W. B. Saunders, 1969.

Neelon, F., and Ellis, G. *A Syllabus of Problem-Oriented Patient Care.* Boston: Little, Brown, 1974.

Peplau, H. Principles of Psychiatric Nursing. In S. Arieti (Ed.), *American Handbook of Psychiatry.* New York: Basic Books, 1969. P. 1840.

Reik, T. *Listening With the Third Ear.* New York: Farrar, Straus and Giroux, 1972.

Roesche, N. *Examination of the Personality.* Philadelphia: Lea & Febiger, 1972.

Ruesch, J. *Therapeutic Communication.* New York: W. W. Norton, 1972.

Ryback, R. *The Problem Oriented Record in Psychiatry and Mental Health Care.* New York: Grune & Stratton, 1974.

Scheflen, A. *Body Language and Social Order.* Englewood Cliffs, N.J.: Prentice-Hall, 1973.

Schell, P. L., and Campbell, A. T. POMR — not just another way to chart. *Nursing Outlook* 20:510–514, 1972.

Schwartz, L. *The Psychodynamics of Patient Care.* Englewood Cliffs, N.J.: Prentice-Hall, 1972.

Stevenson, I. The Psychiatric Interview. In S. Arieti (Ed.), *American Handbook of Psychiatry.* New York: Basic Books, 1969. P. 197.

Stevenson, I., and Sheppe, W. The Psychiatric Examination. In S. Arieti (Ed.), *American Handbook of Psychiatry.* New York: Basic Books, 1969. P. 215.

Sullivan, H. S. *The Psychiatric Interview.* New York: W. W. Norton, 1954.

Sundberg, N., and Tyler, L. E. *Clinical Psychology.* New York: Appleton-Century-Crofts, 1962.

Ten reasons why Lawrence Weed is right. *New England Journal of Medicine,* 184:51–52, 1971.

The Problem-Oriented System — A Multi-Disciplinary Approach. New York: National League for Nursing, 1974.

Traux, C., and Carkhuff, R. R. *Effective Counseling and Psychotherapy.* Chicago: Aldine, 1969.

Weed, L. L. Medical records that guide and teach. *New England Journal of Medicine* 278:593–600, 652–657, 1968.

Weed, L. L. New approach to medical teaching. *Medical Times* 94:1030–1038, 1966.

Wolberg, L. *The Techniques of Psychotherapy* (2nd ed.). New York: Grune & Stratton, 1967.

Wooley, F. *Problem Oriented Nursing.* New York: Springer, 1974.

8 Content and Process of Types of Therapy

MARY JO TRAPP BULBROOK
AND JUDY KEITH

Included in this chapter are both those traditional theories that serve as the foundations of the field of psychiatry and the contemporary theories of psychiatric therapy. For each theory there is first a discussion of its basic concepts and techniques and then an assessment tool especially designed to be used with the accompanying therapy. Each tool provides guidelines for gathering additional base information to supplement the Comprehensive BASIC Assessment System tool discussed in Chapter 7. These assessment tools were developed to act as a bridge between theory and practice for those students struggling to put theory into practice.

The material given here is basically only a general overview of each theory and should be only used as a guide. To gain a greater depth of understanding of each, the student should go to those sources cited for each theory at the end of the chapter.

PSYCHOANALYTIC MODEL

Content

Psychoanalysis was Freud's original creation. Its discovery, exploration, and constant revision formed his life's work. Yet opposition to Freud's theories began from the moment he first attempted to convey them to his colleagues. Freud wrote in a history of the psychoanalytic movement:

> I innocently addressed a meeting of the Vienna Society of Psychiatry and Neurology . . . expecting that the material losses I had willingly undergone would be made up for by the interest and recognition of my colleagues. I treated my discoveries as ordinary contributions to science and hoped they would be received in the same spirit. But the silence which my communications met with, the void which formed itself about me, the

hints that were conveyed to me, gradually made me realize that . . . from now onwards I was one of those who have "disturbed the sleep of the world," as Hebbell says, and that I could not reckon upon objectivity and tolerance. [9, p. 21] .

This reaction of his colleagues, indeed, the reaction of much of the world, was due primarily to the assumptions then held by psychoanalytic theorists concerning the nature of man. The first of these assumptions, less controversial than the others, is that man is a bound energy system in which energy flows, can get sidetracked, or can become damned up. Within the system there is only a limited amount of energy, and if the energy is discharged in one way, there is less energy to be used in another way. If energy is blocked from one channel of expression, it will find another channel, usually along the path of least resistance. Although man's behavior may take many forms, it is basically reducible to common forms of energy. The goal of all behavior is pleasure, or the reduction of tension by the release of energy [8] . This view of man is traceable to the progress taking place in the field of energy dynamics in Freud's time. While still in medical school, Freud came under the influence of a physiologist named Brücke, who viewed the human being as moved by forces according to the principles of the conservation of energy, that is, that energy could be transformed but could not be destroyed. Freud adopted these views and adapted them for his own purposes to explain human behavior [8] .

The second of the psychoanalytic assumptions concerning the nature of man is that man is primarily animalistic, that is, he is shaped by biological needs, sex drives, and aggressive instincts. Freud believed that this view was confirmed by the strong sadistic and destructive drives he observed in his patients. Man is seen as sharing with animals the activation of behaviors that serve homeostatic ends and the need to reproduce the species. On the other hand, man has developed his communication skills, and these have freed him from an entirely instinctual, animal-like existence. As a result, man has developed particular human qualities, such as courage, honor, and loyalty. These vary with different cultures but are almost universally positively regarded [1] . This view, which has been put forth by the ego-analysts, Anatol, Rapaport and Eric Erikson, that there is much that is significant about human behavior that is quite independent of man's instinctual urges, is primarily an extension of Freud's psychoanalytic stance. To put it simply, then, man is by nature animalistic, but over the years he has added a more "human" self. According to Freud, for our society to exist we must surrender most of our instinctual drives for sexual and personal freedom since the basic claims of the individual and the claims of society will always be in conflict. Man must renounce, too, his aggressive, self-assertive, and uncharitable drives or he would be unable to live at peace with others.

Man's behavior, then, is seen as being determined, and he is only to a limited extent master of his life. He is shaped to follow behaviors that gratify his basic biological needs, instincts, and instinct derivations. None of his behavior can be considered accidental.

Another of the assumptions of the psychoanalytic theorist is implied by the assumption mentioned above: Man is an irrational being and most of his behavior is controlled by unconscious motivational and goal-directed determinants. This personal unconscious consists of once conscious experiences that have been repressed, suppressed, forgotten, or ignored and of experiences that were too weak originally to make a conscious impression upon the individual. Consciousness is the *un*usual rather than the usual feature of mental processes. Man constantly both wants and fears things of which he is not consciously aware. These unconscious desires strive for expression but are disguised because they would be unacceptable if they were consciously expressed. The individual never has direct access to the unconscious, but one can see its operation in terms of behavior and symbolism [5]. All acts are considered to have both a commonplace meaning, i.e., a practical meaning that would ordinarily be assigned to the act by others, and a symbolic meaning, one that comes from unconscious urges and can be understood only through analysis.

The final basic assumption of the psychoanalytic theorists concerning the nature of man is that, although man is born with certain structural limitations imposed by genetics, such as physical, maturational, and intellectual ones, early experiences structure later personality trends. Freudians tend to think of a separate history for the various aspects of development. They feel that there is an actual freezing of some aims at the infantile level while other aims develop normally in accordance with the requirements of society.

There has been a tendency on the part of more modern psychoanalytic theorists to play down the past emphasis on heredity and maturation and to emphasize instead the role of environmental and social variables. This has been done by orthodox Freudians and ego-analysts like Erik Erikson as well as those who took the lead in emphasizing social variables, e.g., Karen Horney, Erich Fromm, and Harry Stack Sullivan. Alfred Adler, too, felt that man is inherently a social being motivated primarily by social interests and urges. Since Adler thought that man was basically a conscious planner of his own life and life style, he held to the uniqueness of each personality and of the life goals of the person. This concept of man as a social animal was essentially an optimistic view of man, as opposed to Freud's more pessimistic view, and it caused conflict between the two men. In general, however, all schools of psychoanalytic thought encompass both concepts of heredity and early environment, the differences lying in the amount of relative importance they attach to each.

In order to understand Freud's concept of personality structure, it would first be appropriate to discuss his distinctions among man's levels of awareness, or consciousness. The first level, or conscious level, is the sum total of everything of which we are aware. Freud regarded consciousness as only a relatively small part of the total mental life of the individual — an immediate, constantly changing reflection of everything of which we are aware at a given instant in time. This awareness is limited, however, by both our human capacity for focusing attention and by the raw material coming from outside stimuli and that which we may be remembering from the past [9]. The more attention the individual focuses on past memories, the less attention will be focused on present changes in his surroundings, and vice versa. Too, there are times when an external stimulus may gain added significance by its immediate association with some remembered past incident.

The second level of awareness described by Freud is the preconscious, the reservoir of everything we can remember, even ideas and thoughts, all that is accessible to voluntary recall. For an unconscious element to become conscious, it must first become a part of the preconscious.

This leaves the unconscious area of mental life, the third level of awareness, to contain all those more primitive drives and impulses that influence actions without the individual's being aware of them. These include the ideas or memories with a strong emotional charge that were once present in the conscious but which have since been repressed so that they are no longer available to it, even through introspection or attempts at memory. Freud believed that the individual unknowingly resists bringing these feelings into consciousness. Because these feelings continually strive to become conscious, the individual must expend energy to keep them at the level of the unconscious. Man is thus in a constant state of internal conflict of which he is unaware [4]. The unconscious is that portion of the mind that received most of Freud's attention and the part that he believed to be the primary influence on behavior. In his later writings, however, he enlarged upon this theory by visualizing the individual as made up of three sub-systems; this set of sub-systems forms the basis of his structural theory of personality. The subsystems — the id, ego, and superego — interact to such an extent that it is difficult to discern their separate effects upon the individual's behavior, and hence no clear line exists among them. Since one of the subsystems seldom operates independently of the other two, the individual's behavior is seen as the result of interaction among the three.

Freud conceived of the id as the original system of the personality, consisting of all that the individual brings into the world with him, everything that is inherited, that is present at birth and is laid down in his constitution. It consists also of unlearned physiological motives and unlearned primitive reactions for satisfying them. Within the id Freud included man's instincts, which are core characteristics of personality.

Freud discusses three types of instincts, differing only in content, all having a source (an energy or driving force), an aim, and an object. The *source* of an instinct is within the organism and is expressive of the biological requirements of the organism. An instinct, or innate capacity to react to stimuli in a stereotyped way, is an indication that the organism does not have something it needs, that it is in a state of deprivation, which is experienced as tension or pressure, constant in nature. The tension of deprivation states will always exert an influence on an organism's living [6].

The *aim* of instincts is generally satisfaction, or the reduction of the tension of biological deprivation. The ideal state, quiescence, is never reached because of the constant nature of instinctual demands. This aim to produce consequences that reduce the intensity or quantity of the psychological energy of tension implies some selectivity in the functioning of the instinct.

The *object* of the instinct is that which satisfies or eases the tension of deprivation. There are generally several things or events that can ease the tension of an instinct, and one of these may become particularly important to any one person on the basis of his learning experiences. The range of possible satisfiers are inherent to the nature of the instinct, however, and can be specified. The process whereby an object becomes recognized as an instinctual satisfier for a person is called "cathexis." A cathexis is an investment of energy in an object or idea. When an impulse arises that presses to become a part of the system preconscious but is rejected, no cathexis occurs. The energy connected with the impulse goes back to the unconscious as anxiety since the impulse has not been satisfied. The energy then may become attached to anticathexis, a substitute idea and one that is removed from the original idea. The process that has now occurred is called "repression proper" [2].

The three kinds of instincts Freud identified earlier are all subsumed under the concept of the id: self-preservation instincts, sexual instincts, and the death instinct. The first two are life instincts, and the energy associated with them Freud called "libido."

Freud emphasized the sexual energies and their consequences most, distinguishing between the broad concept of the sexual and the narrow concept of the genital [1]. The sexual instinct received more attention, not because of its greater survival importance, but because it seemed to Freud to be a much greater contributor to conflict than the self-preservation instincts, owing to the fact that it matured slowly and has many parts that could be satisfied in many ways. It can also be more affected by what the individual learns early in life than the other instincts.

Later in his theorizing Freud postulated the death instinct, which he believed to function antagonistically to the life instincts. This instinct is the basic tendency of an organism to push toward death. Freud never developed this idea as he did the life instincts, and, although it is intriguing, everything that can be accounted for by the concept can also be explained by the idea of aggression resulting from frustration of the attempt to satisfy the life instincts [6].

Instincts as they exist in the id are selfish, basic, and uncivilized and are ineffective in the external world. They function according to the pleasure principle, or the tendency to maximize instinctual gratification without regard for external reality. Just on the basis of id alone, the person is only able to satisfy instincts through wish-fulfilling fantasy, or primary process thought, as it is called. The ego, then, must serve the person in the external world through the thought and perceptual processes involved in recognition, remembering, and action relevant to satisfying instincts, or secondary process thought. With experience, this portion of the mind becomes differentiated for the purpose of facilitating reality principle functioning. The major function of the ego is defensive, in that it permits only those forms and portions of instincts unlikely to trigger punishment and guilt to remain in the consciousness.

Punishment and guilt originate in the demands of society. When individuals transgress societal rules, they receive punishment from other people in that society. Young children, who most often break the rules because they have not yet learned those rules, are most often punished. As the punishments accumulate, the child begins to learn the nature of the rules, begins to internalize them, and eventually can feel guilt. In this way, a portion of the mind consisting of the ego differentiates into the superego, the abstract representation of the rules of society, its ideas of good and bad and right and wrong. The superego then is a form of internal control within the individual. Freud believed it to be made up of the conscience — representing those things that the person believes he should not do — and the ego-ideal — representing those things that the person would like to be. Both of these parts are often in conflict with the id impulses [4]. When some instinctual impulse that threatens to produce punishment or guilt arises, anxiety occurs as a warning. In turn, to avoid anxiety, some form of defensiveness occurs to remove the instinctual impulse from consciousness. Therefore, Freud believed, all behavior was in some way defensive. Unlike the ego, the superego does not try to postpone instinctual gratification but rather tries to block it permanently.

Under ordinary circumstances the three systems of personality do not work at cross purposes. They work rather as a team under the executive of the personality, the ego. The person's behavior then is a compromise between the different demands of the three systems [3].

Freud discusses personality development primarily in terms of psychosexual stages: oral, anal, phallic, latency, and genital. The oral stage, during the first year of life, is one in which the erogenous zone is the mouth, and the primary activities are receiving (oral incorporative) and taking (oral aggressive). Feeding is the important area of conflict at this stage.

In the second year of life, the anal stage, the erogenous zone is the anus, and the primary activities are giving (anal expulsive) and withholding (anal retentive). The important area of conflict is bowel training.

The genitalia are the erogenous zones in the third through fifth year of life, the phallic stage. The primary activities of this stage involve heterosexualizing interaction. The conflict is Oedipal.

During the latency stage, the sixth year through puberty, the sexual instinct is latent, and the child learns nonsexually related skills. Freud felt that this stage was essential if the education of children was to take place.

The last stage, the genital, lasts from puberty to death. It is characterized by a mature sexuality that combines all that is learned in the pregenital stages and relies for the most part upon intercourse and orgasm [4].

When the conflict encountered at each stage is of minimal intensity, the stage is passed through successfully. But when parents intensify the conflict, growth is arrested and fixation occurs. This means that the activities of this particular stage will remain unduly important to the person, even after puberty.

In the early stages of development the conflicts and threats to self that create anxiety come from outside the individual. As the superego develops, however, threats to the self also come from within. Freud held that anxiety develops automatically when a person is overwhelmed by stimuli or when the situation is a traumatic one. A person's defense mechanisms, which are designed to cope with these threats and accompanying anxiety, take place primarily at the unconscious level, although they operate to some degree in normal behavioral functioning as well as in pathological ways. The basic mechanisms are: (1) repression, in which a person rejects from consciousness the impulses that provoke anxiety; (2) reaction formation, the conversion of unacceptable hostility into solicitousness; (3) rationalization, in which the individual explains his own behavior so as to conceal the motive it expresses; (4) denial of reality; (5) projection, disguising the source of conflict by ascribing the motives to someone else; and (6) regression, the retreat to an earlier stage of behavior. Three other important mechanisms are: (1) introjection, the opposite of projection; (2) displacement, in which the motive of a goal is disguised by substituting another one for it; and (3) sublimation, in which a sexual drive may be directed into nonsexual channels [10].

Ego-analysts such as Erickson, similar to classic Freudians, differ in the amount of importance they give to functions of the ego. They attribute more conscious control of behavior to the individual. In this way their concepts are an extension of psychoanalytic thought with a major emphasis on the ego functions and ego strength.

The primary goal of Freudian psychoanalytic therapy is to bring into the individual's consciousness the repressed impulses causing his anxiety. These impulses come from the id and are those with which the ego has been unable to deal effectively. The patient, as he is referred to in classic psychoanalysis, is unable to deal with these anxieties alone because repression keeps him unaware of his conflicts and their causes. In the threat-free therapy situation, the individual can express his thoughts without danger of condemnation, and the repressed thoughts will eventually return to consciousness. The conflicts can then be resolved through logical thought, and the patient can explore new courses of action. This does not mean that the patient will be free of all conflicts, but only that his self-awareness will be increased so that he can recognize his psychologically determined wishes and the demands of reality. He can then hope to use his conscious thought to help himself cope with life.

According to the psychoanalysts, there are also several requirements the patient must fulfill. He must wish to be cured, since this is the motivating force in most kinds of psychotherapy. He must be able to form some kind of interpersonal relationship with the therapist, and he must be able to attend to situational events and think somewhat logically about them. Persons who do not possess a reasonable amount of education and fairly reliable character and those with character disorders should be refused.

The basic techniques used in psychoanalysis are free association, interpretation, and working through the transference — the phenomenon wherein the patient *transfers* his neurotic feelings onto the therapist. Free association is the practice of having the individual verbalize whatever comes to mind. Its fundamental rule is that there should be no attempt on the part of the patient to logically organize his thoughts or screen them in any way.

Another major technique used by the psychoanalyst is interpretation or explanation, in which he makes statements that provide the patient with different ways of thinking about his behavior. One method of interpretation used is the dream interpretation. Freud originated this idea, and Jung developed it further. The latent content, which carries the significance of the dream, has hidden and symbolic meaning for the individual and may allow him to bring many conflicts to the surface. Once brought to the surface he may work through them by chaining together associations by means of the process of free association. While the symbols in the dreams may not all be universal, many are thought to be, and these can be interpreted by the therapist and pointed out to the client. Dreams are important because they are a part of nonwaking life when censorship is weakened and the unconscious is more accessible. Dreams may provide a means of understanding the unconscious and also may serve as a point to begin the free association process [2].

Interpretations must be correctly timed to produce the highest therapeutic value. The therapist should not introduce conventional morality into his discussion but should maintain complete affective and intellectual neutrality. As resistances occur on the part of the patient (anything that interferes with the progress of analysis is called "resistance"), the psychotherapist identifies them and explains to the patient why they are occurring. If the patient continues to make avoidance responses, the therapist should continue to point them out and prevent them from reducing anxiety; the patient will then find it harder to deny their occurrence and will more willingly acknowledge them. The patient is then able to work through them in a period of examination and discussion with the therapist [1].

An especially important kind of resistance is known as transference, which generally consists of the individual directing his neurotic emotional feelings toward the therapist as though the therapist were the object that originally caused the feelings. This transference, although difficult to deal with, provides the therapist with a valuable tool. The responses represent basic conflicts and the infantile responses learned with the conflicts. During analysis they occur under different circumstances, and the individual has different sequences with which to respond to them. These responses can be grouped into three categories: (1) the simple friendly feelings toward the therapist that keep the client at his work and are a great help in therapy; (2) the strong affectionate feelings with sexual overtones; and (3) the hostile, resentful feelings that generally follow the positive ones, and the therapist must be very careful not to respond to sexual and hostile affective attacks. Rather, he should calmly point out to the client that they are misdirected and help the client to discover their real origins and purpose. The real neurosis is transformed into a transference neurosis and thereby becomes accessible to modification. Successfully handled, the old, conflicting responses can be brought under control and modified under the new circumstances [7]. Recognizing the inappropriateness of the patient's behavior is an emotional as well as an intellectually insightful experience; without the emotional experience, intellectual insight is not effective [7]. If the patient's behavior toward the therapist is changed, the changes are expected to transfer then to other situations. No special procedures are needed to facilitate this transfer if the therapist successfully resolves the

transference pattern of behavior [1]. If the responses are
changed while they are occurring in relation to the therapist,
they will be permanently changed and can no longer attach
themselves to any object in their old form.

Psychoanalytic Group Therapy for Children
Psychoanalytic activity group therapy is a form of ego therapy
that deals with behavior disorders and character correction by
using action-oriented methods. It is Slavson's belief that therapy
can occur only through the patient living in a world of action
[1]. The main purpose of the activity group is to remove the
patient's resistance not only to the world but to the people in
it who may influence him in a socially desirable way. The therapy group provides a place where distressing, threatening, and
hostile pressures can be removed with an atmosphere of permissiveness. This near total permissiveness, this "unconditional
love," accepting the child fully with all his faults, destructiveness, and hostilities, allowing him to act out his infantile
impulses, all are necessary in order to counteract the inhibitive
and restraining pressures in the child's past experiences and
thereby break down his resistance to the world. When the child
is not censured and his personality is accepted, his attitudes
toward himself are also altered. The dissatisfaction with himself
is replaced by self-tolerance and a hopeful attitude. Only then is
he able to accept others.

Slavson states four needs of clients that are met through
activity group therapy, thereby effecting change. First, every
child needs the security of unconditional love from his parents
and significant others in his life. If love is not forthcoming from
these people, a substitute can be supplied for them through the
activity group. Second, the ego and sense of self-worth that are
usually crushed in problem children must be built up by recognition, acceptance, and encouragement. Third, every child needs
some genuine interest to occupy his leisure time and allow him
creative self-expression. Activity group by its very nature sup-
plies help in this area. Fourth, and most important for improvement in an activity group, every child exhibits "social hunger,"
a desire to be accepted by, or at least not excluded from the group.
The activity group provides the opportunity for significant experiences in group relations, leading to acceptance by the group.

SELECTION AND COMPOSITION OF THE GROUP
The basic requirement for admission to activity group therapy is a
capacity for social hunger. Excluded from activity group therapy

are (1) children with strong sexual ties to their parents; (2) children with marked deviation in conduct or symptoms — the overly sadistic or masochistic, the brain-injured, the physically crippled, and the sexually perverted; and (3) children who are extremely overcontrolled or undercontrolled, especially those with no inner controls.

A balanced group is made up of instigators (children who activate the group either constructively or destructively), neutralizers (those who check aggression and help establish equilibrium), social neuters (those who exert little effect on the group), and isolators (those who stay by themselves, withdrawn from the group). The age distribution within any one activity group should be a two-year span, for example, 8 to 10 years or 9 to 11 years old. The age group for which the activity group is designed is the 8- to 12-year-old. The groups are homogeneous with regard to the sex of the children.

The ideal number of children for an activity group is five or six. The number can be increased to eight in the latter stages of treatment. A roll of eight members usually brings the attendance for weekly sessions to approximately the desirable number.

ROLE OF THE GROUP LEADER
The therapist in activity groups is neutral and permissive. He does not set limits, settle conflicts, or assign tasks; he observes and registers the meaning of the behavior of each child and the interactions of the group as a whole. Since this type of therapy relies primarily on identification and activity rather than on verbalization, the therapist must serve as a desirable identification model and ego ideal. His attitudes and behavior must convey an image of strength, tolerance, and calmness. He prevents failure in whatever the children undertake to do by help and suggestion. In his relations with the children the therapist aims to accomplish three things: (1) to accept the child, (2) but at the same time, not to feed his dependence, and (3) to prevent the jealousy of other children and their consequent aggression.

LENGTH OF SESSION AND DURATION OF TREATMENT
The activity group typically meets once a week for a two-hour session. It is not unusual for treatment to continue for a period of two to three years.

Psychoanalytic Assessment Tool
    I. Conscious level: get answers from patient to following questions
       A. What is going on in your life today?

B. What are you currently aware of?

C. Describe your past memories.

D. Describe your early childhood.

E. Describe your mother and father.

II. Preconscious: get answers from patient

A. Describe all you can remember about your early childhood.

III. Unconscious

A. Identify drives, impulses.

B. Identify ideas, memories with a strong emotional charge.

IV. Investigate personality structures.

A. Id

1. Unlearned physical motives

2. Unlearned primitive reactions

3. Self-preservation instinct (libido: life energy)

4. Sexual instinct (libido: life energy)

5. Death instinct (strive to satisfy pleasure principle)

B. Ego (strive to satisfy reality principle)

1. Thought process

2. Perceptual process

C. Superego

1. What rules does patient live by?

2. What does patient consider good or bad?

3. What does patient feel he should not do?

4. Is patient feeling guilty?

5. Defense mechanism identification (repression, displacement, reaction formation, isolation, undoing, rationalization, intellectualism, denial, projection, regression, counterphobic mechanisms, withdrawal, introjection, identification, acting out, sublimation)

V. Identify psychosexual stages and fixations: oral, anal, phallic, latency, and genital

VI. Relationship with therapist

1. Transference

2. Countertransference

3. Resistances

Techniques of psychoanalysis are: free association, interpretation, and waking through the transference.

REALITY THERAPY
Content
Reality therapy, developed by Glasser [1], is an unconventional approach to psychiatry. The person is not considered to be ill,

but as a person unable to fulfill his needs because he denies the reality of the world around him. Therapy consequently is directed to getting him to give up the denial world, to recognize that reality exists and that his needs must be fulfilled within its framework. Stated again: "A therapy that leads all patients toward reality, or simply REALITY THERAPY" [1, p. 6]. It is important to remember that simply to help a patient face reality is not enough. The person must also learn to fulfill his needs.

Every person has two basic needs: the need to love and be loved and the need to feel that he is worthwhile to himself and to others. The basic thrust of reality therapy is to help patients fulfill these two needs that all persons have, even though they vary in their ability to fulfill them. The needs are fulfilled by being involved with other people, one at the very minimum. The other person must be in touch with reality himself and be able to fulfill his own needs within the world.

Feeling loved and worthwhile are two separate needs, although a person who loves and is loved will usually feel that he is a worthwhile person. Too, one who is worthwhile is usually someone who is loved and who can give love in return. But, to be worthwhile we must also maintain a satisfactory standard of behavior.

Reality therapy depends on the three Rs: reality, responsibility, and right and wrong. Responsibility is considered the ability to fulfill one's needs in such a way that others are not deprived of the ability to fulfill their needs. A responsible person does that which makes him feel his own self-worth, which in turn creates a feeling of being worthwhile to others.

The task of the therapist utilizing reality therapy is to become involved with the patient in such a way that the patient can begin to fulfill his needs. He must build a firm emotional relationship with a patient who has not learned to establish such a relationship and who often avoids such a relationship. The patient is seeking a person who cares about him, one he can care about, and one who will stay with him until he can feel better and fulfill his own needs.

In order to do the above the therapist must be a very responsible person, tough, interested, human, and sensitive. He must fulfill his own needs and be willing to reveal his humanness as it becomes applicable. He should be willing to be tested by the patient and to withstand intense criticism. He must not condone an irresponsible action and should be willing to watch the patient suffer if that helps him toward responsibility.

Development of a therapeutic relationship may take anywhere

from one interview to several months. The progress depends on: (1) the skill of the therapist, (2) his control over the patient, and (3) the resistance of the patient. After the relationship has formed, the therapist confronts the patient with the reality of his behavior. The patient must now face up to the responsibility of his actions. Feelings are unimportant, as is past history. The here and now is emphasized, and how the patient can meet his needs to be worthwhile and loved by being reasonable is determined. The therapist is very directive and active in an attempt to teach the patient the new ways of behaving that will fulfill his needs. Happiness will come to the patient not during therapy but as a consequence of the patient's taking responsibility for himself.

In reality therapy the therapist rarely asks why. The usual question is "What?" What are you doing? Therapy begins with the formation of a relationship and progresses to aiding the patient in seeing the responsibility of his actions. Once the patient admits his behavior is irresponsible, relearning, the last phase of therapy, begins.

Glasser describes the basic concepts of reality therapy in the following way. *Security Person* has an inner core that requires food, shelter, and clothing. Over against this concept are those of *Failure Person, Symptom Person,* and *Negatively Addicted Person.* Failure Identity results in a weakness of man in which he becomes increasingly lonely.

People move into negative energy states in an attempt to reduce pain. First they give up, avoid what is causing pain, which gives temporary pleasure. People are *Failure,* though, at this time and will be less able to withstand any intervening pain. When pain hits again, Failure Person tries to reduce the pain by denying it. *Symptom Person* begins to emerge, as manifested by (1) acting out, (2) emotional upset, (3) psychosis, (4) psychosomatic illnesses. At first man experiences a fleeting pleasure, but he soon runs into difficulty with more pain.

To deal with the pain, people escape into drugs, food, gambling, and so on, and become *Negatively Addicted Persons.* They find pleasure in failure, which is why it is so difficult to change. When someone is this low, his personal world grows smaller.

Success Identity occurs in people when they approach life, its pluses and minuses, with strength. They are rationally motivated and involved; consequently their personal world grows larger. They are positively addicted. Once people reach this state, they have tremendous power and capability. A success identity means people can (1) give and receive love; (2) gain worth and recognition; (3) have fun; and (4) become self-disciplined.

In reality therapy the therapist has a more or less fixed guide in his relationship with the client. The steps to take are: (1) make friends; (2) establish what is being done; (3) determine if it is helping, if it is not, (4) make a plan to do better; (5) get a commitment; (6) don't accept excuses; (7) don't punish but don't interfere with natural or reasonable consequences of patient's actions; (8) never give up.

Reality Therapy Assessment Tool

I. Patient Identification
   A. Name, address, race, birthdate, religion, education, sex, marital status
   B. Chief complaint
   C. Reference source
   D. Family data: members, children, spouse, social and economic situation of the family, educational level, income, housing
   E. Pertinent medical data
   F. Medications
   G. Present life situation
   H. Mental status examination: attention, judgment, insight, mood, intelligence, behavior, appearance
II. Fulfillment of Needs: get answers from patient
   A. Are you loved?
   B. Who loves you?
   C. Whom do you love?
   D. How do you feel about yourself?
   E. What are the things you think are wrong with you according to you or to others?
   F. What are the good things about you according to yourself and others?
   G. Is the person you rely on most responsible?
III. Responsibility-Behavior: get answers from patient
   A. In what ways are you responsible for yourself?
   B. Therapist is to determine age-appropriate and developmental-level responsible tasks.
   C. Are there any things that you should be doing that you are not able to do now?
   D. What is keeping you from doing what you think you should be doing?
   E. What are your goals?

IV. Evaluate Preceeding Data to Ascertain Fulfilling Needs and
   Responsibility
   A. Establish relationship
   B. Confront patient with irresponsibility
   C. Wait until patient admits irresponsibility
   D. Develop with the patient a plan for relearning more
      responsible behavior.

INTERPERSONAL MODEL

Content

Harry Stack Sullivan's theory of personality is both Freudian
and social in nature. He maintained that personality could not
be studied apart from interpersonal relationships. Personality is
the dynamic center of various processes that occur in a series of
interpersonal fields. A child's development comes from his
mother, who is the carrier of the culture. From the moment of
birth she conveys her own reactions to life and to him around
her attitudes. Learning from others he begins to develop his self
system. Sullivan believed that all human beings have major goals
and/or end states. The first goal is acculturation and emphasizes
a relationship with another. These needs are shown as inner tensions, and the way the individual attempts to handle them are
dynamisms [1].

The major processes in Sullivan's personality theory are dynamisms, personifications, and cognitive processes. Dynamisms are
relatively enduring in interpersonal relations, something like a
long-standing habit, and most serve the basic needs of the body.
The most important of the dynamisms is the self-dynamism, a
complex self-definition, mainly unconscious that is derived from
a person's experiences of approval and disapproval from others
and leads him to behave in a way that allows him to avoid the
insecurity of disapproval.

A personification is generally the image that a person has
either of himself or of another person [3].

Cognitive processes are used to describe personal development
as well as mental illnesses. The three modes of experience (cognitive process) are prototaxic, parataxic, and syntaxic. The prototaxic mode is a primitive state in which the person experiences
reality as a stream of raw sensations, images, or feelings with no
sequence or meaning. The parataxic mode of thinking exists
when the person sees causal relationships between events that
are time-related but not logic-related. The highest mode, the
syntaxic, consists of symbol activity, mainly verbal in nature.

These processes are the chief structural features of Sullivan's system [3].

The primary dynamics of Sullivan's system of personality are the tension from the needs of the organism and the tension that results from anxiety. He arranged needs, in order from lower to higher, for energy transformation; for example, the total dissipation of tension is the goal of a personality [2].

Sullivan postulated six stages of development: (1) *infancy,* in which the person is essentially helpless to and through the maturation of language phase; (2) *childhood,* in which a child learns the dimensions of his culture and ending with a need for peers; (3) *juvenile era,* covering the grammar school years, during which the child becomes social, becoming competitive and cooperative; (4) *preadolescence,* ending with the maturation of the genital lust dynamism and marked by the need for a close relationship with a same sex peer; (5) *early adolescence,* extending to the development of stable patterns for satisfying genital drives; and (6) *late adolescence,* extending into full interpersonal maturity [3]. These last two stages allow the adolescent to come to terms with the lust dynamism. When the person has gone through these stages, he has been transformed, largely through inter-personal relations, from an animal organism into a human person [2].

In therapy Sullivan focused on anxiety and the interpersonal context in which it is manifested. The therapist is a participant-observer and transference — the response of the multitude of distortions that develop out of the parataxic interpretation of one's experience — is noted. Therapy focuses on this interrelationship between client and therapist as an exploratory aid to uncover repressed or dissociated material. The therapy then becomes a learning process to help the patient reconstruct his life.

Interpersonal Theory Assessment Tool
   I. Self
      A. Describe yourself; get answers from patient for 1 through 6.
         1. What are you like?
         2. What do you do that wins you approval?
         3. What do you do that gets you disapproval?
         4. Are you anxious?
         5. What is it like being anxious?
         6. Describe your feelings, attitudes.
         7. Identify protataxic, parataxic, and syntaxic cognitive processes in the patient.

B. Identify stage of development.
   1. Infancy
   2. Childhood
   3. Juvenile era
   4. Preadolescence
   5. Early adolescence
   6. Late adolescence
II. Primary Group
   A. Family of orientation: mother, father, siblings
   B. Family of procreation: marriage partner, children
III. Secondary Groups
   A. Church, politics, culture, professional group, work
IV. Therapist-Client Relationship
   A. Goals
      1. Identify the relationship patterns of significant people in the person's life.
      2. Goal of therapy is to dissipate tension.
V. The Patient and Group Participation
   A. What is the structure of the group?
      1. Actors
      2. Roles
      3. Power relations among actors
      4. Rules for interaction
   B. What are the processes of the group?
      1. How are decisions made?
      2. How are conflicts resolved?
      3. Communication patterns
      4. Transmission of emotions
      5. Energy into actions
   C. Describe developmental tasks of the group.
      1. Problems of concern
      2. Direction of change
      3. Behaviors rewarded or punished
      4. Skills and knowledge emphasized
      5. Developmental needs of members
   D. Investigate the physical environment of the group as it influences behavior.

BEHAVIOR MODIFICATION
Content
Behavior modification has been used for a long time by clinical psychologists and others under the guidance of a psychologist. Today the clinical application of operant behavior modification

theory in the practice of nursing is receiving increasing attention in the literature, schools of nursing, psychiatric nursing practice, and other clinical nursing situations. Nurses are turning to this operant learning theory to provide a scientific, researchable foundation for nursing practice and nursing education [1].

Behavior modification is based on three principles: (1) behavior is learned; (2) behavior occurs in a certain setting or situation; and (3) behavior is maintained or altered by its consequences. The basic idea is that once a response is emitted, there are certain environmental consequences that influence the future probability of the response, i.e., whether the response is maintained, increased, or decreased [2].

The goal in behavior therapy is to clearly identify the functional or dysfunctional and adaptive or maladaptive behavior and determine the problem. The problem definition is then behaviorally specified according to frequency, duration, and magnitude, being measured in quantifiable terms as objectively as possible by either the patient or some person in his environment and/or the professional. Data is collected on behavior during the antecedent controlling situation and the environmental consequences of the problematic behavior. It is also noted who has labeled a given behavior problematic. A history of desirable as well as undesirable behaviors is necessary for an effective treatment plan. Questions are asked such as: What is the problem behavior? How often did the patient engage in certain behaviors? In what kinds of situations? What happened following the problem behavior? What were the primary reinforcers or punishers for the client? Who instituted the reinforcement or punishment? [1].

Once the above data is ascertained, the therapist-educator or clinician can develop and implement a treatment plan that indicates clearly what the desired behavior is and the built-in evaluations for achieving the desired change. Whenever possible, goals should be mutually determined by the patient/client and the therapist. This can expedite the treatment process.

So far the discussion has summarized the essential phenomenon of behavior modification. Although stating the theory is easy compared to applying it clinically by a practitioner, the techniques can be mastered under the guidance of an experienced behavioral practitioner. Essentially, four processes are involved in altering behavior: (1) increase the strength of a certain adaptive behavior; (2) teach new behaviors that are not already in a client's repertoire for living; (3) teach new ways of adjusting to the environment; and (4) decrease the strength of his maladaptive behavior [1].

Two primary types of events must be considered: *behavioral responses* and *environmental stimuli. Responses* are small, distinct parts of a person's behavior. *Stimuli* are environmental events that interact with a person's behavior and influence it. A stimulus that follows a response and increases the future probability of that response is called a *positive reinforcer* and is symbolically represented as SR^+. Reinforcement is one of the most direct ways of increasing a behavior. Positive reinforcement involves a desirable consequence following a behavior, i.e., use of attention to elicit appropriate behavior. *Negative reinforcement* is a process of removing an aversive event in order to strengthen behavior, i.e., the pain a child experiences after a fall acts as an aversive stimulus, the removal of which will reinforce the response of asking mother for pain-relieving measures. A stimulus that follows a response and decreases the future probability of that response is called an *aversive stimulus* or *punisher* and is represented by the symbol SR^-. *Punishment*, an environmental consequence immediately following a response, results in a decrease in the future probability of that response. Punishment can be delivered by presentation of an aversive stimulus immediately following a response or by the withdrawal of an ongoing, positive reinforcer immediately following a response [2].

Some environmental stimuli may precede a response and influence it by signaling for the response to occur. These stimuli are called *discriminative stimuli,* e.g., seeing a commercial on TV elicits a desire to buy the product being advertised; this type of stimuli is represented by the symbol SD. A *stimuli-delta,* S, occurs and signals that a response should not occur. If a response does occur, it will not be reinforced, e.g., Mother tells a child she cannot have anything to eat before supper; and when the child approaches Mother to ask her, Mother walks away [2].

Many stimuli are neutral, however, and serve no purpose in relation to the way a person behaves in their presence. In order for a relationship to exist, the responses and stimuli must become linked together in an orderly way. This linking takes place via the process of operant conditioning — responses occur and are strengthened (learned) or weakened (unlearned) according to a plan or program. The interrelationship between a response and the stimuli that effect it is referred to as a *contingency.*

Reinforcement can be maintained by various schedules. Continuous reinforcement occurs when the environment produces a reinforcer every time the response occurs. When the environment produces a reinforcer only occasionally following the response,

intermittent reinforcement occurs. Simple intermittent schedules can be planned on the basis of time (interval) or on the
basis of number of responses emitted per reinforcer (ratio).
Each schedule has its specified applications [2].

Behavioral Group Counseling

Behavioral counselors define behavior as a function of heredity
and environment. They are concerned with observable behavior,
and this constitutes the criterion against which counseling outcomes are assessed. Since most behavior is learned, it can be
unlearned and replaced with more adequate behavior patterns.
The counseling process, then, becomes the process of arranging
learning or relearning experiences to help individuals find more
adaptive ways of coping with difficulties. Social learning principles, e.g., reinforcement, social modeling, cognitive learning
(verbal instruction and role-playing), and emotional learning
(desensitization and relaxation), are all used to help a person
gain a repertoire of appropriate responses so that he can then
choose among alternate ways of behaving in certain situations.

Group counseling is of value because the relationships that
form within the group setting become effective modifiers of
behavior since group members directly experience the results
of their behavior. A number of models and sources of reinforcement within the group act as modifiers of behavior; group membership itself may even act as a modifier. There are numerous
opportunities for behavior to be practiced, changed, and
strengthened and for supervised discriminations and generalizations to occur.

SELECTION AND COMPOSITION OF THE GROUP

Selecting a member for a particular group would depend primarily upon (1) counselor interest in a client's problem type, (2)
competency of the counselor, and (3) ethical considerations.
The individual should be placed in a group setting in which there
are adequate models from which he can learn. Groups are made
up of persons who share a common problem, this being much
more important than personality traits, age, and sex, although
these may occasionally be considered.

ROLE OF THE GROUP LEADER

The group leader, or counselor, aids in the learning process by
arranging conditions under which the client can learn adaptive
behavior. He helps the client set behavioral goals that the client
wants to attain and that the counselor feels will contribute to the

client's welfare. These goals are stated in specific kinds of behavior appropriate to each client's problems so that everyone knows exactly what is to be accomplished. Three categories of goals can be constructed, each calling for a somewhat different approach by the counselor: goals for altering maladaptive behavior, goals for learning the decision-making process, and goals for preventing problems. Only one problem at a time is selected to work on.

DURATION OF TREATMENT AND LENGTH OF SESSIONS
Duration of treatment varies according to the client's problem, but termination always occurs immediately upon achievement of the client's goals. The session itself usually lasts no longer than two hours at a time.

BEHAVIORAL MODIFICATION ASSESSMENT TOOL *
[Clients/patients usually seek help for a defined reason or problem. Before a treatment regimen can be developed, instituted, and assessed, and the client helped, however, the practitioner must accurately diagnose or assess the *real* problem. Applying the theory of behavior modification can effectively provide a framework for therapeutic interaction. The theory is of particular help in dealing with concrete and specific problems that are clearly delineated when the assessment tool below is utilized. The practitioner as usual collects data from the Comprehensive Basic Assessment System first, after which the additional behavioral process information is obtained.]

   I. Behavioral Problem Statement
      A. Define the problem statement.
         1. Client's own definition of problem
         2. History of problem
         3. Date of onset
         4. Related symptoms
         5. Successful relief measures
         6. Unsuccessful relief measures
      B. Define the problem statement by the professional ascertained by Comprehensive Basic Assessment System using problem-oriented system format.
         1. State subjective data.
         2. State objective data.
         3. State assessment.

*Based on the Behavioral Nursing Process outlined in [1, pp. 76–77].

II. Behavioral History
    A. Responses
        1. List age-appropriate responses.
        2. List responses present in client's behavior.
        3. List inappropriate responses present in client's behavior.
    B. Consequences
        1. What reinforces the behavior in question?
        2. What general things serve as reinforcers for the client?
        3. Is punishment affecting the behavior? How?
        4. What in general has served as punishment for the patient?
    C. Control
        1. Can the stimulus surrounding the problematic behavior be controlled?
        2. Can the consequences surrounding the problematic behavior be controlled?
III. Baseline Data
    A. Define the problem objectively.
    B. Determine the rate of a response of the behavior.
    C. Validate potential reinforcers from baseline data
IV. Assessment
    A. Define new problems.
    B. Restate problem as needed.
    C. Determine type of learning problem.
        1. Response too frequent
        2. Response too infrequent
        3. Response does not occur
        4. Response inappropriate
V. Treatment/Intervention
    A. State behavioral goal.
    B. Develop plan to accomplish goal.
    C. Implement plan.
VI. Evaluation
    A. Was the desired behavioral goal reached?
    B. If the desired behavior goal was not reached, reevaluate steps I through V to determine probable inaccurate data.
    C. Make necessary changes in steps I through V.
    D. Reevaluate alternate plan.

CLIENT-CENTERED THERAPY
Content
Client-centered therapy was developed by Dr. Carl Rogers, a phenomenological theorist. His theory is that (1) meeting man's

basic needs of love, belonging, security, and affection, provides him with control over his antisocial emotions; (2) man's behavior is not determined by outside forces but through a thoughtful and conscious process; and (3) inherent in man is an actualizing tendency to develop all his capacities for self-maintenance and enhancement. The goal of man's behavior is to develop fully and be free of external controls.

Rogers has built his theory of personality structure around three main concepts: the organism, the phenomenal field, and the self. The *organism* is the total individual in which changes in any one part may produce changes in any other part. The organism is all the thoughts and behaviors and the physical being of a person. The organism acts in a holistic fashion to the phenomenal field, as an organized entity in attempting to satisfy a person's needs. The organism has a desire to develop fully and be free of external controls. Finally, it acts in a way that allows some experiences to become symbolized in the consciousness while others are ignored — this is a product of learning.

The *phenomenal field* is the constantly changing external and internal experiences of the person. This includes all going on within the organism that might reach consciousness. The organism reacts to the field as it is experienced and perceived. What might be actual reality is not important here since it is what the individual *perceives* to be occurring that is his reality.

Seemingly, the most important concept in Rogers' theory of personality is the concept of the *self*. The self is a differentiated part of the phenomenal field, composed of a series of perceptions and values about the person himself, the *I* and *me*. It is the center of the structure around which the personality evolves. For Rogers it is an organized conceptual Gestalt, consisting of the individual's perception of himself alone and of himself in relation to other persons and to objects together with the values attached to these perceptions. The self-concept is not always in awareness but is always available to awareness.

The self develops out of interaction with the environment and in the process tends to integrate the values of others that are consistent with the self and distorts inconsistent ones in order to maintain a consistency within the self. It is not necessarily coexistent with the physical organism. Whether or not an object or an experience is regarded as a part of the self depends to a considerable extent upon whether or not it is perceived as within the control of the self. Those things that one controls are seen as a part of the self, but when even such an object as a part of one's body is out of control, it is experienced as being less a part of the self. Rogers feels that perhaps it is this gradient of autonomy which first gives an infant an awareness of self when he for the first time becomes aware of a feeling of control over some aspect of his world of experience [4]. It is important to note here that within Rogers' framework the self is always in process, growing and changing as a result of its continuing interaction with the phenomenal field. Thus the personality in turn continues to interact and produce changes in the individual.

A healthy personality is what Rogers calls a fully functioning individual [5]. Under proper growth conditions the human is capable of being open to all his experiences, having no need to apply defensive mechanisms. He will, since he is aware of his experiences, be able to symbolize them accurately. He will be in a constant state of change, able to deal in adaptive and creative ways with new situations because he will have no need to deny or distort experiences. He will be socially effective because of the rewarding character of reciprocal positive regard and will live each moment to its fullest. He trusts his own judgments and choices and depends less upon others' approval or disapproval. Within the individual there is a basic congruence between the phenomenal field of experience and the conceptual structure of the self.

Psychological maladjustment occurs when the individual denies significant sensory and visual experiences to awareness; consequently these experiences are not symbolized and organized into the Gestalt of the self's structure. In other words, there is a state of basic incongruence and the individual perceives much of his behavior as out of control. Conscious control becomes more difficult as the individual strives to satisfy needs that are not consciously admitted and to react to experiences that are denied to the conscious self. The individual feels anxious, unsure of his direction, and feels that he is not integrated or united.

There are several concepts that play an important part in Rogers' theory of learning and human development [1]. First, Rogers recognizes that the individual is in a constant transaction in a changing world; this produces various responses within him in addition to the response produced by processing going on within the individual himself. Rogers labels as experiences these subjectively observable responses (which are potentially available to awareness at any one point in time). These are divided into nonsymbolic responses and awareness and symbolic responses. The organismic experience represents the nonsymbolic subclasses of responses under the concept of experience. The concept includes all interoceptive, proprioceptive, extroceptive, and affective responses that represent the data by which the environment and its effects on the individual become available to the person's awareness. Situational events are important only in that they evoke responses; it is the individual's perception of events that is crucial to eliciting subjective responses, or organismic experiences.

With the symbolic and awareness responses the individual does not learn to be aware — this is inborn — but the *focus* of one's attention is a product of learning. The person is only aware of what is symbolized, though there may be varying degrees of awareness, as implied above. These symbolizations (images and thoughts) will represent the antecedent events accurately unless certain kinds of learnings occur that produce distortions and hence interfere with effective behavior.

Another important concept in Rogers' theory is the capacity of the individual to resolve, through thoughts and emotions, incongruities among responses. The individual not only learns new responses in new situations but automatically tries to fit these into existing patterns of behavior. This response organization determines which thoughts about oneself will become habitual. Only new images and thoughts that are consistent with the existing whole unit can become a part of it, and this unit influences which behaviors the individual will perform. People choose to behave in ways that are consistent with their self-concepts and reject those that are not. Thus a change in self-concept may produce an important change in one's entire self-organization. Because the self undergoes constant change and actively influences the occurrence of other responses, Rogers speaks of the self as "process' [2].

The final major learning concept involves the actualizing tendency, the prime initiator of behavior, residing within the person. All of the more specific drives or motivational events such as need reduction, drive reduction, and tension reduction are manifestations of this major drive. This is the tendency to maintain oneself — maintaining one's physical integrity through breathing, eating, drinking, and avoiding being hurt or damaged in some way — or enhancing oneself through learning new skills or tasks and seeking out pleasurable and satisfying things. Behavior thus has a directional trend in this urge to develop and mature and grow.

Maslow's [3] theory is built entirely upon this tendency toward actualization of inherent potentialites but is somewhat different from that of Rogers, emphasizing sometimes the physiological organism and sometimes the phenomenal self. The first is actually a survival tendency rather than a fulfillment tendency. This survival is prepotent over the actualization tendency in that a certain amount of satisfaction of the former is necessary before an individual can engage in any real expression of the latter. However, the survival tendency can, according to Maslow's theory, only maintain life, not enhance it in any way. Maslow [3] classified the actualization tendency as growth motivation and the survival tendency as deprivation motivation. Rogers made no such distinction. He only identified what he believed was an underlying theme in behavior — that the direction of every person's life is not only to keep himself alive but to accomplish something, exercise his potentialities, and attempt to mold his environment into achievements for his enhancement. Behavior may thus be thought of as one functional unit since it all serves the same purpose.

Rogers' theory concerning human growth and development holds that from birth the infant's behavior is directed toward the need to satisfy the organism in interaction with reality, which for the individual is what *he* experiences. It is this perceived reality that affects behavior, regardless of whether that perception is in fact an accurate one. As the individual interacts with his perceived reality, he interacts as a unit and begins to evaluate his experiences as to whether they meet his self-actualization needs. As he goes through this evaluating process, the individual begins to attend to those experiences he evaluates as positive and avoid those he evaluates as negative. Out of this interaction with perceived reality — these self experiences — the self of the individual develops.

As this awareness of self develops, the person also becomes aware of the positive and negative responses of others to his behavior. He then begins to avoid those behaviors that do not elicit responses satisfying to him. In this way he has acquired a need for positive regard [2]. This leads him to judge his behavior according to the values of others, whether or not it is satisfying to him. In the development of the unhealthy personality, the evaluation of others becomes so important to the person that his behavior is dominated by what others think; even his liking or disliking himself is based on the evaluation of others. This sequence will not happen if the individual always feels loved by others, even though they do not accept some of his behavior, because the "conditions" of worth do not develop. If the child always feels loved, he experiences unconditional positive regard and hence experiences only conditional self-regard. These conditions lead to the development of a healthy personality, or a fully functioning individual as described in the preceding section.

Rogers' Theory of Counseling

Rogers' theory of counseling consists of three main parts: condition, process, and outcomes. If certain conditions exist, then a definite process is set in motion, which in turn leads to certain outcomes or changes in the client's personality and behavior. Rogers has set forth six general conditions that seem to him to be necessary to initiate constructive personality change and which, taken together, seem to be sufficient for the process. These conditions must continue over a period of time. Among these conditions are that two persons must be in psychological contact, with the first (the client) being in a state of incongruence, vulnerability, or anxiety. The therapist must experience an unconditionally positive regard for the client. He must also experience an empathetic understanding with the client and unconditional positive regard must be at least minimally achieved. Rogers believes that if these conditions exist and continue over a period of time, the process of constructive personality change will follow [5]. Since these necessary and sufficient conditions are so important to Rogers' psychotherapy process, it would be well to explore in greater detail their meaning and the terms used in them.

The first condition, that of psychological contact, is met when both client and therapist are aware of being in personal and psychological contact with each other. The second condition, the incongruent state of the client, refers to a discrepancy between the actual experience of the client and his self-picture insofar as it represents that experience. When the individual is not aware of such incongruence in himself, he is merely vulnerable to the possibility of anxiety and disorganization. An experience could occur so suddenly or so obviously that the incongruence could not be denied, making the person vulnerable.

The third condition is that the therapist should be, within the confines of the relationship, a congruent, genuine, integrated person. This means that the therapist is freely and deeply himself, with his own actual experience accurately represented by his awareness of himself. This includes being himself even in ways that may not be usually regarded as ideal for psychotherapy. He should never deceive the client as to himself.

To the extent that the therapist finds himself experiencing a warm acceptance of each aspect of the client's experience as being a part of that client, he is experiencing unconditional positive regard, the fourth condition. In this way no conditions are placed upon acceptance, no "ifs" attached to the liking. It involves as much a feeling of acceptance for the client's expression of negative, defensive feelings as for his expression of positive, mature, and confident feelings. It means caring for the client as a separate person with permission to have his own feelings and experiences.

The fifth condition is that the therapist experience an accurate, empathetic understanding of the client's awareness of his own experience. It means sensing the client's anger, fear, or confusion as if it were the therapist's own, yet without the therapist's own anger, fear, or confusion getting bound up in it. When this condition is met, the therapist's remarks fit in closely with the client's mood and content, and his tone of voice conveys his ability to share the client's feelings.

Finally, the sixth condition involves the client's perception of the therapist's acceptance and empathy. Unless there is some communication of these attitudes, they do not exist in the relationship so far as the client is concerned and the therapeutic process cannot be initiated.

Although these conditions are stated as if they were all-or-none elements, Rogers states that the second and sixth conditions exist on a continuum [5]. He also maintains that when the preceding conditions exist and continue, a therapy process with the following characteristics is set in motion:

1. The client feels increasingly free to express his feelings in a variety of ways, feelings that refer more and more to the self rather than the nonself.
2. The client more accurately symbolizes his experiences and realizes the incongruity between some of his experiences and his self-concept. He is aware of this incongruence as a threat.
3. The client's self-concept becomes reorganized to include experiences and feelings that were previously denied or distorted.
4. The client can then become more accepting of the therapist's unconditional positive regard, and he feels an unconditional, positive self-regard, experiencing himself as the focus of evaluation.

Although there is no clear distinction between process and outcome, it would be expected that after the process has been gone through the client will become a more fully functioning person [5].

As can be seen, the nature of the relationship between client and therapist is of major importance in the establishment of the counseling process. Since the client comes to the counselor for help, the responsibility for the relationship is the client's; it is the client himself who has the answers to his own problems. The counselor generally sets specific time limits for the sessions; he may even set a specific number of sessions in which to work so that the client may sense a need to make each session as profitable as possible.

In general, the client-centered approach does not believe that the counselor should bring information, as such, into the counseling process. It does not deny the importance of information; rather it holds the view that the client should be the one who brings information gathered outside of counseling into the counseling process. The counseling experience thus becomes one of helping the client sift through the information gathered, with the emphasis placed on the client's *feelings* about that information [1]. The emphasis in the counseling process is on the individual and not on the particular concern or problem. The entire human being requires attention, not just one particular aspect. The specific concerns will be solved as a by-product of the individual's growth toward self-actualization.

Client-Centered Group Therapy

At the core of Rogers' rationale for change in client-centered therapy is the theory of self-structure, which develops out of the individual's interaction with the environment, at times incorporating the value of others. The individual strives for consistency and behaves in ways that are consistent with his self-concept. Experiences that are inconsistent with the self-structure are perceived as threats and are defended against by means of denial or misperception of the experience. In order to change this process of threat and defense, the self-concept must become more congruent with the individual's actual experiences. But, changes in the self-concept are resisted because they tend to violate the conditions of worth and the need for positive self-regard.

The client-centered group provides a climate in which there is less threat, less need for the defenses against anxiety that make the person ineffectual in living with himself, and others, and less need to resist change. The individual becomes increasingly free to examine himself, knowing that he will be understood and accepted, not only by the therapist but by others who are honestly sharing their feelings and are also searching for a more satisfying way of life. The intense relationships that often develop as a part of the basic encounter group release the individual from socially learned restraints that keep him from fully experiencing himself and those around him.

The group situation also provides an immediate opportunity for finding more satisfying ways of relating to people. Since the discrepancies in the perception of the self are primarily products of the experiences the individual has had with important others in his life, he is in need of the group experience. It will bring him closer to others and help him discover those denied aspects of himself which are important in his relationship with others. As a member of a group, he learns what it means to give and receive emotional support and understanding in a new and more mature way, and he may achieve a more mature balance between independence and a realistic dependence on others.

In this kind of climate, the individual is free to get on with what Rogers believes is an inherent tendency to move in directions of growth, health, adjustment, socialization, self-realization, independence, and autonomy; Rogers calls this tendency "self-actualization." This, along with the construct of "self," is a primary motivating factor of behavior in the client-centered approach to group therapy, a dominant factor that can be relied on to affect growth and change in the client's behavior.

SELECTION AND COMPOSITION OF THE GROUP

The selection of members for a client-centered therapy group is relatively simple, the criteria being that (1) the individual is likely to benefit from the experience, and (2) that the group will be likely to benefit from his presence in it. Since Rogers feels that it is impossible to say who will gain and who will not, it is usually left to the individual to decide whether or not he feels he will profit from the group experiences. It is felt, however, that certain persons do tend to disrupt a group and that it is best not to include disturbed but psychologically sophisticated people who might use their knowledge of psychodynamics to hurt others in the group, and extremely hostile and aggressive people who make it impossible to achieve the climate of freedom and acceptance that is essential to the growth of individuals in the group. It is also not desirable to place persons in the same group who have continued close daily contact outside the group, as this may restrict the amount of freedom to disclose one's self in the group setting.

ROLE OF THE GROUP LEADER

The group leader takes an active role both in helping to establish a warm, supportive climate and in helping to establish the group's responsibility for its own direction. The leader attempts to understand what a group member is saying and feeling, to communicate that understanding to the group, and to make it easier for a group member to explore himself more fully. He does this best by making statements that show acceptance of what is said, restating content, and clarifying feeling. It is important that he not dominate the group while doing this. He may delay his responses slightly in order to give group members an opportunity to take the role of therapist. If important feelings go unrecognized or if other group members tend to deny feelings of a member, however, the leader must come in with a response. The leader must be able to recognize and objectively deal with the cross-currents of feeling that develop within the group, and he must be able to clarify his own feelings toward group members so that he can respond to each person with consistent understanding.

SETTING OF THE GROUP AND MEDIA USED
Groups meet in a comfortable, quiet room, neither too cramped nor too spacious, where everyone can sit in a circle or around a table, and interruptions can be avoided. Structure and the use of media is avoided since the group determines its own direction.

LENGTH OF SESSIONS AND DURATION OF TREATMENT
Groups usually meet twice a week for a period of one hour, although longer time periods are used. There is much flexibility and adaptation to the circumstances and needs of the group. In marathons, weekend encounter sessions, and daily groups, this time period is modified considerably.

The decision to terminate is left to the group, but most groups average approximately 20 meetings.

PREFERRED SIZE OF THE GROUP
Groups are normally composed of about six people in addition to the therapist, since small groups allow a maximum of personal interaction. One or two more may be added, but Rogers feels that more than this slows the group down and increases the number who remain uninvolved in the group process.

Client-Centered Therapy Tool
I. Data Base
   A. Phenomenal field: get answers from client
      1. Describe those forces or external experiences currently going on in your life.

2. Describe those forces or external experiences that are significant in your past.
3. What things are going on inside of you that are causing you difficulty?
4. What things are going on inside of you that caused you difficulty in the past?
5. What things are going on inside you that are important to you right now?
6. What things in the past were important to you?

B. Self: get answers from client
   1. Describe yourself.
   2. What do you like?
   3. What do you dislike?
   4. How do others see you?
   5. What is of value to you?
   6. What values do you reject?
   7. What things do you have control of in yourself?
   8. What is others' evaluation of you?
   9. Do you feel loved?
   10. Do you feel worthwhile?

C. Organism
   1. Thoughts
   2. Behaviors (good: helpful; bad, get you in trouble)
   3. Defense mechanisms
   4. Physical pertinent biological data

D. Is there congruence between the phenomenal field of experience and the conceptual structure of self?

E. Relationship checklist: answers from both therapist and client
   1. Are you in personal and psychological contact with each other?
   2. Is there a discrepancy between the actual experience of the client and his self-picture insofar as it represents that experience?
   3. Is the therapist a congruent, genuine, integrated person?
   4. Is the therapist experiencing warm acceptance of the patient (unconditional positive regard)?
   5. Is the therapist experiencing an accurate, empathetic understanding of the client's awareness of his own experience?
   6. Is the client perceiving the acceptance and empathy on the part of the therapist?

EXISTENTIAL THERAPY

Content

The existential approach is consistent with the phenomenological viewpoint. Existentialists identify the following characteristics of man. Man is aware of his continuously occurring, changing behavior during interaction with surrounding events. Self-awareness gives him his personal sense of identity of being, which in turn makes him capable of being selective in what he responds to and how he responds. Thus he is continuously expressing his behavioral possibilities, molding his environment to himself.

Self-awareness leads to the recognition that the individual could lose his identity if he lost all significant relationships with his environment. This leads to anxiety, a response characteristic of all men and not necessarily a basis for pathology. It occurs when the person sees a threat to his importance, welfare, or actual existence. Anxiety leads to a restriction of behavior, which in turn leads to guilt, also a normal affective response.

Existentialists believe that man is in a constant state of transition, emergence, and actualization and that he has worth and dignity.

Existentialists are steeped in the phenomenological approach, seeming to have an aversion to formal, abstract theorizing. According to many existentialists, intuitive understanding is the only important psychological knowledge, and intuition is the antithesis of abstraction. There are some assumptions that existentialists hold concerning personality, however. Maddi [2] has presented the existential position in terms of core and peripheral characteristics of personality. "Being-in-the-world" is the basic core characteristic of personality, emphasizing the unity of person and environment, since both are personally or subjectively defined in this heavily phenomenological position. Person and environment are essentially one and the same because both are human creations. *Being* is the sum total of intuitive sensory experiences, combined with memories, fantasies, and anticipations. *World* is the environment a person creates for himself through exercising the capacities that produce being.

Being-in-the-world has three components: the construed biological and physical world, the construed social world, and the internal dialogue of relationship to oneself. It is assumed that behind these three components are man's biological, social, and psychological needs. Although these three sets of needs are similar to Maslow's [3] theory, Maddi does not propose them as being organized into a hierarchy. Once it is assumed that man's needs are biological, social, and psychological, it follows that the ideal is to be an expression of all three, a merging that produces a unitary whole [2].

Existentialists define two basic personality types: the individualist and the conformist [1]. The individualist defines himself as someone with a mental life through which he can understand and influence his social and biological experiences. In his world view, society is the creation of men and, as such, properly in their service. His functioning has unity and shows originality and change. His biological and social experiencing shows subtlety, taste, intimacy, and love. Although he may experience doubt as a natural concomitant of being his own measure of meaning, he does not let this emotion undermine his decision-making process.

The conformist defines himself as nothing more than a player of social roles and an embodiment of biological needs. In effect, he inhibits expression of symbolization, imagination, and judgment (the psychological needs), which has the effect of making his functioning fragmentary and stereotyped. His biological experiencing is isolated and gross, his social experiencing is contractual rather than intimate, and he feels worthless and insecure. He stresses materialism, and pragmatism in his world view. It is obvious which of the types is the existentialist's ideal and which is the epitome of maladjustment.

Existential Therapy Assessment Tool
I. Data Base
   A. Self-awareness of client
1. What is causing you trouble? How?
2. What are your biological needs?
3. What are your social needs?
4. What are your psychological needs?
5. Do you consider yourself to be a conformist or an individual?
6. What are you responding to now?
7. How do you respond?
8. Are you at terms (congruent) with your environment?
9. What significant relationship do you have with the environment?
10. Are you anxious?
11. Describe your anxiety.
12. Is there a threat to your importance?
13. Is there a threat to your welfare?

14. Is there a threat to your actual existence by yourself (suicide) or others?
15. Describe your memories.
16. Describe your fantasies.
17. What are you anticipating in life?
18. What is stopping you from getting what you want in life?

B. Directions for therapist
1. Discern your intuitive response to the patient.
2. Stay in the here and now.
3. Flow with the patient.
4. Share with the patient what you are experiencing.

ADLERIAN THERAPY

Content

A few major concepts sustain the theoretical structure of Adlerian theory. Four underlying principles in the Adlerian approach to counseling explain the techniques and therapeutic results of this therapy. Alfred Adler believed first that all human qualities are expressive of social interaction, since man is primarily a social being who seeks relationships with other humans. The desire to belong, to have some significance in the immediate environment is the prime motivating force behind human action, although individuals seek their belonging and significance in different ways. Humans sometimes develop devious means to find significance or have a distorted view of their possibilities to do so. Adler emphasizes that human problems are of a social nature. Although an individual's behavior may seem inappropriate, it is reflecting his belief that this is his way to find his significant place in society.

The second principle holds that all human action has purpose. The individual sets his own goals: both immediate ones, i.e., for the present field of action, and long range ones, goals for his entire life. These goals form the basis of his personality or life style. Life style is the individual's consistent and particular approach to the work, problems, and challenges of life. It makes no difference whether the individual is aware of his goals or not; he always acts in accordances with his life goals and does only what he really intends to do [3].

The third principle of the Adlerian approach concerns itself with the individual's phenomenological field. The therapist does not deal with the way events appear externally, but with the way the individual perceives those events, their meaning for him.

Adler himself wrote "A man is not determined by his environment, but by his estimate of it" [1]. Each person explains his experiences so that they fit in with his own particular life style; so, in order to understand behavior, one must consider the individual's own private logic.

The last basic principle of the Adlerian model is the belief in unity of the personality. The holistic view of man sees the indivisibility of the individual, who is more than the sum total of all of his physical, mental, and emotional processes and functions interacting with each other.

Analysis and guidance toward new behavior is the focus of this holistic approach. The therapist primarily decides what is inappropriate and what is causing the client social problems, and he determines the therapeutic objectives at the beginning of therapy. Adlerian therapists feel that since clients are generally unaware of what is disordered in their behavior patterns, the therapist must help guide the client in the analysis of his problem and help him change his behavior.

One of the first tasks of therapy is to uncover the client's neurotic life style. Symptoms as such are not attended to, since the therapist is primarily interested in the goals that these symptoms serve. Since behavior is understood in terms of its social purposes, the therapist is able to use symptoms to pinpoint the social consequences sought by the client. The therapist is then equipped to help the client understand and change his inappropriate life goals, and thus change his inappropriate behavior and more basically, his life style. This redirection of goals requires a restoration of the client's faith in himself, his own abilities and strengths, and his own self-worth. The success of therapy depends to a great extent upon the ability of the therapist to provide this kind of encouragement.

In the therapy process an effort is made to provide, as in most other approaches, an atmosphere of acceptance and positive regard for the client. The focus is on the here and now since little time is used in delving into the past. It is felt by Adlerian therapists that going into the past only gives the client an excuse for behaving inappropriately. The aim is rather to help the client take responsibility for his actions in the present no matter what has happened in his past.

Dinkmeyer and Carlson [2] have set forth five specific techniques used in the Adlerian approach that enable the therapist to accomplish the above-mentioned tasks: (1) those techniques that focus on the content of the communication, (2) those eliciting affect, (3) those designed to facilitate an awareness of the client's own part in transactions with others that may be causing him difficulty, (4) techniques for analyzing the goals and dynamics of behavior, and (5) those designed to facilitate new goals and new behavioral responses. The utilization of these techniques must be accomplished with sensitivity to the human relationship involved, for it is through this therapist-client relationship that change is facilitated. This relationship shows the client an alternative way of behaving, a healthy way, which he can then transfer outside the therapy situation.

Theoretical Rationale for Change

Before we explain the techniques and therapeutic results of group counseling in the Adlerian tradition, there will be a brief review of some basic principles in Adlerian psychology. First, from the Adlerian point of view all human qualities are expressions of social interaction, and all human problems are of a social nature. The desire to belong is the prime human motivation. Second, all human actions have a purpose. The individual sets his own goals, which then form the basis of his personality, his life style. The third principle is the belief in the unity of the personality. The holistic view of the man sees the indivisibility of the individual, who is more than the sum total of all his physical, mental, and emotional processes and functions.

Since the individual's problems and conflicts are thus seen in their social nature, the group is ideally suited, not only to reveal the nature of a person's conflicts and maladjustments, but to offer corrective influences. In addition, since mistaken concepts and values are at the root of social deficiencies and emotional maladjustments, the group can serve as a value-forming agent, influencing the convictions and beliefs of its members.

Group Therapy

There are four phases in Adlerian group counseling. The first of these is the establishment and maintenance of a proper counseling relationship, which means winning the clients' cooperation for the task of working toward common goals. Many times, confidence in the therapist and his ability is enhanced in a well-functioning group, as is confidence in the outcome of therapy. The distrust that a client may have can vanish under the impact of the faith exhibited by other group members.

The second phase involves the analysis of the life style of the client. In the group setting, the client is seen in action and his goals and movements become obvious in the interaction with his fellow group members. This phase also involves a study of the client's formative years and family constellation, for that is when and where he developed his concept about himself and about life.

The third phase of counseling involves interpretation of the client's movements and intentions. All of the experiences the client reports are used to explain his goals and movements, with constant reference to his basic life style. The group facilitates this insight because, as the person learns about other members, he learns about people in general and more about himself in particular. Insight, however, is not a basis for adjustment; it is only a mechanism for change.

The most decisive change necessary for a lasting therapeutic effect is for the client to give up the faulty premises upon which the individual operates and reorient himself toward a new life style, the fourth phase. As mentioned earlier, this redirection of mistaken goals requires a restoration of the client's faith in himself, the realization of his own strength and ability, and the belief in his own dignity and worth. This important process of restoration is called encouragement. Since each member of the group enjoys social equality, the need for emotional isolation and competitiveness is removed, and the individual can be himself without fear or danger. In this sense, the group itself provides a subtle encouragement for each member. The success of therapy depends, to a large extent, on the ability of the counselor and the group to provide this encouragement.

SELECTION AND COMPOSITION OF THE GROUP

No one who wishes to join a group is turned away because a refusal would be contrary to the Adlerian therapist's belief in democratic premises. Dreikurs states that no rigid criteria about the composition of the group or member selection has ever been formulated. Group counseling may be done with adults, children, adolescents, and families. When counseling children, however, it is advisable to have an even number of boys and girls in the group, and too divergent an age range should be avoided. Homogeneous grouping with regard to problems is not necessary and may even be less therapeutic.

ROLE OF THE GROUP LEADER

The job of the therapist leading the group is to help the individual substitute realistic for unrealistic life goals and to instill social interest and feeling. This involves assuming an active, teaching role in which the counselor establishes himself as the group leader, even though the democratic atmosphere still prevails. This is especially true in group counseling with children, where it is important that the counselor be kind, but firm, and without the destructiveness of familiarity. The group counselor must assume the responsibility of serving as an interpreter and guiding agent in the psychological process of change. It is his function to direct the group's interaction through the four phases of counseling described above.

SETTING OF THE GROUP
The setting for the Adlerian group should be a private place where it is possible for the participants to sit close together in a circle or semicircle so they can face each other. No special media are involved.

LENGTH OF SESSION AND DURATION OF TREATMENT
Most groups meet once or twice a week for approximately one and one-half hours. Duration of treatment depends entirely upon the successful redirection of the client.

PREFERRED SIZE OF THE GROUP
Ten to twelve clients is generally accepted as the maximum size, with six to eight being the minimum. The size of the group often depends upon the skill and experience of the counselor.

Adlerian Theory Assessment Tool
I. Patient Interview
   A. What is the nature of the problem?
   B. Identify what patient does in relationship — a key technique.
   C. When did the problem arise?
   D. Relationship of siblings (if any)
   E. Environmental influence
      1. Relatives
      2. Other people in the house
      3. Neighbors
   F. Describe your daily routine.
   G. Describe your social relationships.
   H. What is your interest in the future?

CARKHUFF MODEL
Content
Perhaps the most outstanding eclectic therapist of our time is Robert R. Carkhuff. At the least, he is the theoretician who has

most recently attempted to make eclecticism more than the stepchild of therapy, to make it a model built around a central core of conditions that he believes are shared by all interview-oriented approaches [1].

Carkhuff's goals of counseling are: (1) fostering client exploration of his problem; (2) furthering the client's understanding of himself; and (3) helping the client to act on his understanding. He feels that most theories include only one or two of these goals; e.g., primarily relying on insight, as do the psychoanalytic theories; on emotional catharsis, as do the nondirective theories; or on action, as do the behavioral theories. Carkhuff's theory attempts to integrate all of these emphases within one counseling model. Carkhuff divides therapy into two major phases, the downward and inward phases — involving the building of a therapist-client relationship and the exploration of the problem with some understanding taking place — and the upward and outward phases — involving a reintegration with the world through further understanding and constructive action on the part of the client.

In order to help a client experience both phases and make effective changes in his life, Carkhuff's model makes use of the facilitative conditions of a central core; these conditions are considered to be critical to the process. The first three conditions are facilitative responses intended to be the building blocks of trust in the client-therapist relationship; the last three are action-oriented conditions.

The first of the core conditions necessary for trust in the client-therapist relationship is respect, or positive regard. It manifests itself in the warmth and caring of one person for another and must be communicated so that the client can develop high self-regard. According to Carkhuff this communication of respect seems to break the isolation of the client and form the basis for empathy. It is automatically communicated over a continuing period of interaction if the therapist himself has a deep sense of respect for all of his own feelings and experiences as well as those of others, including the feelings of anger and hurt as well as the more pleasant ones.

The second facilitative condition, empathy, involves an understanding by the therapist of the experience of the client and a communication of this understanding to the client. It is more than an intellectual understanding, an awareness of the client on a deeply human level.

The third condition — concreteness — is largely under the therapist's direct control and involves the direct and complete expression of specific experiences and feelings, regardless of their emotional content. The specificity encourages accuracy on the part of the therapist, clarification and correction of misunderstandings, and direct attention to feelings and experiences that might otherwise be expressed in vague terms less easily dealt with.

On one level, genuineness is one of the bases of the client-therapist relationship, making it a part of the downward and inward phase of therapy. However, Carkhuff makes a distinction between this level of genuineness and the construct of facilitative genuineness that is an outward dimension [1] and the first of the three action-oriented conditions. Negative genuineness in regard to the client is potentially destructive. The therapist must therefore make an effort to express his genuineness in a constructive manner so the client can use it to grow and change. Although the therapist may choose to withhold some very genuine responses from a client who cannot yet make use of them in a constructive way, the emphasis must be toward a more genuine, full sharing, relationship that can be changed.

Confrontation, or telling it like it is, is aimed at bringing the client into more direct contact with himself, his strengths and his weaknesses [1]. This, the second action condition, is a constructive attack because it is directed at incongruence and destructive discrepancies between what the client says and what he does, between client fantasy and reality. Its goal is to bring about a congruence and unity within the client. It is a challenge to the client to make use of his resources and grow toward deeper insight and constructive action; this makes it part of the upward, outward phase of therapy.

Immediacy is the last of the six core conditions and the third action condition. It is the expression of what is going on in the here and now.

Carkhuff has systematically scaled the core helping conditions. At level 1 none of the conditions are communicated in a response to any noticeable degree. At level 2 some of the conditions are communicated and some are not. At level 3, called the "interchangeable level" because it exists when either the helper or helpee could have made the response, all of the conditions are communicated at a minimally facilitative level. At level 4 all of the conditions are communicated fully, simultaneously, and continually. At level 5, the highest level of communication, all of the conditions are communicated fully, simultaneously, and continually.

The philosophical underpinning of this model is the concept

that any helper can only help a client up to that helper's own level. This means that only a therapist functioning at high levels can facilitate the higher functioning of the client, that the therapist cannot facilitate the growth of a client to levels higher than those at which he himself is functioning. At the minimally facilitative level of communication and functioning, level 3, the therapist's response is interchangeable with that of the client. At the levels 4 and 5, however, the therapist's response adds to and expands upon the client's response, enabling the client to move on to deeper levels of self-exploration and upward to action [1]. If the therapist is functioning below level 3 he has nothing to offer the client and can hinder the client's exploration and growth by his lack of understanding and incongruence.

In Carkhuff's model the therapist cannot be effective unless he is a fully functioning person, finding fulfillment in a creative life. To be able to help a client live effectively, the therapist must be able to say, "I am living effectively." Carkhuff believes, then, that counseling and therapy are a way of life.

Carkhuff Model Assessment Tool
  I. Client Exploration of His Problem
     A. What is client's problem in his own words?
     B. How do others see client's problem?
     C. How does therapist see client's problem?
     D. Restate the problem.
 II. Furthering Client's Understanding of Himself
     A. Client describes self.
     B. Therapist describes client.
     C. Therapist shares perception of client with him.
     D. Client's response to therapist's perception recorded.
III. Helping Client to Act Upon His Understanding
     A. Develop plan to act on problem.
     B. Evaluate plan effectiveness.
     C. Recycle through III A and III B to reassess the problem and develop a new plan, if needed.

GESTALT THERAPY
Content
In Gestalt theory, Fritz Perls [4], building a great deal upon Freudian theory, emphasizes conscious and unconscious processes and uses the traditional psychoanalytic defenses such as repression, to explain the causes of neuroses. Gestaltists nonetheless are phenomenological and use words such as *enhancement,*

intimacy, actualization, creativity, ecstasy, and transcendence to describe what is ideal in the human personality. Gestalt theory holds that the basic tendency in every individual is to strive for balance, to aim at reducing tension or providing pleasurable feelings. Perls also says that every organism has self-actualization as its goal. In striving for balance in relation to demands from the environment, the organism is not a passive receptor or reactor but an active perceiver and organizer of its perception into an internal reality.

Perls sees the ego (the awareness of self and nonself) as serving an organismic function, performing an integrative function as it relates the actions of the organism to its needs; e.g., when the self contacts the outside world, the ego establishes the boundary between the personal and impersonal field. It structures the environment, or the impersonal field, in terms of the organism's needs as it perceives them.

A person in conflict or neurosis rejects parts of himself, causing divisions within the personality and avoiding an experiencing of those parts. Perls talks about five layers of neurosis [5]. Many people spend much of their time on the first, or phony, layer, on which games are played and roles are lived; in the process much of the individual is disowned, with the resultant creation of voids. The person constantly harasses himself with the "topdog/underdog game," the topdog being what the person thinks he should be and the underdog the promiser, the maniuplator, the saboteur.

The second layer is the phobic layer. As a person becomes aware of phony behaviors and manipulations, he begins to get in touch with the fears that maintain them. He begins to want to avoid new behavior or has fantasies about what the consequences might be if he behaved in a genuine way.

The third layer is the impasse; here the person is caught, not knowing what to do or where to move. He experiences the loss of environmental support but does not have the support of a belief in his own resources.

The fourth layer is an implosive one. With grief and despair or self-loathing come a fuller realization of how the person may have limited or restricted himself, after which he may begin to experiment with new behavior. The fifth, or explosive layer, then emerges as the previously unused energies are freed in such a way as to make the greatest impact.

The Gestalt theory of personality thus is built around the ideal of a fully functioning, whole and spontaneous, and sensorily aware person, one who has freedom in movement, is expressive, is flexible in relating, and has closeness with others, intimacy, competency, immediacy, creativity, and self-support. It is Rogers' fully functioning individual, Maslow's self-actualized person, the existentialist's authentic being.

Gestalt therapy was developed from Gestalt psychology (the *Gestalt* being the meaningful, organized whole of an organism and its background), which was essentially a learning theory. In this theory the process by which the organism finds its satisfactions in the environment can be conceptualized as essentially that of a Gestalt formation in which there are a number of sub-wholes. Organismic needs lead to sensory motor behavior. Once a need that has the qualities of a good Gestalt is formed, the need that has now become the foreground is met through the sensory motor behavior and a balance is achieved — the organism is free to form new Gestalts [6]. This balance is what Perls felt to be the motivation for behavior rather than self-actualization, as such.

When needs are not recognized and expressed, the flexible harmony and flow between the organism and environment field is disturbed and the formation of new Gestalts is interfered with. The mentally healthy person has a permanent, meaningful, emerging, and receding figure and ground characterized by attention, interest, excitement, concentration, and concern. The neurotic or psychotic person, on the other hand, has a rigidity or lack of figure formation characterized by confusion, boredom, compulsions, fixations, extreme anxiety, and self-consciousness.

According to Perls the most important thing about the figure-ground formation is that if a need is genuinely satisfied, the situation changes, permitting the needs of the next highest in the dominance hierarchy to organize behavior and perception [5]. Hence change is effected in the individual through focusing the awareness of the person on himself and his needs as he sees them in the here and now.

In the Gestalt theory then, growth and learning occur through physical and mental assimilation of fragmented parts from the environment, through awareness, and because of the formation of complete and comprehensive Gestalts, all of which allow needs to come to the forefront and be met in a need hierarchy similar to Maslow's.

The position of self in the theory also puts a great deal of emphasis on the here and now of the individual's existence. "Present-centeredness" is reflected in the technical repertoire of Gestalt therapy in two main ways. One is the request of the therapist that the client attend to and express what enters his present field of awareness. This will very often be coupled with the instruction to suspend reasoning in favor of pure self-observation. The second is having the client bring into the present the past or future or fantasy in general by means of an inward attempt to identify with or relive past experiences or a reenactment of the scenes with gestural and postural participation, e.g., with psychodrama [1].

The aim of Gestalt therapy is to enable the individual to act on the basis of all possible information, perceiving not only the relevant factors in the external field but also relevant information within. The client is directed to attend, at any given moment, to what he is feeling, what he is doing, and what he wants, the goal being uninterrupted awareness. In this way he can discover *how* he interrupts his own functioning. *What* is being interrupted, or resisted, is the awareness of the needs that organize his behavior. Present awareness then becomes a tool for uncovering those needs and the ways in which the individual prevents himself from experiencing them.

Because of the importance of awareness, the Gestalt therapist calls the client's attention to the way in which he blocks his communications, either with his internal self-system or with the interpersonal system. This awareness can be facilitated by directing the client's attention to what his body is doing, what his mind is doing, and what is or is not going on between people [1].

The therapist uses certain rules and games of Gestalt therapy to help facilitate awareness [2]. The first of these is the principle of the here and now, already mentioned indirectly. To stay in the here and now is a discipline to which we are not accustomed and are inclined to resist, so the therapist must point out to the client how easily he leaves it and help him to stay in it.

The I-and-thou rule strives to drive home the idea that true communication involves both sender and receiver, since the client often behaves as if his words were aimed at no one particular. He is asked to be aware of the distinction between talking *to* and talking *at* or *about* another individual.

The rule about it-and-I language deals with the semantics of responsibility and involvement. By the technique of changing an "it" to "I," the client learns to identify more closely with a behavior and to assume responsibility for it. Instead of "*It* is trembling," (meaning a hand), for example the client is encouraged to say "I am trembling."

The rule concerning the client's need to ask questions involves discouraging a kind of "give-me" or "tell-me" passivity on the part of the client. The therapist may request that the client change his question into a statement if careful listening reveals that the question is not really necessary or that it represents laziness on the part of the client.

In *Gestalt Therapy Now* [2], edited by Fagan and Shepherd, Levitsky and Perls have set forth the games of Gestalt therapy. They are proposed by the therapist when the moment seems appropriate, either in terms of the individual's or the group's needs. Some of them are useful warm-ups at the beginning of a session and others facilitate the awareness or integration processes. They include, among others, games of dialogue between disowned parts, rehearsal of roles, taking responsibility, and a game of "secrets," which permits exploration of feelings of guilt and shame.

Perls felt that awareness in and of itself is curative. Since the focus in Gestalt therapy is upon integration, however, the therapy process is a step-by-step effort by the client to reown the disowned parts of his personality until he becomes strong enough to continue his own growth [3].

Dream work is an important part of integration. The therapist attempts to have the client relive the dream in the present, usually acting it out. He is asked to play the part of various objects or persons in the dream, since it is believed by Gestaltists that these different parts are projections of the self. In acting out the dream then, the client can identify with the alienated parts of himself and integrate them into a whole. After the acting out, the interpretation of the dream is left to the client himself.

As in Rogers' client-centered approach, as well as in self-theory in general, the client has the answers to his own problems. It is he who sets the real goals of therapy, and it is he who provides the motivation and assumes the real responsibility for his own therapy. The therapist is by no means passive, however; he sets the emotional tone of the sessions, tries to keep the client in the here and now, is aware of the incongruence in the client and may make the client confront it, is empathetic and supportive in many ways, but, most of all, is constantly helping the client to accept both himself and the responsibility for his own actions, so that he may become a balanced, integrated, fully functioning person.

Rationale for Group Therapy

Perls believed that individual therapy should be the exception rather than the rule, that the group setting was much more feasible and efficient in affecting change in the individual. First of all, the client can learn much in a group from indirect participation —

the therapeutic value of listening to others; and in addition, abstract problems can more quickly and readily be brought to earth. Finally, there is an advantage of directness in a group; there is more immediate and fuller feedback, resulting in the expansion of the individual's awareness of himself.

SELECTION AND COMPOSITION OF THE GROUP
Perls felt that the only requirement for group membership was the client's readiness to be open with a group. If the client is not ready for the openness, then individual therapy is indicated. The group is heterogeneous in makeup. Basically, group therapy is designed for those who are dissatisfied with some aspect of themselves and are willing to expend some effort to either become different or to be more content with the way they are.

ROLE OF THE GROUP LEADER
The Gestalt therapist works almost exclusively in the present, becoming aware of the way in which each client blocks out portions of himself or his environment and focusing on that particular problem. The therapist's role is an active one, and much of his activity is devoted to discerning body awareness as well as listening to the client's words. As the therapist becomes aware of discrepancies, he translates these into suggestions and experiments for the client.

Perls' approach to group therapy is somewhat different from that of the standard Gestalt group. He prefers to play down the interaction of the group. The invitation to participate is an invitation to work with the therapist, to occupy the "hot seat." The therapist then helps the client learn (through directed awareness, the acting out of dreams, conversing with parts of himself) how the client is out of contact with reality, where and what the actuality now is, and how to keep in contact with it.

Gestalt Therapy Assessment Tool
I. Self
    A. Describe ego as organismic function, establish boundary between the personal and impersonal field.
    B. Distinguish five layers of neurosis.
        1. Phoney layer: topdog/underdog game
        2. Phobic layer: identification of fears
        3. Impasse: not knowing what to do or where to move; loss of environmental support
        4. Implosive: grief and despair on how limiting the self is
        5. Explosive: unused energies freed

C. Investigate positives.
   1. Spontaneity
   2. Sensory awareness
   3. Freedom in movement
   4. Expressiveness
   5. Flexibility in relating
   6. Closeness with others
   7. Intimacy
   8. Competency
   9. Immediacy
   10. Creativity
   11. Self-support
D. Relate negatives.
   1. Rigidity
   2. Confusion
   3. Boredom
   4. Compulsions
   5. Fixations
   6. Extreme anxiety
   7. Self-consciousness
E. What is figure/ground in client's life now? In the office at this moment? Here and now?
   1. What are you feeling?
   2. What are you now aware of?
   3. What are you doing?
   4. What do you want?
   5. What is keeping you from what you want?
F. Describe fantasies, dreams.
G. Identify blocks to communication, either within internal self or with interpersonal system.
   1. What is his body doing?
   2. What is his mind doing?
   3. What is or is not going on between people?
H. Rules of Gestalt therapy: identify and focus attention on:
   1. Here and now
   2. I and thou
   3. It-and-I language (semantics of responsibility and involvement responsibility)
   4. Questions become statements.
I. Games to try
   1. Dialogue between disowned parts
   2. Rehearsal of roles
   3. Taking responsibility
   4. Secrets (explore feelings of guilt and shame)

5. Lived dreams in present
J. Therapist
   1. Set emotional tone of sessions.
   2. Keep in here and now.
   3. Be aware of incongruences.
   4. Be empathetic and supportive.
   5. Help client accept responsibility for self and own actions, to become a balanced, integrated, fully functioning person.
K. Evidence of resistances
   1. Introjection: accepts values of others without question
   2. Projection: sees own qualities only in others
   3. Retroflection: does to himself what he wants done by others
   4. Confluence: loss of I-Thou boundaries, almost symbolic
   5. Deflection: maneuvers for turning aside from direct contact

TRANSACTIONAL ANALYSIS
Content
Eric Berne, the originator of transactional analysis (TA) therapy, set forth his theory in easily-understood terms in his article, "Transactional Analysis: A New and Effective Method of Group Therapy," which was published in the *American Journal of Psychotherapy* in 1956.

In transactional analysis, a reality-oriented therapy, each individual has at his disposal a limited repertoire of ego states: Child, Adult, and Parent. *Structural analysis* is learning to identify these ego states. These three ego states are systems of feelings and the patterns of behavior that stem from them. The Parent is derived from external events occurring from birth to age five, i.e., the feelings, attitudes, behavior, and responses of parents or parental surrogates. It is composed of a critical parent and a nurturing parent. The Adult of an individual begins to develop at about the age of 10 months. It autonomously collects and objectively processes data, estimates probabilities, and makes decisions. The Child is comprised of an individual's feelings, attitudes, and behavior patterns from birth to age five. It has three parts: adapted child, little professor, and natural child. It is important to emphasize that the Parent can function as either an ego state or an influence. It is parental influence that determines whether the adapted Child (functions as the parent would have liked) or the natural child (free from parental influence) is the active ego state [3].

Exclusion and contamination of an ego state are examples of structural pathology or anomalies of psychic structure. The constant Parent, the constant Adult, or the constant Child occurs when there is defensive exclusion of the other two ego states. All the overt responses of an individual come from the excluding ego state and the other two states are almost impossible to reach. Contamination is best illustrated by prejudice or delusion. In the state prejudice, part of the Parent intrudes into the Adult and is included in the Adult ego boundary. In functional pathology, an individual is capable of either stubborn persistence in an ego state or of shifting rapidly from one state to another, or both.

Transactional Analysis Proper
Transactional analysis proper consists of determining which ego state is functioning in a transaction between two people. A transaction is the basic unit of social exchange that occurs when people talk or interact in any manner with each other. There are three types of transactions: complementary, crossed, or ulterior. Complementary transactions are those in which the lines of communication are parallel; thus the response complements the stimulus and communication can continue indefinitely. Communication is broken down if the lines become crossed, which occurs when the response does not complement the stimulus. For instance, if an Adult stimulus elicits a Child-to-Parent or Parent-to-Child response, a crossed transaction results. There are two types of ulterior transactions. The first is the angular transaction in which an Adult-to-Adult stimulus hides a stimulus directed to the Child. The desired response comes from the hidden stimulus. The second, a duplex transaction, occurs when the overt stimulus and response are Adult-to-Adult, i.e., on a psychological level. Complementary and crossed transactions are simple ones; ulterior ones are complex and are the bases for games. The more skilled one becomes in picking up the clues, not only of words used, but of voice tone, body gestures, and facial expressions, the more adept one becomes at identifying the stimulus and response as coming from the Parent, Child, or Adult [2].

Recognition Hunger and Strokes
Berne's transactional analysis is based primarily upon a reinforcement theory of learning — individuals develop concepts about

themselves very early in life according to how and why these concepts are reinforced. They develop because of the basic human need for reinforcement, or *strokes* in TA terms [1]. Every person has the biological and psychological need to be touched and recognized by others. These needs may be appeased with strokes, or reinforcement, given either in the form of actual physical touch or in some verbal form.

Infants need the actual physical touch of others, without which they will not grow and develop normally. This need of reinforcement is generally met in the everyday intimate trans-actions of feeding, diapering, and fondling that nurturing parents give their babies.

As the child grows older, the early primary hunger for actual touch becomes the hunger for recognition and other, more subtle, forms of reinforcement that are cognitively oriented, primarily verbal. These positive strokes usually take the form of complementary transactions that are direct and appropriate to the situation. They leave the individual feeling good and important and help him develop the "I'm OK, you're OK" position. In a decision-making situation, the individual will operate from the Adult ego state if he has developed this psychological position. If individuals do not get enough positive strokes, they provoke negative ones and develop mental disturbances, oper-ating from one of the other three psychological positions, i.e., either I'm OK, you're not OK; I'm not OK, you're OK; or I'm not OK, you're not OK [4].

Time-Structuring
Berne believes that, important as recognition is, it is not enough since the individual has a greater problem in the structuring of his time, or structure hunger. There are six choices open to an individual as to how he structures his time: withdrawal, rituals, pastimes, activities, games, and intimacy. *Withdrawal* can be mental, indulging in fantasies, or it can be physical: sleep or isolation. *Rituals* are fixed, predictable ways of behaving toward others; greetings and farewells are examples of transactions that are rituals. Rituals serve to pass time without a person getting close to anyone. *Pastimes* are less stereotyped than rituals and are pleasant forms of filling time and getting to know people, for example, conversations about football, cooking, and auto-mobiles. Pastimes may lead to intimacy with others but are also useful in maintaining superficial relationships in social situations. *Activities* are commonly referred to as work, and the transac-tions involved are based on accomplishing something. Activities

are ways of keeping busy in a satisfying and productive manner but may also be used to avoid contact with others. Dr. Berne has devoted an entire book, *Games People Play* [2], to the subject of *games*. The following is his description of a game:

> A game is an ongoing series of complementary ulterior transactions progressing to a well-defined, predictable outcome. Descriptively it is a recurring set of transactions, often repetitious, superficially plausible, with a concealed motivation; or, more colloquially, a series of moves with a snare, or "gimmick." Games are clearly differentiated from procedures, rituals, and pastimes by two chief characteristics: (1) their ulterior quality and (2) the payoff. Procedures may be successful, rituals effective, and pastimes profitable, but all of them are by definition candid; they may involve contest, but not conflict, and the ending may be sensational, but it is not dramatic. Every game, on the other hand, is basically dishonest, and the outcome has a dramatic, as distinct from merely exciting, quality [2, p. 48].

Essentially then, games are unconscious transactions that serve to keep people apart and enable them to avoid intimacy. *Intimacy* exists independently from the other forms of time-structuring. It is, unfortunately, threatening to many people in our culture. It is an honest expression of feelings of love and trust, a game-free relationship of giving and sharing, made possible by the absence of a fear of being vulnerable [2].

Game Analysis and Basic Life Positions
Game analysis is a useful therapeutic tool when coupled with an understanding of structural and transactional analysis. The purpose of game analysis is to help the Adult understand what the Child and Parent are doing and why. Games are designed to defend one of the four basic life positions that an individual assumes in relation to how he feels about himself and others. The four basic life positions are as follows [4]:

1. I am OK, you're OK.
2. I am OK, you're not OK.
3. I am not OK, you're OK.
4. I am not OK, you're not OK.

Position 1 is the only constructive, healthy position. Number 2 is essentially one of paranoia, number 3 is depressive, and number 4 is futile. The last three positions are unconscious and are assumed early in life, probably by age three, by the individual's Adult. The first position is a conscious decision based on the premise that transactions with others are mutually beneficial, and in treatment, it is referred to as "getting well." The second position leads to the alternative of "getting rid of people," which ranges from socially acceptable political actions to the extremes of homicide or infanticide. The third position may result in a complete withdrawal from society by institution-alization in a mental hospital or prison. With severely depressed individuals, the ultimate form of withdrawal is suicide. Because a person in the fourth position goes through life with a feeling of hopelessness and despair, this position may also ultimately lead to suicide. Game analysis helps an individual to understand his predominant ego state when he is playing games, his basic life position, and the games he is playing to defend that position. He is then able to begin relinquishing his games and undertake a more constructive way of life by activating his Adult and gaining insight into the feelings he has been deriving from his games. It is well to remember that some games are harmless, but that some are dangerous and a few are lethal. For an in-depth study of these games, examples of which are life games, marital games, underworld games, and so on, see Eric Berne's book *Games People Play* [2] .

Transactional Trading Stamps
Transactional trading stamps are feelings that are collected from something that happens to an individual as a result of what someone else does to him or he does to himself. These feelings become rackets when an individual purposely uses them to collect "red" or "brown" trading stamps. Red stamps are for angry feelings stored in a person's Child that he releases when someone does something that he feels justifies his expressing these angry feelings. If a person stores up enough of these red stamps, he may feel justified in killing someone. Brown stamps are for guilty or bad feelings and are collected by people to justify doing something free of guilt — they feel that they then have the right to do what they want to do. "Gold" stamps are good feelings an individual saves to have reasons for being happy or having a good time.

Script Analysis
Script analysis is the uncovering of the unconscious life plan of an individual based on decisions made by the Child early in life as to how his life should be lived. These decisions are in turn based on the verbal and nonverbal messages a child gets from his parents or parental surrogates. Scripts can be constructive or tragic depending upon the basic life position of an individual.

People with tragic scripts usually spend their lives waiting for something wonderful to happen to them. When the something wonderful doesn't occur, these individuals have four alternatives of action, depending upon their basic life positions: (1) they can get rid of the people they feel are responsible for the failure; (2) they can withdraw from society through institutionalization or living in isolation from others; (3) they can commit suicide; or (4) they can get better.

Goal of Transactional Analysis

The goal of transactional analysis is to help the individual achieve the position "I am OK, you're OK." The therapist gives patients permission to become members of society by helping them to accept with satisfaction what the world and intimate relationships with others can offer them. The therapist aids individuals in achieving the goal of transactional analysis by helping them to do the following [2].

1. Replace any unhealthy parent part.
2. Be a nurturing parent to yourself.
3. Educate your Adult to facts about yourself.
4. Get the little kid to feel that it's OK to change.
5. See in your own way; not how you were *taught* to see.
6. Feel as you want to feel, not as your Parent *tells* you to feel.
7. *Your* Adult can make your decisions.
8. Remember, you are already OK. [2]

In summary, Berne's transactional analysis, which term refers to the system as a whole, is divided into four phases: structural analysis, learning to identify the ego states of Child, Adult, and Parent; transactional analysis, determining which ego state is active in each of the persons involved in any transaction; game analysis, analyzing a series of ulterior transactions with a gimmick that lead to a usually well-concealed but well-defined payoff; and script analysis, determining which decisions the individual made in childhood that are still governing the way in which he lives his life [3].

Transactional analysis is contractual. No matter how sick the client may be, it is thought that his Adult can be reached in order to make a realistic treatment contract. Contract negotiations concerning a treatment goal are, in many cases, the first steps a patient takes in confronting unrealistic Child fantasies or perfectionistic Parent standards. In the following steps the Adult can learn to operate in the executive position, and the individual can become responsible for his own life and actions.

Rationale for Transactional Analysis (TA) Group Therapy
The TA group provides opportunities for clients to distinguish among their ego states. They discover what kinds of transactions and strokes each member seeks. They learn, too, how their Adult, rather than their Parent, can bridge the gap between reality and the needs of their Child, establishing open and authentic communication between the affective and intellectual components of the personality. Such insights allow the client to learn how he can relate to others with more inner freedom.

Script analysis, the last phase of TA, is usually done only if analysis of transactions and games fails to free the client from inappropriate transactions and decisions. Once a losing lifescript is discovered, clients, with more or less assistance from the therapists, can make effective redecisions about their lives and can redirect otherwise creative scripts by learning and testing new ways of relating to others. In this way they turn the losing lifescript into a winning one.

SELECTION AND COMPOSITION OF GROUP
Except under special circumstances, no particular criteria are used in selecting members for a TA group. Patients are generally picked at random, in their order of application or in some other way that would increase the heterogeneity of the group. It is felt that selecting patients to insure homogeneity in the group is deleterious to therapeutic progress. Oftentimes the patients in clinics or institutions are assigned to a group on the basis of extrinsic factors by someone other than the therapist, thus relieving the therapist of the problems of going through complicated rationalizations for assigning a particular patient to one group or another. Patients with proper preparation can even be assigned to established groups in this way.

The selection of a particular group for a particular patient is done only in the case of certain remittent schizophrenics or psychotics following shock treatments. In these cases the group should be one in which the therapist functions primarily as Parent rather than Adult.

ROLE OF THE GROUP LEADER
Transactional analysis leaders actively enter their groups to identify transactions among members in addition to several other kinds of therapeutic operations. These other activities include the following:

Interrogation: Questioning is used to help the therapist document points that promise to be clinically decisive.

Specification: Information is categorized in order to fix it in both the therapist's and the client's minds so that it can be referred to later.

Confrontation: Therapist uses information previously elicited and specified in order to disconcert the client's Parent or Child by pointing out inconsistencies.

Explanation: Therapist attempts to strengthen, decontaminate, or reorient the client's Adult.

Illustration: An anecdote or comparison that is given after a successful confrontation for the purpose of reinforcing the confrontation and softening its possible undesirable effects.

Interpretation: Deals with revealing the pathology of the Child.

Crystallization: Statement is made of the client's position from the Adult of the therapist to the Adult of the client concerning how healthy the client is.

The therapist may also choose at times to use support, reassurance, persuasion, and exhortation, and to give permission to the client to act in a more healthy manner.

MEDIA AND SETTING OF THE GROUP

The meeting place should be selected to keep external disturbances at a minimum but with physical comfort in mind. The therapist may require a tape recorder or a chalkboard to diagram transactions.

LENGTH OF SESSIONS AND DURATION OF TREATMENT

The group should meet at a regular time, usually weekly, and for a specified duration. One and a half hours seems to be an optimal time for a session. There is no optimal length of time a group may meet. Termination for individuals within the group may be accidental, resistant, or therapeutic.

PREFERRED SIZE OF GROUP

The preferred size of the group is eight, although any number from six to ten is acceptable.

Transactional Analysis Assessment Tool
  I. Structural Analysis
    A. Parent
      1. Words (*should, don't, ought, honey,* etc.)
      2. Gestures and postures (pointing a finger, consoling, rolling eyes, etc.)

    3. Tone of voice (sneering, supportive, sympathetic, condescending)

    4. Facial expressions (scowl, frown, smile)

B. Adult

    1. Words (*how, when, who, what, why,* etc.)

    2. Gestures and postures (straight, not stiff, eye-to-eye contact)

    3. Tone of voice (clear, calm, confident, inquiring)

    4. Facial expression (thoughtful, attentive, quizzical, lively, confident)

C. Child

    1. Sample words (*gosh, wow, can't, won't, mine, wish, want*)

    2. Gestures and postures (slumped, joyful)

    3. Tone of voice (giggling, gurgling, whining, manipulating, belly-laughing)

II. Transactional Analysis Identification of Predominant Ego State Functioning (identify Stimulus and Response)

A. Complementary: message gets predicted response

B. Crossed: unexpected response

C. Ulterior: involves two or more ego states by using overt adult-to-adult message and psychological secret

III. Strokes (identify sources, kind, and maintaining consequences of reinforcement)

IV. Time Structuring (identify how individual spends his time)

A. Withdrawal

B. Rituals

C. Pastimes

D. Activities

E. Games

F. Intimacy

V. Game Analysis

A. Identify ulterior transaction with payoff (bad feelings)

B. Payoff: red, brown, gold stamps

C. Identify kind of game

VI. Script Analysis (uncovering unconscious life plan)

A. I am OK, you're OK: healthy

B. I am OK, you're not OK; distrustful and paranoid

C. I am not OK, you're OK: feeling low/depressed/suicidal

D. I am not OK, you're not OK: unhealthy

Therapist can give life script questionnaire to patient developed by Bulbrook based on the work of Steiner, McCormick, and others. The following are terms used in the questionnaire.

BP = Basic position (of child)
C = Contract (agree only to goals that you and client can see him reach in treatment)
CI = Counterinjunction (from parent's Parent "Do . . .")
D = Decision (e.g., "I'll probably never make it")
G = Game (favorite)
P = Program (how to obey injunction)
PI = Parental Injunction (message from parent's child "Don't . . .")
R = Racket (bad feelings)

QUESTIONS

1. What do you think of yourself: BP, D
2. How do you see yourself: BP, D
3. How would your mother describe you to someone: PI, CI
4. How would your father describe you to someone: PI, CI
5. How would any significant other describe you to someone: PI, CI
6. What is your best or worst feature: BP, D
7. What is (was) your mother like: PI, CI
8. What is (was) your father like: PI, CI
9. What names have you been called: BP
10. Describe your reaction to the names: BP, D
11. What did your parents want you to be in life: PI, CI, BP
12. When was your best time in life: BP, D
13. When was your worst time in life: BP, D
14. What is the favorite story you remember as a child: P
15. What was the best part of it: P
16. Describe what life will be like for you in the future: C
17. When and how will you die: P, D
18. What do you want to happen in life: D, C
19. What would you like to change about yourself: D
20. If you could change something by magic what would it be: D, C
21. Describe your sister(s)/brother(s):
22. How do you relate to them:
23. What is (was) your grandmother like:
24. What is (was) your grandfather like:
25. Have you been seriously ill:
26. Have your parents been ill:
27. How will you die:
28. What do you want people to say about you:

CRISIS INTERVENTION

Crisis intervention as a treatment modality has been developed within the past few decades and is based on a broad range of theories of human behavior. A person in crisis is confronted with a problem that he cannot readily solve by using his usual coping mechanisms. Consequently his anxiety and tension rise and he becomes less able to find a solution. He becomes and/or feels helpless. Crisis treatment offers immediate help to reestablish the client's equilibrium; it does not primarily attempt to reconstruct the personality.

Crisis intervention evolved from the type of brief psychotherapy that developed as the result of increased demand for mental health services and the lack of personnel trained to meet the need. Its roots are in psychoanalytic theory, but it differs from psychoanalysis in terms of goals and other factors. It is limited to removing or alleviating specific symptoms and assisting the individual in his ability to function above the precrisis level.

Crisis is characteristically self-limiting and lasts from four to six weeks. The client usually seeks help immediately or 10 to 14 days after the crisis. Therapy sessions range from one to six sessions.

Caplan [2] identifies four developmental phases in a crisis: (1) an initial rise in tension as habitual problem-solving is applied: (2) lack of success in coping with the increase in discomfort; (3) further increase in tension and emergency problem-solving levels; (4) disorganization and crisis if problem continues and cannot be resolved or avoided.

Jacobson, Strickler, and Morley [3] state that crisis intervention can be approached in two ways: generically and individually. The generic approach focuses on the characteristic course of a particular kind of crisis, while the individual approach focuses on the psychodynamics of each individual in crisis. The former is generally carried out by a nonmental health professional for crisis in specific situational events (threats to biological, psychological, or social integrity) and maturational events (normal growth and development) occurring to a particular population group. The individual approach differs in that its emphasis is on assessment and treatment by a professional of the interpersonal and intrapsychic processes of the person in crisis.

Aguilera and Messick [1] define the steps in the crisis intervention technique that can help the client. The first phase is the assessment of the individual and his problem, determining the precipitating event and the resulting crisis. The therapist used active focusing techniques to isolate the problem. If the patient is at high risk of committing suicide or homicide, he is considered for hospitalization.

Following the assessment, phase two is planning the intervention, trying to bring the client back to a precrisis level of equilibrium. It is important to note how much the crisis has affected the person's life and the effect it is having on others in the environment. The client's strengths and the skills that had been used successfully in the past are ascertained. Intervention is the third phase, followed by resolution of the crisis and anticipatory planning, the fourth phase.

During intervention, Morley and Messick [5] suggest that the therapist (1) help the individual to gain an intellectual understanding of his crisis; (2) help him bring into the open his present feelings to which he may not have access; and explore his coping mechanisms and reopen the social world.

Aguilera and Messick [4] developed a paradigm of the effect of balancing factors in a stressful event.

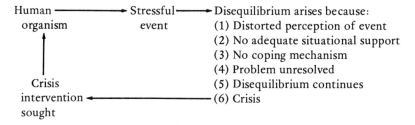

In crisis intervention the client is assessed, after which he is treated by assisting him to have a realistic perception of the crisis and to develop situational supports and/or reactivate old or develop new coping mechanisms. Since therapist contact is very active, flexible, and directed to the immediate crisis situation and is not a thorough diagnostic evaluation, a modified assessment tool is indicated. The therapist must continually keep in mind that the treatment time is limited and the goal explicit. His energy should be directed to returning the client to his precrisis level.

Crisis Intervention Assessment Tool
   I. Identifying the Precipitating Event
      A. Why did you come here today?
      B. When did things start to go wrong for you?
      C. What is different in your life now that concerns you?
      D. How do others see your situation?

E. What do you think is needed to change things for you?

F. If things don't change, what do you think will happen?

II. Identify Coping Mechanisms

A. Has this situation or another ever happened to you?

B. How did you handle it?

C. How do you usually handle situations that cause you stress?

D. Have you applied the same helpful solutions that worked before? If not, why not?

E. What would make you feel better?

F. Have you tried any of the things that usually make you feel better?

III. Identify Support System

A. Who do you turn to in times of stress?

B. Have you turned to them this time?

C. Did that person help?

D. Have you sought help from any other person?

E. How does your family support you?

IV. Level of Stress

A. Have you ever thought of hurting yourself or another?

B. What have you thought of doing to yourself?

C. Can you tell the difference in you now?

D. What specifically is different in your concentration? Attention? Insight? Mood? General activity? Physical appearance? Rapport? Motor activity? Thought process? Thought content? Intellectual functioning? Judgment?

Compare therapist's assessment with client's assessment

V. General Data

A. What is your general health?

B. Are you on any medications?

C. How is the problem affecting your normal routine?

VI. Resolution of Problem

A. What are the client's assets?

B. How does he feel generally about himself?

C. Identify feelings.

D. Examine alternative plans to meet problems.

E. Offer emotional support.

F. Review plans.

G. Evaluate progress in relation to goal.

H. Develop termination plans.

VII. Identify Process in Client/Therapist Interaction During Interview

REFERENCES
Psychoanalytic Model
1. Ford, D. H., and Urban, H. B. *Systems of Psychotherapy: A Comparative Study.* New York: Wiley & Sons, 1963.
2. Freud, S. *A General Introduction to Psychoanalysis.* New York: Washington Square Press, 1924.
3. Hall, C. S., and Lindzey, G. *Theories of Personality.* New York: Wiley & Sons, 1970.
4. Hansen, J. C., Stevic, R. R., and Warner, R. W. *Counseling: Theory and Process.* Boston: Allyn and Bacon, 1972.
5. King, P. T. Psychoanalytic Adaptations. In B. Stefflre (Ed.), *Theories of Counseling.* New York: McGraw-Hill, 1965.
6. Maddi, S. R. *Personality Theories: A Comparative Analysis.* Homewood, Ill.: Dorsey Press, 1972.
7. Patterson, C. H. *Theories of Counseling and Psychotherapy.* New York: Harper & Row, 1973.
8. Pervin, L. A. *Personality: Theory, Assessment and Research.* New York: Wiley & Sons, 1970.
9. Stafford-Clark, D. *What Freud Really Said.* New York: Schocken Books, 1965.
10. Shertzer, B., and Stone, S. C. *Fundamentals of Counseling.* Boston: Houghton Mifflin Co., 1968.

Psychoanalytic Group Therapy for Children
1. Slavson, S. R. *A Textbook in Analytic Group Psychotherapy.* New York: International University Press, 1964.

Reality Therapy
1. Glasser, W. *Reality Therapy.* New York: Harper & Row, 1965.

Interpersonal Theory
1. Freedman, A., Kaplan, H., and Sadock, B. *Modern Synopsis of Comprehensive Textbook of Psychiatry.* Baltimore: Williams & Wilkins Co., 1972.
2. Hall, C., and Lindzey, G. *Theories of Personality.* New York: Wiley & Sons, 1970.
3. Sullivan, H. S. *The Interpersonal Theory of Psychiatry.* New York: W. W. Norton and Co., 1953.

Behavioral Modification
1. Loomis, M. E., and Horsley, J. A. *Interpersonal Change: A Behavioral Approach to Nursing Practice.* New York: McGraw-Hill Book Co., 1974.
2. Schaefer, H. H., and Martin. P. L. *Behavioral Therapy.* New York: McGraw-Hill Book Co., 1975.

Client-Centered Therapy
1. Ford, D. H., and Urban, H. B. *Systems of Psychotherapy: A Comparative Study.* New York: Wiley & Sons, 1963.

2. Hansen, J. C., Stevic, R., and Warner, R. W. *Counseling: Theory and Process.* Boston: Allyn and Bacon, 1972.
3. Maslow, A. *Toward a Psychology of Being.* New York: Van Nostrand, 1968.
4. Rogers, C. R. *Client-Centered Therapy.* Boston: Houghton Mifflin, 1951.
5. Rogers, C. R. Necessary and Sufficient Conditions of Therapeutic Personality Change. In B. N. Ard, Jr. (Ed.), *Counseling and Psychotherapy.* Palo Alto, Calif.: Science and Behavior Books, 1966.

Existential Therapy

1. Ford, D. H., and Urban, H. B. *Systems of Psychotherapy: A Comparative Study.* New York: Wiley & Sons, 1963.
2. Maddi, S. R. *Personality Theories: A Comparative Analysis.* Homewood, Ill.: Dorsey Press, 1972.
3. Maslow, A. *Toward a Psychology of Being.* New York: Van Nostrand, 1962.

Adlerian Therapy

1. Adler, A. *The Individual Psychology of Alfred Adler.* New York: Basic Books, 1956.
2. Dinkmeyer, D., and Carlson, J. *Consulting.* Columbus, Ohio: Charles E. Merrill Publishing, 1973.
3. Dreikurs, R., and Grunwald, B. *Maintaining Sanity in the Classroom.* New York: Harper & Row, 1971.

Carkhuff Model

1. Carkhuff, R., and Berenson, B. *Beyond Counseling and Therapy.* New York: Holt, Reinhart & Winston, 1967.

Gestalt Therapy

1. Enright, J. B. An Introduction to Gestalt Techniques. In J. Fagan and I. L. Shepherd (Eds.), *Gestalt Therapy Now.* New York: Harper & Row, 1970.
2. Levitsky, A., and Perls, F. S. Rules and Games of Gestalt Therapy. In J. Fagan and I. L. Shepherd (Eds.), *Gestalt Therapy Now.* New York: Harper & Row, 1970.
3. Patterson, C. H. *Theories of Counseling and Psychotherapy.* New York: Harper & Row, 1973.
4. Perls, F. S. *Gestalt Therapy Verbatim.* Moab, Utah: Real People Press, 1969.
5. Perls, F. S. Four Lectures, In J. Fagan and I. L. Shepherd (Eds.), *Gestalt Therapy Now.* New York: Harper & Row, 1970.
6. Polster, I. Introduction: A Contemporary Psychotherapy. In P. D. Pursglove (Ed.), *Recognitions in Gestalt Therapy.* New York: Harper & Row, 1968.

Transactional Analysis

1. Berne, E. *Transactional Analysis in Psychotherapy.* New York: Grove Press, 1961.

2. Berne, E. *Games People Play.* New York: Grove Press, 1964.
3. Berne, E. *Principles of Group Treatment.* New York: Oxford University Press, 1966.
4. Harris, T. A. *I'm OK — You're OK. A Practical Guide to Transactional Analysis.* New York: Harper & Row, 1969.

Crisis Intervention

1. Aguilera, D., and Messick, J. *Crisis Intervention, Theory, and Methodology.* St. Louis, Ill.: C. V. Mosby, 1974.
2. Caplan, G. *Principles of Preventive Psychiatry.* New York: Basic Books, 1964.
3. Jacobson, G., Strickler, M., and Morley, W. E. Generic and individual approaches to crisis intervention. *American Journal of Public Health* 58:339–342, 1968.
4. Messick, J., and Aguilera, D. A schema, the psychiatric nurse on the community mental health team. *Journal of Psychiatric Nursing* 4:431–439, 1966.
5. Morley, W., and Messick, J. Crisis paradigms of intervention. *Journal of Psychiatric Nursing* 5:537, 1967.

SELECTED READINGS
Psychoanalytic Model

Adler, A. *Understanding Human Nature.* Greenwich, Conn.: Fawcett Publications, 1927.
Freud, S. *The Problem of Anxiety.* New York: Norton, 1936.
Freud, S. *An Outline of Psychoanalysis.* New York: Norton, 1947.
Hilgard, E. R., and Bower, G. R. *Theories of Learning.* New York: Appleton-Century-Crofts, 1966.
Horney, K. *Our Inner Conflicts.* New York: W. W. Norton & Co., 1945.
Jung, C. G. *Two Essays on Analytical Psychology.* Princeton, N.J.: Princeton University Press, 1953.

Reality Therapy

Bratter, T. E. Reality therapy: A group psychotherapeutic approach with adolescent alcoholics. *Annals of the N.Y. Academy of Sciences* 233:104–114, 1974.
Brook, P., Degun, G., and Mather, M. Reality orientation: A therapy for psychogeriatric patients: A controlled study. *British Journal of Psychiatry* 127:42–45, 1975.
Glasser, W. *Schools Without Failure.* New York: Harper & Row, 1969.
Glasser, W. *Mental Health or Mental Illness.* New York: Harper & Row, 1970.
Glasser, W. *The Identity Society.* New York: Harper & Row, 1972.
Lee, R. E. Reality orientation: Restoring the senile to life, Part 1. *Journal of Practical Nursing* 26:28–29,35,37, 1976.
Lee, R. E. Reality orientation: Restoring the senile to life. Part 2. *Journal of Practical Nursing* 26:30–31, 1976.
Letcher, P. B., Peterson, L. P., and Scarbrough, D. Reality orientation: A Historical study of patient progress. *Hospital and Community Psychiatry* 25:801–803, 1974.

Miller, M. A. Remotivation therapy: A way to reach the confused elderly patient. *Journal Gerontological Nursing* 1:28–31, 1975.

Nelson, P. Involvement with Betty: An experience in reality therapy. *American Journal of Nursing* 74:1440–1441, 1974.

Settle, H. A pilot study in reality orientation for the confused elderly. *Journal Gerontological Nursing* 1:11–16, 1975.

Interpersonal Theory

Havens, L. *Approaches to the Mind, Movement of the Psychiatric Schools from Sects Towards Science.* Boston: Little, Brown and Co., 1973.

Mullahy, P. *Psychoanalysis and Interpersonal Psychiatry: The Contributions of Harry Stack Sullivan.* New York: Science House, 1970.

Sullivan, H. S. *Conceptions of Modern Psychiatry.* New York: W. W. Norton and Co., 1953.

Sullivan, H. S. *The Psychiatric Interview.* New York: W. W. Norton and Co., 1954.

Sundberg, N., and Tyler, L. *Clinical Psychology.* New York: Appleton-Century-Crofts, 1962.

Behavior Modification

Ainslie, G. Specious reward: A behavioral theory of impulsiveness and impulse control. *Psychological Bulletin* 82:463–496, 1975.

Ayllon, T., and Michael, J. The psychiatric nurse as a behavioral engineer. *Journal of the Experimental Analysis of Behavior* 2:323–334, 1959.

Berni, R., and Fordyce, W. *Behavior Modification and the Nursing Process.* St. Louis: C. V. Mosby, 1973.

Bidder, R. T., Bryant, G., and Gray, O. P. Benefits to Down's syndrome children through training their mothers. *Archives of Disease in Childhood* 50:383–386, 1975.

DeBow, M. *Behavior Modification: A Significant Method in Nursing Practice.* Englewood Cliffs, N.J.: Prentice Hall, 1973.

Erickson, M. H., and Rossi, E. L. Varieties of Double Bind. *American Journal of Clinical Hypnosis* 17:143–157, 1975.

Flannery, R. B., Jr. Behavior modification of geriatric grief: A transactional perspective. *International Journal of Aging and Human Development* 5:197–203, 1974.

Lovaas, O. I., Schreibman, L., and Koegal, R. L. A behavior modification approach to the treatment of autistic children. *Journal of Autism and Childhood Schizophrenia* 4:111–129, 1974.

Maurer, A. Corporal punishment. *American Psychologist* 29:614–626, 1974.

Rachman, S., and Hodgson, R. Synchrony and desynchrony in fear and avoidance. *Behaviour Research and Therapy* 12:311–318, 1974.

Rokeach, M. Long-term value change initiated by computer feedback. *Journal of Personality and Social Psychology* 32:367–376, 1975.

Schwitzgebel, R. K. Learning theory approaches to the treatment of criminal behavior. *Seminars in Psychiatry* 3:328–344, 1971.

Shapiro, D., and Surwit, R. S. Operant conditioning: A new theoretical approach in psychosomatic medicine. *International Journal of Psychiatry in Medicine* 5:387, 1974.

Skinner, B. F. *Science and Human Behavior.* New York: The Free Press, 1953.

Skinner, B. F. *Contingencies of Reinforcement.* New York: Appleton-Century-Crofts, 1969.

Skinner, B. F. *Beyond Freedom and Dignity.* New York: Bantam Books, 1971.

Wenrich, W. W. *A Primer of Behavior Modification.* Belmont, Calif.: Brooks/Cole Publishing Co., 1970.

Whaley, D., and Malott, R. *Elementary Principles of Behavior.* New York: Appleton-Century-Crofts, 1971.

Wolper, J., Salten, A., and Reyna, Z. J. *The Conditioning Therapies.* New York: Holt, Rinehart & Winston, 1966.

Wolpe, J. *The Practice of Behavior Therapy.* New York: Pergamon Press, 1969.

Yates, A. *Behavior Therapy.* New York: Wiley & Sons, 1970.

Client-Centered Therapy

Abramowitz, C. V., Abramowitz, S. I., Roback, H. B., and Jackson, C. Differential effectiveness of directive and nondirective group therapies as a function of client internal-external control. *Journal of Consulting and Clinical Psychology* 42:849–853, 1974.

Hart, J. T., and Tomlenson, T. M. *New Directions in Client Centered Therapy.* Boston: Houghton Mifflin, 1970.

Kilmann, P. R., and Howell, R. J. Effects of structure of marathon group therapy and locus of control of therapeutic outcome. *Journal of Consulting and Clinical Psychology* 42:912, 1974.

Loesch, L. C., and Loesch, N. A. What do you say after you say MM – HMM? *American Journal of Nursing* 75:807, 1975.

Maddi, S. R. *Personality Theories: A Comparative Analysis.* Homewood, Ill.: Dorsey Press, 1972.

Miller, B. V. The preschool child's perception of adult approval in nondirective statements. *Journal of Abnormal Child Psychology* 2:63–66, 1974.

Morrison, T. L., and Newcomer, B. L. Effects of directive vs. nondirective play therapy with institutionalized mentally retarded children. *American Journal of Mental Deficiency* 79:666–669, 1975.

Narr, R. Client-centered psychotherapy: Comment and critique. *American Journal Psychoanalysis* 35:79–81, 1975.

Patterson, C. H. *Theories of Counseling and Psychotherapy.* New York: Harper & Row, 1973.

Pervin, L. A. *Personality: Theory, Assessment, and Research.* New York: Wiley & Sons, 1970.

Rogers, C. R. *Client-Centered Therapy.* Cambridge, Mass.: Riverside Press, 1951.

Rogers, C. R. *On Becoming A Person.* Boston: Houghton Mifflin, 1961.

Rogers, C. R. Theory of Therapy. In B. N. Ard, Jr. (Ed.), *Counseling and Psychotherapy.* Palo Alto, Calif.: Science and Behavior Books, 1966. Pp. 43–74.

Rogers, C. R. *Person to Person: The Problem of Being Human.* Moab, Utah: Real People Press, 1967.

Rogers, C. R. *Freedom to Learn.* Columbus, Ohio: Merril Publishing Co., 1969.

Rogers, C. R. *Encounter Groups.* New York: Harper & Row, 1970.

Rogers, C. R. *Becoming Partners: Marriage and Its Alternatives.* New York: Delacorte Press, 1972.

Snygg, D., and Combs, A. W. *Individual Behavior.* New York: Harper & Row, 1959.

Existential Therapy

Adamson, J. D. Letter: Existential encounter with the patient. *American Journal of Psychiatry* 131:509–510, 1974.

Buber, M. *I and Thou.* New York: Charles Scribner's Sons, 1958.

Buckley, F. M. A phenomenological approach to psychotherapy. *Psychiatric Communications* 16:31–40, 1975.

Frankel, V. E. *The Doctor and the Soul.* New York: Knopf, 1955.

Frankel, V. E. *Man's Search for Meaning.* Boston: Beacon Press, 1959.

Freedman, A., Kaplan, H., and Sadock, B. J. *Modern Synopsis of Comprehensive Textbooks of Psychiatry.* Baltimore: Williams & Wilkins Co., 1972. Pp. 149–151.

Gabel, P. Freud's death instinct and Sartre's fundamental project.*Psychoanalytic Review* 61:217–227, 1974.

Garfield, C. A. A psychometric and clinical investigation of Frankel's concept of existential vacuum and of anomia. *Psychiatry* 36:396–408, 1973.

Good, L. R., and Good, K. C. A preliminary measure of existential anxiety. *Psychological Reports* 24:72–74, 1974.

Greaves, G. Toward an existential theory of drug dependence. *Journal of Nervous and Mental Disease* 159:263–274, 1974.

Havens, L. L. The existential use of the self. *American Journal of Psychiatry* 131:1–10, 1974.

Illie, P. U. *An Existential View of Self and Society.* Madison: University of Wisconsin Press, 1967.

Kempler, W. Experiential psychotherapy with families. *International Journal of Group Psychotherapy* (1965), pp. 57–71.

Marcel, G. *The Mystery of Being.* Chicago: Henry Regnery, 1960.

May, R. *Psychology and the Human Dilemma.* New York: Van Nostrand, 1966.

May, R. *Love and Will.* New York: Dell Books, 1969.

May, R. The Existential Approach. In S. Arieti (Ed.), *American Handbook of Psychiatry.* New York: Basic Books, 1969. Pp. 1348–1362.

May, R., Angel, E., and Ellenberger, H. F. *Existence: A New Dimension in Psychiatry and Psychology.* New York: Basic Books, 1962.

Miller, M. H. Beginning at the beginning in psychotherapy: An existential point of view. *Canadian Psychiatric Association Journal* 18:459–465, 1973.

Pishkin, V., and Thorne, F. C. A factorial study of existential state reactions. *Journal of Clinical Psychology* 29:392–402, 1973.

Roiphe, A. A writer looks at the void. *American Journal of Psychoanalysis* 35:35–55, 1975.

Sanborn, P. *Existentialism.* New York: Pegasus, 1968.

Sartre, J. P. *Being and Nothingness* (translated by H. Barnes). New York: Philosophical Library, 1956.

Scher, J. M. Space and space making in ontoanalysis. *Existential Psychiatry* 1:20–29, 1956.

Scher, J. M. Ontoanalysis: Man as rhythm in the world. *Existential Psychiatry* (Winter, 1967), pp. 459–470.

Schmidt, K. T. On existentialism and existential psychiatry. *Virginia Medical Monthly* 97:448–451, 1970.

Siomopoulos, V. The existential hero: Schizophrenic or the forerunner of a new affectivity? *Psychoanalytic Review* 62:429–436, 1975.

Thorne, F. C. The existential study: A measure of existential status. *Journal of Clinical Psychology* 29:387–392, 1973.

Thorne, F. C., and Pishkin, V. A comparative study of the factorial composition of responses on the existential study across clinical groups. *Journal of Clinical Psychology* 29:403–410, 1973.

Tillich, P. *The Courage to Be.* New Haven, Conn.: Yale University Press, 1953.

Watson, J. Existentialism: Its relevance for practice and education. *Supervising Nurse* 6:21, 23–27, 1975.

Adlerian Therapy

Dreikurs, R., and Grey, L. *A Parent's Guide to Child Disciplines.* New York: Hawthorn Books, Inc., 1970.

Berenson, B., and Carkhuff, R. (Eds.) *Sources of Gain in Counseling and Psychotherapy.* New York: Holt, Rinehart & Winston, 1967.

Carkhuff, R. *Helping and Human Relations.* New York: Holt, Rinehart & Winston, 1969. Vol. 1.

Carkhuff, R., and Berenson, B. *Beyond Counseling and Therapy.* New York: Holt, Rinehart & Winston, 1967.

Gestalt Therapy

Alban, L. S., and Groman, M. D. Dreamwork in a Gestalt therapy context. *American Journal of Psychoanalysis* 35:147–156, 1975.

Bornstein, P. H. I: language-induced anxiety. *Psychological Reports* 35:453–454, 1974.

Boylin, E. R. Gestalt encounter in the treatment of hospitalized alcoholic patients. *American Journal of Psychotherapy* 29:524–534, 1975.

Fagan, J., and Shepherd, J. L. *What is Gestalt Therapy?* New York: Perennial Library, 1973.

Fagan, J., and Shepherd, I. L. *Life Techniques and Gestalt Therapy.* New York: Harper & Row, 1970.

Kempler, W. *Principles of Gestalt Family Therapy.* Costa Mesa, Calif.: Kempler Institute, 1974.

Nelson, W., and Groman, W. D. The meaning of here-now, there-then in Gestalt therapy. *American Jornal of Psychoanalysis* 34:337–346, 1974.

Perls, R. S. *The Gestalt Approach and Eye Witness to Therapy.* Palo Alto, Calif.: Science and Behavior Books, Inc., 1973.

Perls, F. S., Hufferline, R. F., and Goodman, P. *Gestalt Therapy: Excitement and Growth in the Human Personality.* New York: Dell Publishing Co., 1951.

Polster, I., and Polster, M. *Gestalt Therapy.* New York: Brunner Mazel Publishers, 1973.

Stevens, J. *Awareness: Exploring, Experimenting, Experiencing.* Moab, Utah: Real People Press, 1971.

Transactional Analysis

Agel, J. *The Radical Therapist.* New York: Ballantine Books, 1971.

Appell, L., and Baskin, D. Transactional analysis: Improving the nurse/patient relationship. *Journal of Practical Nursing* 25:24–26, 1975.

Berne, E. *The Structure and Dynamics of Organizations and Groups.* Philadelphia: J. B. Lippincott Co., 1953.

Berne, E. Transactional analysis: A new and effective method of group therapy. *American Journal of Psychotherapy* 12:735–743, 1956.

Berne, E. *What Do You Say After You Say Hello?* New York: Grove Press, 1972.

Ernst, F. *Handbook of Listening Transactional Analysis of the Listening Activity.* San Francisco, Calif.: Transactional Publishers, 1971.

Freed, A. *T.A. for Kids and Grown-ups Too.* San Francisco, Calif.: Freed, 1971.

Freed, A. *T.A. for Tots and Other Prinzes.* San Francisco, Calif.: Freed, 1973.

Friedman, F. B. Using TA to Become OK. *Journal of Practical Nursing* 25:18–19, 1975.

Gowell, E. C. Transactional analysis strategies for dealing with pain. *Journal of Psychiatric Nursing* 12:25–30, 1974.

Ikemi, Y., and Sugita, M. The oriental version of transactional analysis. *Psychosomatics* 16:164–170, 1975.

James, M. *Born to Love — Transactional Analysis in the Church.* Reading, Mass.: Addison-Wesley Publishing Co., 1973.

James, M., and Jongeward, D. *Born to Win.* Reading, Mass.: Addison-Wesley Publishing Co., 1971.

Jesness, C. F. Comparative effectiveness of behavior modification and transactional analysis programs for delinquents. *Journal of Consulting and Clinical Psychology* 43:758–779, 1975.

Jongeward, D., and James, M. *Winning With People.* Reading, Mass.: Addison-Wesley Publishing Co., 1973.

Klingbeil, G. A., and Alvandi, O. M. Concepts of transactional analysis and anxiety with persons in crisis. *Journal of Psychiatric Nursing* 13:5–10, 1975.

Lange, S. Transactional Analysis and Nursing. In C. E. Carlson (Coor.), *Behavioral Concepts and Nursing Intervention.* Philadelphia: J. B. Lippincott Co., 1970.

McCormick, P. *Guide for Use of a Life Script Questionnaire in Transactional Analysis.* San Francisco, Calif.: Transactional Publishers, 1971.

McCormick, P., and Campos, L. *Introduce Yourself to Transactional Analysis (A TA handbook).* Stockton, Calif.: San Joaquin TA Study Group, 1969.

Meininger, J. *Success Through Transactional Analysis.* New York: The New American Library, 1973.

Selavan, A. Hypnosis and transactional analysis theory. *American Journal of Clinical Hypnosis* 17:260–262, 1975.

Steiner, C. *Games Alcoholics Play: The Analysis of Life Scripts.* New York: Grove Press, 1971.

Steiner, C. *Scripts People Live By.* New York: Bantam Books, 1974.

Wagner, F. The stroke bank. *Nursing Care* 7:26, 1974.

Crisis Intervention

Appley, M. *Psychological Stress.* New York: Appleton-Century-Crofts, 1967.

Block, H. An open ended crisis group for the poor who are sick. *Archives of General Psychiatry* 18:178, 1968.

Caplan, G. *An Approach to Community Mental Health.* New York: Grune & Stratton, 1961.

Caplan, G. *Principles of Preventive Psychiatry.* New York: Basic Books, 1964.

Dixon, M. C. The training of telephone crisis intervention volunteers. *American Journal of Community Psychology* 3:145–150, 1975.

Donner, G. Parenthood as a crisis. *Perspectives in Psychiatric Care* 10:84–87, 1972.

Engel, G. Grief — grieving. *American Journal of Nursing* 64:93–98, 1964.

Ford, D., and Urban, H. *Systems of Psychotherapy.* New York: Wiley & Sons, 1963.

Glasser, P., and Glasser, L. *Families in Crisis.* New York: Harper & Row, 1970.

Jacobson, G. Crisis Theory and Treatment Strategy. *Journal of Nervous Mental Disease* 141:209–218, 1965.

Langner, T., and Michael, S. *Life Stress and Mental Health.* New York: Free Press, 1963.

Langsley, D. G., and Kaplan, D. *The Treatment of Families in Crisis.* New York: Grune & Stratton, 1968.

Levine, S., and Scotch, W. *Social Stress.* Chicago: Aldine, 1970.

Lieb, J., Lipsiteb, L., and Slaby, A. *The Crisis Team — A Handbook for Mental Health Professionals.* New York: Harper & Row, 1973.

Martin, D. *Learning-Based Client-Centered Therapy.* Monterey, Calif.: Brooks-Cole, 1972.

Parad, H. (Ed.). *Crisis Intervention, Selected Readings.* New York: Family Service Association of America, 1965.

Parad, H. *Crisis Intervention.* New York: Family Service Association of America, 1970.

Patterson, V., and O'Sullivan, M. Three Perspectives on Brief Psychotherapy. *American Journal of Psychotherapy* 28:265–277, 1974.

Rapoport, L. The state of crisis, some theoretical considerations. *Social Service Review* 36:211–217, 1962.

Rapoport, R. Normal crisis, family structure and mental health. *Family Process* 2:68–80, 1964.

Realich, F. The concept of normality. *American Journal of Psychotherapy* 6:551–576, 1952.

Schneidnim, E. *The Psychology of Suicide.* New York: Science House, 1970.

Sifneos, P. *Short Term Psychotherapy and Emotional Crisis.* Cambridge, Harvard University Press, 1972.

Small, L. *The Briefer Psychotherapies.* New York: Brunner Mazel, 1971.

Tanley, J. C. Use of the A-B variable in a crisis phone setting. *Journal of Clinical Psychology* 30:285–289, 1974.

9 From Theory into Practice: Undergraduate Students

MARY JO TRAPP BULBROOK

One of the joys of teaching, facilitating, and guiding the learning process of students is to participate in and witness their growth. The high I get from the sharing of experiences with students (not unlike my experiences with clients), ranks at the top of my list of pleasant encounters.

Material in this chapter includes case studies of undergraduate nursing students and the assessment tool they utilized. The three patients discussed, A., R., and B. are real people — only their names and the places and dates have been changed to protect their anonymity. All the students were in their junior year in an integrated four-year nursing program and got their experience in a Veterans Administration (VA) hospital. The clinical experience was obtained under my supervision in an in-patient, short-term facility situation.

ASSESSMENT TOOL

The assessment tool used by these undergraduate students was adapted from an assessment tool utilized at Texas Women's University, Dallas Center, Academic Year 1975–1976.

  I. Data Base
    A. Patient profile
      1. Name, age, sex, religion, date, voluntary or involuntary entrance into system, referred by
      2. Chief complaint
      3. Past experience with problem
      4. Individual's status on health-illness continuum
      5. Individual medical history
    B. Mental status examination
      1. Attitude, appearance, and general behavior
      2. Affect, mood, and emotional responsiveness

3. Memory
   a. Remote past
   b. Present past
   c. Immediate impressions
4. Orientation: time, place, persons, self
5. Intellectual functioning
   a. General information (days of week, where sun sets, etc.)
   b. Calculations
   c. Symbolization (abstractions, e.g. "A rolling stone gathers no moss")
   d. Reasoning and judgment (Why are laws necessary?)
6. Insight
7. Mental trend
   a. Thought content: perceptions, misperceptions, illusions, hallucinations
   b. Thought processes: stream of thought, talk, psycho-motor activity
C. Self-description
   1. Source of worry
   2. Outstanding characteristics
   3. Difficulties to overcome
D. Choices
   1. Most important turning point in life
   2. Illustration of success and failure
   3. Main resources of help in times of need
E. Sociocultural profile
   1. Family of orientation
   2. Birth and development
   3. Education and training
   4. Work record
   5. Recreation and interest
   6. Marital and family data
      a. Present family interaction
      b. Major events in course of marriage
F. Evaluator's profiles
   1. General response to individual
   2. General impressions
   3. Describe your assets or limitations in handling individual
II. Problem Asset Lists
III. Initial Plans (S.O.A.P.)
   S = subjective data
   O = objective data
   A = assessment
   P = plans (goals)

IV. Orders (Nurse, social worker, physician, psychologist, other)
 V. Progress Notes (S.O.A.P.)
VI. Discharge Planning
    A. Overall statement
    B. Problem/asset list
    C. Summary of each problem, identification, treatment,
       outcome, follow-up treatment
    D. Summary (follow-up plans and recommendations)

GUIDE FOR DISCUSSION

The following general guide and questions can be used as the
basis for a study and discussion of any case a student will see.
It has been followed, for the most part, in the case studies that
follow.

General Guide

The following are things the student should do to generally
strengthen his or her background in the field: Review literature
on etiology of drug abuse, neurotic behavior, psychotic break,
and psychosomatic disorders. Read material on charting according to problem-oriented method. Study nursing interventions
that beginning practitioners can use in psychosocial nursing for
the patient's condition. Review drug therapy utilized in psychiatric conditions, emphasizing nursing management, and review
symbols used in administration of drugs. Also review how to
assess the prognosis of each client from the data available and
back up statements with alternative review.

Reviewing Accuracy of Case Information

DATA BASE REVIEW

1. Has the precipitating event that led to hospitalization been
   identified?
2. Are dates, places, names, and other identifying data clear?
3. Is the recorder's writing style clear and accurate?
4. Is student aware of the effect of his or her behavior on the client?
5. Does the data base have the essential elements?
6. Is verbal and nonverbal behavior described, illustrating a clear
   picture of the events?

PROBLEM LIST

1. Are all the problems identified in the data base?
2. Are the problems general or specific? Do they clearly document the current and past status of clients?

3. Do the problems reflect all the content recorded in the data base?
4. Are the client's assets listed?

INITIAL PLANS

1. Is the S.O.A.P. in the initial plans accurate for each category?
2. Does the subjective information reflect the client's statements?
3. Does all the data deal with a particular problem reflected in the data base?
4. Is the assessment clear and accurate and based on subjective and objective data?
5. What other assessment(s) can be made from the data?
6. Are the plans realistic?
7. Is any other plan of action useful?

NURSING ORDERS

1. Are the nursing orders clear and related to the problem?
2. What other orders can be determined?

PROGRESS NOTES

1. Do the problems listed correspond to the original problem listing?
2. Are the problems dated and is progress or lack thereof clearly identified?
3. Review progress S.O.A.P. and determine its accuracy.

DISCHARGE SUMMARY

1. Have all the problems been reviewed and their current status determined?
2. Is a plan(s) identified for client follow-up?
3. Is the follow-up comprehensive, dealing with major needs in a realistic fashion?
4. Has the recorder summarized important material clearly and accurately?
5. What additional data can be added?

DATA BASE: A.

A. is a 45-year-old white male. His diagnosis, as stated in his chart, is depression and anxiety. He entered the hospital with complaints of nervous depression, back and head pain, excessive weight loss, and a history of cardiovascular disease.

A. related that prior to hospitalization he had become very depressed, with excessive weight loss, head and back pain, and high blood pressure. He said that he couldn't eat or sleep, so he went to the hospital in his home town, feeling that his problem was physical. For economic reasons, he was sent to this Veterans Administration (VA) hospital. No physical cause was found for his illness, so he was sent for psychiatric evaluation. He agreed that he should stay there for help.

A. was asked to describe his emotional status just prior to hospitalization. He said that after a year of school at a nearby junior college and working full-time as a policeman to support his wife and four children, his motor just ran down. He said that he progressively began to feel depressed and would have periodic crying spells to get his pent-up feelings out. He could not talk to anyone including his wife about how he felt. He has had previous experience with depressed feelings at different times throughout his life. He said that his first experience was at age 19 when he was in college. After being forced to drop out of school to work on his father's farm when he was 14, he always had had a powerful drive to get through college in order to escape a life of menial labor. At 19 he obtained a high school equivalency degree and left home to start business school. He was also working full-time and taking part in many church activities. When I asked him to explain why he became depressed, he expressed two reasons. The first was the death of his mother, who died of cancer when he was 14. They had been very close, and he became very bitter, not being able to understand why God had taken her away. The other was frequent feelings of loneliness. After finishing school, A. entered the armed services and a year later, at the age of 21, he married. They had two children but the marriage didn't work out, and they were divorced. A. said that he had badly wanted it to work out because he loved his two boys very much and wanted to be with them. It was difficult for him to see his children after the divorce, and the feelings of depression again arose. Because of the way he was feeling he couldn't keep up with his job so he quit it and moved away. A few years later he married again. This marriage brought him out of his depression. His wife had two young children from her previous marriage who, A. said, took the place of his own two sons. Two years ago he decided to return to school to further his education. He had always wanted a college education so that he could give his family the life he had never had. After starting school full-time and at the same time working as a policeman full-time, the feelings of nervousness and depression again arose. This time physical symptoms — high blood pressure, headaches, back pain, and an inability to sleep — came with it. This time he sought medical help. A. says he feels much better at the present time, although he frequently wakes up at 2:30 in the morning and can't get back to sleep.

Psychological Profile

A.'s dominant emotions and behaviors seem to be ones of aloofness. The nurse mentioned that on a group picnic he would not participate in the games the other patients were playing but tended to remain an observer. He also is uncomfortable when discussing his inner feelings and tries to keep the conversation on a more superficial level. He seems to have trouble with interpersonal relationships and told me during our last meeting that he was a little uncomfortable talking to me. He said he usually cannot talk about his feelings. I have noticed some fluctuation in his behavior. On some days he seems quite happy and friendly, yet on others he appears quieter and depressed. On the depressed days, he has a very tired, tense look on his face, as though he has a lot on his mind. He carries on a conversation with emotions and behavior appropriate to the subject being discussed.

A. seems to be highly intelligent. He has a good vocabulary and has no trouble communicating. His memory is intact. He remembers how long he has been in the hospital and how he got there. He discusses past experiences without any apparent lapses in memory. He has no suicidal tendencies or grandiose ideas. He carries on a conversation in a very logical manner and stays on the subject; his thought processes and content therefore seem normal.

The patient does not have any misperceptions or illusions. He is aware he has a problem and says he wants to do something about it. The nurses feel he needs some insight into his feelings and the cause of his problems. He does not have hallucinations. Attention is good and he has no trouble concentrating on what is being said. He is fully oriented, knowing where he is and what is going on.

A.'s main source of worry seems to be finishing school. He expresses a great desire to finish college so that he not only can provide a good life for his family, but get a feeling of self-satisfaction as well. He states that he is a religious man and an ambitious one. He told me that he had a hard time talking to others about his feelings and wished he could overcome this. He said that although his wife knows when he's feeling depressed and would like him to talk about it, he just can't.

A. mentioned only one time that he felt he had failed. This was his divorce from his first wife. He had always wanted a family and not being able to make it in this marriage was quite a disappointment to him. He said that this had been a very bad time in his life and had been hard for him to get over.

Sociocultural Profile

A. grew up on a farm with six brothers and sisters. His father knew nothing but menial labor. He had little schooling and the family was quite poor. After his mother died, his two youngest sisters were put in an orphanage because his father could not afford to care for them. He said that he and his father were not very close because of what he felt was his father's ignorance. A. did not feel that he could talk to his father about anything because his father had nothing to offer him. He mentioned being quite independent after his mother died and that he pretty much took care of himself. No bitterness was felt toward his father or his father's life style, but he said that he was determined to offer his own family a better life.

A.'s work record is quite good. He was a wholesale shoe salesman for a large company for many years but quit because he didn't like the traveling. He has worked for the police department for the past 18 years. For recreation, A. enjoys hunting, fishing, and being with his family.

He is very happy with his wife and family. He has been married for 20 years and feels that there are no conflicts in his home life.

Nurse's Profile of A.

At the beginning of our relationship, there was not much real communication between A. and me. Because he was rather aloof I stayed rather aloof. I expected him to make the first move and open up to me. When he did not, I was quite surprised and didn't really know how to handle it. When I urged him to express his feelings about certain events, communication got better. I feel that I have made some progress in getting A. to open up to me and express some of his feelings. I'm not sure how he feels about me. He said that even though it helps him to talk to me about his feelings, he still feels a little nervous about it. He also said that he had told me many things he had not been able to talk about before. Although he was initially aloof, I think he now feels more comfortable around me and more willing to talk. My first limitation with this patient was that I was not quite sure of my role with him. I was afraid to make the first move in forming a relevant relationship. On the other hand, this might have been an asset. I think this relationship needed a little time to form since Mr. A. seems to have a difficult time talking to people and needs more time to feel comfortable before opening up.

PROBLEM LIST
Active problems as of April 2, 1978, were:

Depression
Physical complaints
Trouble with interpersonal relationships
Sleeplessness
Overachievement
Trouble verbalizing feelings

Inactive problems were pneumonia, broken left hand, hemorrhoid and fistula.

Problem 1. Depression
S: Patient said he was depressed and didn't feel like doing much.
O: Patient hasn't attended occupational therapy or corrective therapy this week. Not talking much; looks tense and tired; often found staring into space.
A: Patient has a serious history of depression.
P: Initiate activities and therapy to bring patient out of depression.

NURSING ORDERS
1. Talk with patient on a one-to-one basis.
2. Have patient attend group therapy to obtain insight into feelings.
3. Get patient involved in enjoyable activities to get his mind off his problems (e.g., cards, walks).
4. Administer medication to reduce signs and symptoms of depression.

Problem 2. Physical Complaints
S: Patient says he entered the hospital with high blood pressure, head and back pains, and excessive weight loss (down from 160 to 130 pounds).
O: Blood pressure was 200/120. No other physical problems were found, and patient was transferred to psychiatric ward.
A: Weight loss and somatic aches and pains due to depression. Possible problems with hypertension.
P: Observe, report, and record signs or symptoms of physical problems.

NURSING ORDERS

1. Check blood pressure weekly and report or record signs of hypertension.
2. Obtain weight status weekly.
3. Note and record recurrence of head and back pains.

Problem 3. Trouble with Interpersonal Relationships

S: Patient has a hard time talking to others about his feelings. He says he can't talk to his wife either, although he knows he should.
O: Patient appears aloof and talks mainly on a superficial level. Patient appears fidgety and nervous when talking about deeper feelings. Hasn't mentioned any close relationships.
A: Patient is unable to form close emotional relationships.
P: Help patient open up and form a close relationship.

NURSING ORDERS

1. Establish rapport on a one-to-one basis.
2. Urge patient to express feelings.
3. Put patient in group therapy to help him understand why he has trouble with this and help him overcome it.
4. Try to make patient feel comfortable about verbalizing his feelings by displaying understanding and genuine interest.

Problem 4. Sleeplessness

S: Patient says he wakes up at 2:30 A.M. most mornings and can't get back to sleep.
O: Patient appears tired in the morning, sleeps during the day.
A: Drinks excessive amounts of coffee. A habit of sleeping during the day instead of at night is forming.
P: Promote better sleep patterns.

NURSING ORDERS

1. Do not allow patient to sleep during the day.
2. Have patient participate in relaxation therapy.
3. Have patient on a sleep machine one hour each day.
4. Urge patient to cut down on coffee drinking.
5. Administer medications.

Problem 5. Overachievement

S: Patient says he feels compelled to finish college yet must work full-time to support his family. Patient agrees he can't cope with it, but when he leaves the hospital he will continue in the same way.

O: Patient has had previous problems with depression under similar circumstances, yet won't change life style. He has rejected sharing his feelings of depressions with his wife.

A: Patient cannot set his own limits.

P: Help patient to set his own limits and slow down. Increase his desire to share his feelings with his wife.

NURSING ORDERS
1. Help patient get insight into his feelings and understanding of what he can cope with.
2. Get patient into group therapy.
3. Work with couple to encourage them to be supportive of each other.

Problem 6. Trouble Verbalizing Feelings

S: Patient said he kept feelings bottled up inside and couldn't talk about them. He said that when things got bad he'd have crying spells to get feelings out. Patient said he was nervous talking about his feelings.

O: Patient appeared to fidget when talking and talks on a superficial level most of the time. He tries to stay aloof.

A: Patient feels uncomfortable when verbalizing feelings and keeps them inside instead of letting them out.

P: Help patient learn to verbalize feelings.

NURSING ORDERS
1. Urge patient to express feelings.
2. Establish a comfortable, therapeutic relationship with patient on a one-to-one basis so he will feel more at ease verbalizing his feelings. Don't push too hard.
3. Get patient involved in group therapy to help him learn to show his feelings.

PROGRESS NOTES as of April 26, 1978
Problem 1. Depression

S: Patient says he is feeling much better because he is taking it easy and has less time to think about his problems. He says the environment and the people on the ward have taken his mind off himself.

O: Patient appears more lively. Smiles and talks more; participates in games more than before.

A: Cutting down on activities and pressures has relaxed patient. Drug therapy has somewhat relieved his anxious and depressed state of mind. He has obtained limited insight into the cause of his problems, although he is still planning to go back to the same life style that put him into the hospital.

P: Initiate therapy to help patient cope with his chosen life style when he leaves the ward.

NURSING ORDERS

1. Continue medications to calm patient and reduce symptoms of depression.
2. Have patient continue in group therapy in order to give him more insight into problems which in turn will enable him to decide what to do about them.
3. Continue meeting with the patient on a one-to-one basis.

Problem 2. Physical Complaints

S: Patient says he feels much better. He no longer has head or back pain and says he has regained his normal weight of 165 pounds.
O: Patient appears healthy. Blood pressure is 100/80.
A: Because of the patient's improved state of mind, somatic aches and pains have subsided.
P: Continue reporting and recording signs and symptoms of hypertension.

NURSING ORDER

1. Continue taking blood pressure weekly.

Problem 3. Trouble with Interpersonal Relationships

S: Patient says he feels better after talking to the doctor or me but that he initially finds it hard to do. Patient says he doesn't talk to his wife because he feels that his problems are his burden, not hers.
O: Patient has opened up more than before. He has appeared happier and more outgoing after our sessions. He seems more relaxed and willing to talk now. He interacts more with other patients, discussing himself with other patients a little more frequently.
A: The environment and people in the hospital promote in him more expression of his feelings and closeness with others.
P: Initiate further opening up of patient so that he will feel more comfortable in forming relationships.

NURSING ORDERS

1. Continue meeting with patient on a one-to-one basis to initiate this opening up.

2. Have the patient continue in group therapy so he can obtain further insight into his feelings.

Problem 4. Sleeplessness

S: Patient says he's sleeping better. He usually wakes up about 5:00 A.M. but then goes back to sleep.

O: Patient appears more rested in the morning and seldom sleeps during the day.

A: Reduced depression and inner turmoil are promoting better sleep patterns. Sleeping less in the day is helping him sleep at night.

P: Promote sleeping for the entire night without awakening.

NURSING ORDERS

1. Cut out any sleeping in the day.
2. Continue medications.
3. Continue relaxation therapy.

Problem 5. Overachievement

S: Patient says he still feels compelled to finish college and still must work full-time to support his family. He can see that his previous life style was too much for him, but he still plans to continue with it when he leaves the hospital.

O: Although patient has had previous problems with depression under similar circumstances, he will not slow down.

A: Patient still cannot set his own limits.

P: Increase patient's awareness of his coping abilities.

NURSING ORDERS

1. Continue helping patient to get insight into his feelings and why he pushes himself so hard.
2. Discuss priorities with patient: What is more important, goals or mental health?
3. Continue patient in group therapy to help with above.

Problem 6. Trouble Verbalizing Feelings

S: Patient says he is aware that it is better to verbalize feelings but has a hard time doing it.

O: Patient appears more relaxed when talking to me and verbalizes more quickly and easily. Patient still interacts somewhat superficially with other patients.

A: Patient still feels a little uncomfortable verbalizing his feelings.

P: Continue helping patient to verbalize his feelings more easily.

NURSING ORDERS
1. Continue relationship on a one-to-one basis.
2. Continue group therapy to encourage patient to verbalize his feelings and gain more insight into them.

DISCHARGE SUMMARY: April 30, 1978
Problem 1: Depression
PATIENT'S RESPONSE

The patient responded well to the plan devised to help his depression. He did gain insight into the cause of his depression through group and individual therapy. Medication decreased the signs and symptoms of depression. When the patient left the hospital he was in good spirits, no longer depressed. The relaxed life style and therapeutic environment of the hospital also contributed to this response to therapy. In the hospital there were none of the pressures that seem to have caused A.'s past depression. I feel that if he returns to the original pressure-filled life style, the depression will return.

Problem 2. Physical Complaints
PATIENT'S RESPONSE

The patient's physical complaints, which I feel were secondary to his depression, disappeared quickly along with his depression. They should not be a potential problem unless the depression recurs.

Problem 3. Trouble with Interpersonal Relationships
PATIENT'S RESPONSE

The patient responded well to the plan for dealing with this problem of interpersonal relationships. He became quite verbal with me and was willing to express his feelings. He formed better relationships with me and other patients during the latter part of his hospitalization. Promoting a closer relationship with his wife as a base would encourage closer relationships with other people. Perhaps Mr. A. and his wife should meet with a marriage counselor after his discharge to help promote a closer, more sharing relationship.

Problem 4. Sleeplessness
PATIENT'S RESPONSE

The patient also responded well to ideas for taking care of his insomnia. He was having no trouble sleeping just prior to discharge. It should not be a problem as long as his nervousness and depression stay under control.

Problem 5. Overachievement
PATIENT'S RESPONSE

The patient did not respond very well to the therapy for the problem of overachievement. He says that he still plans to continue going to school full-time and that he must work in order to support his family. I feel that most of his problems, the depression, physical complaints, and sleeplessness, come from the stressful situation that A. puts himself in. Unless he can slow down and set some limits, this same problem may arise again. I would advise therapy on an out-patient basis for him so he can get more help with this problem. He still needs to gain insight into why he cannot set limits, and then learn to set them. He also needs help to learn to be satisfied with himself as he is, and not push himself so hard.

Problem 6. Trouble Verbalizing Feelings
PATIENT'S RESPONSE

The patient responded well to the therapy outlined for helping him learn to verbalize his feelings. He became much more verbal toward the end of his stay at the hospital. He mentioned not being able to talk to his wife about his problems because he felt that it was his burden, not hers. It would probably be beneficial, as mentioned earlier, for the patient and his wife to go through counseling together to promote a closer relationship.

DATA BASE: R.

R., a 26-year-old white man, was admitted to the hospital psychiatric floor on June 29, 1978. This patient would be placed in the area of "protected poor health in a favorable environment" in Dunn's High-Level Wellness Continuum. The patient described his problem as a withdrawal from everything after failing a class in biology at the university. He said he didn't eat; his friends tried to help him but couldn't. He went to the health service and then was admitted to a state mental hospital where he was treated for "nerves." His parents came to get him and brought him back to San Antonio for treatment at the VA hospital.

The patient said he knew after taking the first test in the biology class that he would fail the course. The professor gave him a chance to withdraw, but the patient elected to continue the class. He stated that he wrote out a precise answer, but the professor labeled the answer as too vague.

The patient said he doesn't get along well with either parent. R. feels that his father has one type of attitude toward him and another toward his brother. He feels that his father treats him in a cold manner, using intellectual statements in conversation, while his brother has a warm relationship with him.

Individual Psychological Profile
EMOTIONAL AND BEHAVIORAL ATTITUDE

Patient has been silent in the group sessions during the day, and has not expressed any open anger or hostility. At one point however, when I was doodling on a piece of paper he abruptly took the pencil from me and stated, "That will put a stop to that." He explained that my action reminded him of a test at the hospital. During activities he plays as if he is interested in the game and its outcome.

CENTRAL ORGANIZING PROCESSES

R. has a college education and appears very intelligent. He discusses school, biology classes, and anthropology. His memory is intact. He talks about his high school play and how he memorized lines for *Bus Stop*. He feels that school represents a lot of memory work and asked "Where will I ever use the stuff I learn?"

PERCEPTIONS

Patient is alert and oriented to time. He said he is ready to go now, but Dr. S. thought therapy would take six months. Patient stated he has four and a half more months to go. R. likes the hospital and said, "I live the life of Riley here." R. stated that he had gotten "involved with a social worker in Dallas." Another time he was talking about a line from *Alice in Wonderland*. When asked if that had any meaning, he responded, "Only if you put your arms around me and hug me."

SELF-DESCRIPTION

R. describes himself as an other-directed person. I had a difficult time understanding that statement.

Patient has good qualities, e.g., persistence in school work.

He worries since he has been in the hospital that he will not be accepted into medical school, which is his goal. He has discussed this problem with the doctor.

R. has said that he thinks his sister looks at him as she would her father.

ILLUSTRATION OF SUCCESS AND FAILURE
On probation at school upon his return to the university in
1978, he failed the biology class, withdrew from school, and
then went to the hospital. When he goes on pass, he visits his
sister and brother who live in Houston.

Sociocultural Profile
R. was born in Oregon and lived near his grandparents for two
years. When he was three, the family moved to Washington.
R. stated that moving when he was young was traumatic for him.
When R. was five he moved into the middle child position when
his sister S. was born. He feels that children have to work through
their feelings and decide how they feel about their siblings.

   R. finally graduated from high school and progressed to college
which he expressed as "following in my brother's footsteps." He
went to the university and majored in premed for two years and
anthropology for one year before going into the U.S. Army, during which time he worked with computers. His brother had
attended the same university and majored in business. His brother,
now 28, works with their father on a newspaper (following in the
father's image). R. feels that his father treats him in a more dif-
fuse manner than he does his brother. There have been underlying problems in the family. S., who is now 20, was married and
had a son. R. stated that his parents interfered in his brother's
marriage, which subsequently ended in divorce. His father has
epilepsy and feels guilty about this condition.

   For recreation, R. likes to play pool, ping-pong and poker,
and travel. On weekends, he likes to go to Greenville Avenue
and listen to music, meet people, and drink. He has used drugs
and has taken LSD a few times.

Nurse's Profile of R.
I have found the patient to be interesting to talk with since he
has a broad education. During the first interactions, however,
I felt uncomfortable because he wouldn't talk, although even
no communication is some communication since it reveals something about the patient. Patient thought that I would be embarrassed if I worked with him. He questioned me with "Do you
think I'm interesting to talk to?" and "Do you like to listen to
other people's problems?" Patient seemed a little distressed and
stated, "It's just a personal thing with me."

   I feel I can best help this patient by listening to him and keeping him involved in activities. I feel also that he should recognize
the limit of our relationship, that it will only be a therapeutic one.

Behavior

In this section will be described the behavior of my patient over the month of July in a variety of situations. This will give some idea of his actions and thoughts.

R. exhibits some weird behaviors, e.g., he will stare into space "and just smile." One day in the canteen he just looked at certain spots on the table (as if they were targets), and then looked at another student and me with a smile on his face. We never really know what he is thinking. When he kept staring at the other student she asked what was he thinking of. He said that he was just looking at the shadows in her glasses.

Patient walks around with a very rigid posture. He occasionally will sit with his eyes half-closed and a blank look on his face. From this it would seem that the patient is in his own little world. If his group is doing therapy on fantasy, the leader must remind the group (with him especially in mind) that the session is about fantasy, not true experiences, and they will return to reality.

Patient seems to be preoccupied with Dracula. He read me an article about Dracula from the November, 1977 issue of *Reader's Digest.* He also keeps asking me about or commenting on my necklace. He asked me if I was religious, and if I was, he wouldn't mention it again. He looks at me in a bizarre manner and smiles very inappropriately, then says something about biting the neck.

In one conversation I asked him what he wanted to do when he got out. The patient crossed his legs, his left hand trembled, and he gave a deep sigh with an inappropriate smile. I told him that I got the impression that he was nervous and regarded the subject as a joke. He laughed and then said, "I want to be a lifeguard." "Do you swim?" He then switched the subject and asked me, "How do elevators work?" All this took only a few seconds.

I told him I didn't know how elevators worked. "Getting back to the subject," I said, "what kind of meaning does a lifeguard hold for you?" "They save lives," he responded. Patient seems preoccupied with occupations that save lives, e.g., doctors and now lifeguards. If he has a low self-esteem, these positions are important because they imply the ability to help another person and have authority over people.

At another time I walked up to R., who was sitting on a table against the wall and below a window. I sat on the window ledge, which was about two inches higher than the table. The patient then moved from the table to the ledge. I felt that this was his way of being on an equal level with others, a way to decrease his level of inferiority.

In interpersonal relationships, people usually have to come to him. When in a group (R., S., and me) he usually has to be asked a question before he will talk; he very seldom initiates a conversation. He responds to verbal speech, but shows a slight hesitancy, blinking his eyes in an attempt to concentrate before giving you an answer. He shows a slight blocking in thought, although he then responds in a very intelligent manner.

R. responds to messages from other patients. When R. saw another student and me at the elevator, he seemed pleased to meet us. R. told us that he missed us and C. and R. exchanged a hug. Another time S. was talking to us. He leaned on R. and put his arm around R.'s shoulder. R. in turn placed his arm around S. and commented that he was glad to have friends.

R. has cut his hair and now combs his hair when walking down the hall. I felt this to be an improvement — he was taking an interest in his appearance. He responds quite well to positive remarks, e.g., "I like the shirt you are wearing today."

PROBLEM LIST
Active problems as of June, 1978, were:

Schizophrenia diagnosis
Drug abuse
Parent/patient relationship
Hypertension
Four operations on right ear, some loss of hearing
Was failing in school and dropped out
Problems with interpersonal relationships

There was one inactive problem — glossitis. As assets there were the facts that he was intelligent, going to college, and that he had some past education in college and the armed services.

INITIAL PLANS as of July 20, 1978
Problem 1. Schizophrenia
 S: Patient stated, "I am a schizophrenic."
 O: Patient smiles and laughs at inappropriate times; he can sit in his own little world very quietly with a blank expression and eyes half-closed. Patient has responded in conversation, expressing an ambivalent attitude. At times patient will block out the topic being discussed and continue talking about another topic. Patient has a very rigid appearance.

A: Diagnosed by physician as schizophrenic.
P: (1) Decrease ambivalence.
   (2) Promote proper stream of thoughts.
   (3) Attempt to influence autistic behavior.
   (4) Maintain touch with reality.
   (5) Maintain medical regimen — drugs for disorders.
   (6) Increase self-esteem.
   (7) Maintain therapeutic environment.

Problem 2. Drug Abuse
S: "I have done a few trips with LSD."
O: Three or more years of moderate use of marijuana.
A: Patient takes drugs not prescribed by physician.
P: (1) Promote ventilation of feelings.
   (2) Increase self-esteem and maintain touch with reality.

Problem 3. Parent/Patient Relationship
S: "I do not get along with either parent." "I'm resentful but everything is OK now."
O: I have never seen parents visit with patient. Chart states that parents said in an interview, "We find his behavior irritating and don't want him discharged."
A: Patient does not get along with parents.
P: (1) Promote ventilation of feelings.
   (2) Alleviate ambivalent feelings.

Problem 4. Hearing Loss
S: "I've had four operations on my right ear."
O: Chart showed four operations on the right ear. Result was equal lateralization when a tuning fork was used. Report from a doctor confirmed that some surgery had been done although he could not determine what.
A: Patient has had some problems with hearing.
P: (1) Prevent further deterioration of hearing.
   (2) Maintain medical regimen.
   (3) Evaluate hearing: consult ear, nose, and throat specialist, give mastoid series.

Problem 5. Interpersonal Relationships
S: "I have a hard time with people because I can't trust them."
O: Patient is withdrawn from the group; must be asked to join in some activities. Sits silently in group and will respond only when spoken to. Will hug other patients only if they initiate the action. Talks about inappropriate things in conversations.

A: Patient has difficulty developing a relationship with another person.

P: (1) Maintain involvement in activities.

(2) Increase self-esteem.

(3) Maintain therapeutic relationship.

(4) Promote proper termination of therapeutic relationship.

PLAN 6: INCREASE PATIENT'S SELF-ESTEEM
Provide activities that he can accomplish: things or games in which there is no score and no winner or loser, just play. Compliment patient when he shows increased interest in his appearance.

PLAN 7: MAINTAIN THERAPEUTIC ENVIRONMENT
Orient to hospital unit, discuss with patient the activities that are provided. Let patient know that you are interested in his therapy.

Problem 2. Drug Abuse
PLAN 1: PROMOTE VENTILATION OF FEELINGS
Talk with patient. Let him verbalize what he feels.

PLAN 2: INCREASE SELF-ESTEEM AND MAINTAIN TOUCH WITH REALITY
Follow steps outlined in Plans 4 and 6 of Problem 1.

Problem 3. Parent/Patient Relationship
PLAN 1: PROMOTE VENTILATION OF FEELINGS
Talk with patient, let him verbalize his feelings.

PLAN 2: ALLEVIATE AMBIVALENT FEELINGS
Point out discrepancies in feelings, talk with patient.

Problem 4. Hearing Loss
PLANS 1 AND 3: EVALUATE HEARING AND PREVENT FURTHER DETERIORATION
Consult ear, nose, and throat specialist. Have mastoid series done by doctor's order.

PLAN 2: MAINTAIN MEDICAL REGIMEN
Give medication per doctor's order. Facilitate wax removal.

NURSING ORDERS
Problem 1. Schizophrenia
PLAN 1: DECREASE AMBIVALENCE
When talking with patient, point out discrepancies of feelings, encourage ventilation of feelings.

PLAN 2: PROMOTE PROPER STREAM OF THOUGHTS
In conversation keep patient on the subject and when he abruptly switches to another topic, bring him back into the conversation with "Getting back to what we were talking about . . ."

PLAN 3: ATTEMPT TO INFLUENCE AUTISTIC BEHAVIOR
When patient seems to be in his own little world, communicate reality by talking with him and getting him involved in activities. Orient him to the here and now.

PLAN 4: MAINTAIN TOUCH WITH REALITY
Communicate reality to him by talking with him. If he is talking about inappropriate subjects of the past, orient him to time — "That happened in the past, but now . . ."

PLAN 5: MAINTAIN MEDICAL REGIMEN
If Artane, which reduces rigidity, is prescribed I give frequent mouth care. Hard candy, chewing gum, and increased fluid intake usually afford some relief from dryness. Be alert for dry mouth. If patient complains about urinary hesitancy, advise him to micturate when he takes the drug.

Haldol reduces agitation. Watch for signs of overdose: severe extrapyramidal reactions, hypotension, and sedation.

Prolixin may cause fluctuations in blood pressure. Also watch for extrapyramidal reactions.

Problem 5. Interpersonal Relationship
PLAN 1: MAINTAIN PATIENT'S INVOLVEMENT IN ACTIVITIES
Play pool, ping-pong, volleyball, catch with him. Take walks with him. Keep him doing physical activity, reduce his rigidity.

PLAN 2: INCREASE SELF-ESTEEM
Involve patient in activities that he can accomplish. Set him to those tasks that do not involve a winner/loser situation or promote failure.

PLAN 3: MAINTAIN THERAPEUTIC RELATIONSHIP
Develop a rapport with the patient.

**PLAN 4: PROMOTE PROPER TERMINATION OF
THERAPEUTIC RELATIONSHIP**
Talk with the patient, discuss with him your leaving, prepare for
your departure from him so that he will not feel deserted or that
he has had another failure with an interpersonal relationship.

PROGRESS NOTES as of August 20, 1978
Problem 1. Schizophrenia
S: "I'm a schizophrenic. I'll get my book and show you." "I'm
   not taking any medication now. I feel better."
O: Patient presented me with book by Sigmund Freud and read
   the section on schizophrenia. Medications have been discontinued. Patient appears less rigid, more spontaneous speech
   is noticed, and he smiles in a more appropriate manner.
A: Patient doing better since medication discontinued. He seems
   to want reassurance about the label *schizophrenic* by identifying symptoms in the book.
P: (1) Observe patient for return of bizarre behavior.

Problem 2. Drug Abuse
S: "I have not had any drugs in 5 months."
O: Patient has been in hospital since June, no new data.
A: Patient has not taken any drugs.
P: (1) Continue previous plan.
   (2) Allow patient to ventilate feelings about taking drugs.

Problem 3. Parent/Patient Relationship
S: "This weekend I went out with my sister to Canton where
   she bought a plant. I also went to the zoo. My parents were
   out of town."
O: Patient had good eye contact when discussing family.
A: Patient is making contact with his family.
P: (1) Previous plan continued.
   (2) Allow patient to ventilate feelings about his family.

Problem 4. Hearing Loss
S: "I had some testing done on my ears." "I can hear, but I have
   a ringing in my ears. In order to hear, it depends on the fre-
   quency of the sound, high or low pitch."
O: Testing results in chart.
A: Patient still has some trouble with hearing.
P: (1) Continue previous plan.
   (2) Evaluate testing results (impression from audiology) and
       decide further treatment.

Problem 5. Interpersonal Relationships

S: "I went to a mental hospital because I could not get along with friends — girls. Three girls I went with dropped me. All three girls got married to other guys. I have trouble accepting compliments — I'm embarrassed."

O: While patient talked he had good eye contact; folded his hands on table. He stood in the doorway and smiled; put his hand over his face while he made statement of embarrassment.

A: Patient has difficulty accepting other people's remarks and developing trust relationships.

P: (1) Continue previous plan.
(2) Allow patient to ventilate feelings about this subject.
(3) Increase self-esteem.

DISCHARGE SUMMARY: September 1, 1978

R., a 26-year-old white male, underwent an acute emotional change while attending the university. Patient had gone to university, but dropped out because of failing grades and lack of motivation. He was evaluated at the University Health Center and sent to a state mental hospital for "nerves." The patient was discharged into his father's custody prior to his admission to this hospital on June 29, 1978. Physical findings included: height, 6'2"; and weight, 183 pounds; blood pressure of 130/90; long hair; full beard; shaky tremor; disturbed mumbling, red tongue; eyes fluttering; inappropriate appearance; catatonic, slow, rigid behavior. Patient was alert and oriented, but speech production was poor with poor articulation.

The program at the hospital involved antischizophrenic medication, occupational therapy, CT and group therapy. Patient has now been taken off self-medication and seems to be improving somewhat in his behavior — smiling more appropriately, less rigid, and with more spontaneous speech. Patient is well oriented and has good intellectual functioning.

He has been evaluated by the ear, nose, and throat department for his hearing loss and "ringing in the ears." He had a mastoidectomy on his right ear at El Paso, Texas. He has also had three other operations on the right ear. Allergies include dust, pollen, animals, and cedar.

Patient had seen a psychologist for his inferior feelings while attending university prior to his admission into the Army. During his three years of service, he worked on computers. After discharge from the Army, he attended the university during the fall semester of 1978 until he failed an examination in biology, had problems with friends, and exhibited the bizarre behavior that led to his present hospitalization.

During an interview with R.'s parents, they denied patient is sick now. They feel he has made much improvement but they find his behavior irritating and don't want him discharged.

Problems during hospitalization were: (1) schizophrenia; (2) drug abuse; (3) family conflict; (4) ear problems; and (5) interpersonal relationships. Plans for discharge are:

1. Help patient find employment. Discuss with social worker patient's interests and assets in finding work that he is capable of doing. Get patient involved in the education necessary for attainment of realistic goals.
2. Discontinue drugs for present time. Have patient visit day center for evaluation of nondrug therapy. If symptoms of schizophrenia reappear, place patient on medications of doctor's orders.
3. Discuss family conflict and resolve ambivalence and resentment. Help patient find own apartment away from family. Discuss with social worker plans for housing close to work or school, its cost, and community centers available in area.
4. After patient receives disability payments, he may be able to get a hearing aid to improve hearing. Test results from audiology department and consultations with doctor from that department indicate that hearing aid would help.
5. Get patient involved in some group activity in order to increase his contact with others. Help him with development of interpersonal relationships.

DATA BASE: B.

B., a 44-year-old black male, was admitted to the hospital originally for an attack of pain in his right shoulder and arm in June, 1978. A previous hospital history concerning this problem was obtained from a hospital in Fresno, California. The client had been x-rayed and received physical therapy for this condition, but according to B. the therapy did not do any good. He visited this hospital, but when test results were negative, the neurologic staff suggested psychiatric treatment for a psychosomatic disorder. At this time (September, 1978) the client wears a sling on his left arm, and has occasional swelling of the phalanges and some triceps degeneration. It has been suggested that further neurologic testing and lumbar puncture may produce positive results, in which case, it would be found that B.'s problem is *not* one of psychosomatic origin, as diagnosed in June, 1978, but of neurologic origin.

At this time, I have not assessed the health or health attitudes of his family members. B. radiates happiness. He smiles frequently, is courteous, and engages readily in conversation. Talking with him in more depth, however, reveals that he resents being placed in a psychiatric unit. He has demonstrated appropriate behaviors in all the situations for which I have made observations.

The patient is very intelligent and interesting, as is reflected by his conversations. He not only discusses current political and social events, but he is capable of recalling past situations, ideas, feelings, and persons. He has well-organized speaking traits, such as developing situations in chronological order and using rising inflections of voice. In talking with the client no noted misperceptions or irregularities of thought processes have been observed. Cognizant of his surroundings, B. maintains good eye contact and does not interrupt when others are talking. He is very attentive and supportive of other patients who frequently come to him rather than the staff for help.

B. considers himself a well-disciplined individual. At this time the limitation in mobility of his arm is his main worry. He would like to recover from this disorder, but he stated that this may not be possible and that he will therefore adapt his activities to meet this impairment.

B. has developed a successful business in California, dealing with some nationally reputable companies. When questioned about his feelings about this psychiatric experience in relation to his business affairs, B. did show some concern. He stated that his situation may hinder his business but did not appear overwhelmed at this possible consequence. B. is very angry over having been diagnosed as a psychiatric patient and having to spend three months in a psychiatric unit. He is currently considering suing the hospital.

Further investigation revealed no remarkable "turning point" in his life. He could not pinpoint any particular event to indicate such.

B. was born in Iowa on December 20, 1937. Both parents are living. I have not obtained information regarding his birth position in the family. He has spoken of one brother who is currently "minding the business." The client has stated that he has a college education, with a B.S. degree in science.

His military involvement consisted of 8 years' service in the Navy.

B. is divorced, although he still lives with his ex-wife. The events that led up to the divorce include a time-consuming job. He revealed that upon completion of his overseas tours of duty he would not spend time with his wife. He admitted to having other female companions although "there was no particular one." His wife suspected infidelity and sued for divorce. B. did not contest. He allots $75.00 weekly for child support. His ex-wife does not work; he said, "She doesn't have to." His only daughter is presently a junior in college and his five sons live at home. The client said that he maintains a good relationship not only with his ex-wife but also with his children. He also said that his ex-wife would like to remarry him. Upon asking him his feelings on this subject, he replied that although he still loved her, he was not interested in getting remarried. He doesn't want to get "tied down" again.

My response to the client is: I like him. He appears to be an intelligent individual with no emotional disorders that I can perceive. I am inexperienced, however. I feel that a good rapport has been established between the client and myself. I feel somewhat limited by my inexperience and hope that my methods of interviewing won't turn off the client. I feel that his disclosures will help in the further assessment of his situation and therefore benefit me in planning an approach of problem-solving and possible instruction.

PROBLEM LIST

As of September, 1978, B.'s active problems (the second of which was also a problem for the hospital) were as follows.

Neurologic disorder of right arm
Contemplation of lawsuit against the hospital
Living with ex-wife

Problem 1. Neurologic Disorder of Right Arm

S: Patient stated, "I have had extreme, constant pain in my muscles and between my shoulders since May."

O: Neurologic testing upon admission to the hospital revealed no remarkable damage. The suggestion was made that this was a psychosomatic disorder and treatment thereof was suggested. Patient was recommended for psychiatric consultation and therapy because of a diagnosis of character disorder with underlying hostility and some paranoid ideations. A second neurologic test in September revealed slight impairment and dysfunction. At this time B. voiced resentment at being placed in a psychiatric unit and began proposing legal action against the hospital. Further investigation of the arm problem on October 1 revealed definite atrophy of the triceps muscle of the right arm and clubbing of the fingers of the right hand. On October 10 he was released from the care of a psychiatrist and transferred to a medical unit for further exploration of his neurologic malfunction.

A: Since hospitalization in June, 1978, progressive deterioration of muscle tone and function, along with circulation impairment, has occurred.

P: Get patient to show increased circulation in the right arm, increase muscle tone, and provide a decrease in pain.

NURSING ORDERS
1. Increase circulation and muscle tone.
   a. Have patient do active range-of-motion (ROM) exercises twice a day for 10 minutes on right arm and hand.
   b. Have patient massage right arm and hand with long strokes toward midline.
   c. Supply hand roll to prevent palmar flexion.
2. Decrease pain
   a. Assess pain status.
   b. Obtain order from doctor to administer analgesic(s) whenever necessary, and possibly 45 minutes before ROM exercises.
   c. Observe patient after administration of medication to assess any alleviation of discomfort; note progress of patient with exercises after analgesic increased.
   d. Position arm to a more comfortable level.

Problem 2. Contemplation of Lawsuit Against Hospital

S: "If my situation is cared for I'll reconsider suing, but if nothing is done, I'll have to sue. It's only right for the damage that has been brought against me. My lawyer has told me that there will be an investigation."

O: Condition was inappropriately diagnosed as a psychosomatic disorder and the client was placed on a psychiatric unit. Little testing was performed since admission in June. Analgesic has been assessed as ineffective. Student's assessment of patient's behavior helped in evaluating mental condition.

A: Hospitalization on psychiatric unit for psychosomatic medical disorder has produced resentment in the patient. Psychiatrist identified, with the aid of student's observations, that the patient has been incorrectly labeled.

P: Client's resentment will be decreased with proper care, which in turn will lessen possibility of lawsuit.

NURSING ORDERS
1. Decrease resentment which in turn will lessen probability of lawsuit.
   a. Agree with patient that injustice has been done.
   b. Assure him that everything is presently being done to improve his situation.
   c. Establish and maintain good rapport with him.
   d. Allow him to ventilate his feelings about treatments and the general situation.
   e. Include patient in all planning for his physical care.

Problem 3. Living with Ex-wife
S: "I still love my wife, but I don't want to get remarried."
O: Information not available at present because I never observed patient with his wife.
A: Inadequate data to determine scope of problem, if there is one at all.
P: Observe interactions with wife.

PROGRESS NOTES as of October, 1978
Problem 1. Neurologic Disorder of Right Arm
INCREASE CIRCULATION AND MUSCLE TONE
S: "It really hurts to move this thing."
O: ROM exercises, massage, and hand roll not implemented upon advice of doctor. Approval from neurologist must be sought before initiating these three plans. Arm and muscle are visibly becoming smaller.
A: Problem of disorder; atrophy is increasing.
P: Await further film study and neurologic test results and seek approval for interventions mentioned in O above.

DECREASE PAIN IN RIGHT ARM
Obtain order from physician for stronger analgesic.

S: "The pain is constant; it's a stabilizing pain between my shoulders."
O: Analgesic, Tylenol No. 2, switched per order of doctor to Talwin 50 mg. plus Tylenol.

A: Patient's pain has decreased after increase in analgesic, as stated by him.

P: Continue with this regimen; observe patient closely for continued alleviation of discomfort and any side effects.

Problem 2. Contemplation of Lawsuit Against Hospital

S: "If my situation is cared for I'll reconsider suing, but if nothing is done I'll have to sue. It's only right for the damage that has been brought against me."

O: Patient has been allowed to ventilate his feeling about this and has been assured that an injustice has been done. He has also been assured that everything possible has been done to improve his current problem. Presently he is in a medical ward.

A: Client is still considering the lawsuit. He feels that the mistake of three months prior has caused him physical impairment, but plan is working.

P: Continue with this plan. Continue education and planning with client.

Problem 3. Living with Ex-wife

S: "I still love my wife, but I don't want to get remarried."

O: Have been unable to observe any interactions between patient and his ex-wife.

A: Problem status cannot be assessed because observations of client and his ex-wife cannot be made.

P: Converse with client in more detail about his present feelings toward his ex-wife, and the results of societal pressure on this situation.

DISCHARGE SUMMARY
Problem List
PROBLEM 1. NEUROLOGIC DISORDER OF RIGHT ARM
Disorder is causing atrophy of triceps muscle, pain, and immobilization. Although ROM exercises were suggested by the student nurse, none was implemented for fear of a possible increase in pain and further damage. Pain assessment was made and medication was changed from Tylenol No. 2 to Talwin 50 mg. plus Tylenol. It was gathered from subjective data that pain was relieved by this increase and Talwin was therefore continued as part of the drug regimen. Further evaluation of the medical problem is being made.

PROBLEM 2. CONTEMPLATION OF LAWSUIT
AGAINST THE HOSPITAL

The patient is justified in feeling that an injustice has been per-
petrated on his mental capacities and physical condition. Plans
were implemented to reduce his anxieties and assure him that
although a mistake had been made everything possible was being
done to correct that mistake. It was thought that by doing this,
the possibility of legal action against the hospital and staff was
lessened. At the time of discharge, however, the client is still
considering initiating legal action.

PROBLEM 3. LIVING WITH EX-WIFE

B. is planning to get an apartment of his own upon discharge. He
states that this situation with his ex-wife allows him a freedom
not obtainable while being married. He also says that he still
loves her.

Because of his arm problem he may experience some inter-
ference with daily activities by living alone. It is suggested that
he and his ex-wife receive counseling concerning their current
situation.

Mr. B. will be seen by his doctor as an out-patient, for further
testing and evaluation every month. The drug regimen for pain
relief will be continued and assessed by the doctor monthly for
analgesic effectiveness and any side effects.

COMMENT BY THE EDITOR

The case B. was one of the most unusual experiences I have
encountered as an instructor. It is a dramatic illustration of how
mislabeling a patient can begin a chain of misunderstandings.

When B. was sent to the psychiatric unit, the staff viewed him
cautiously. They interpreted his comments and behavior as sus-
picious since he was supposed to be "crazy." After a few sessions
of this the patient became hostile and developed what the psychiatrist called "hospital-induced neurotic manifestations." The
speck traveled from the eye of the beholder to the eye of the
patient.

The student and I were outsiders to the unit and were thus
somewhat protected from the "paranoia" that can develop
in-house. Our contacts with B. contradicted what the staff
reported, but independently they did coincide with the psychiatrist's findings. Because of our observations the psychiatrist
gradually gained confidence and began a review of the neurologic
condition with another neurologic team.

After three months of needless delay and misplacement on the psychiatric ward, the patient's problem was identified as a terminal degenerative nerve disease. He was discharged with the knowledge that the pain and loss of function would increase.

I stayed in contact to provide support to him. We explored alternative ways of conditioning to deal with the pain and the outcome of his illness. I have never encountered a more beautiful man, one who exhibited care and love for others while stoically enduring suffering himself. While he was in the psychiatric unit he gave love and support to many patients. I was drawn to him like a magnet. It was interesting to see the staff change their pattern of behavior toward him when his condition was identified. His love was clearly visible when he was approached with an open mind.

His case emphasizes the real danger in prejudging a person on "other"-supplied information. Too many persons were influenced by the initial and incomplete prejudiced assessment.

10 From Theory into Practice: Graduate Students

MARY JO TRAPP BULBROOK

The graduate students contributing to this chapter show varying amounts of expertise, depth, and originality in their dealings with theory and practice. Each student first developed an eclectic conceptual framework and assessment tool to guide her behavior when she began to develop her therapeutic skills. This material was then applied to a clinical situation, using the problem-oriented system discussed in Chapter 7.

As in Chapter 9, the patients and situations discussed are real. These particular patients were seen in different types of mental health clinical settings. Any information that could aid in identification has been changed.

The experiences of both undergraduate (Chapter 9) and graduate students have been included in this book to provide real examples of personal growth struggles experienced by nurse therapists at different levels of education and experience. Some contributions are more sophisticated than others, but all provide the reader with data to critique and incorporate into his or her own learning process, if so desired.

GUIDE FOR EVALUATING GRADUATE STUDENTS' CASE STUDIES

This guide can be utilized by instructors as well as students in evaluating the following cases. The implications of some of the questions transcend the data in the presentations, providing a framework for exploration of issues facing the psychosocial nursing profession.

Review in depth the etiologies and therapeutic interventions from the diagnostic categories discussed; also include variations from the various theoretical formulations.

How did the psychosocial nursing interventions differ between graduate and undergraduate students? Analyze the differences and similarities of the assessment techniques between the students. Compare the consistency of the students' conceptual framework assessment tools and case studies.

What is the theory of crisis intervention as opposed to long-term personality reconstruction?

Research and discuss the implications of financing various treatment modalities for mental health case providers. Analyze the national impact of National Institute of Mental Health priorities on the delivery of services.

Determine the prognosis of the individuals discussed. Discuss in depth the long-term considerations of their care and the analysis of any personal reconstruction needed.

What are the legal steps and requirements for practice for nurses who wish to become psychotherapists? Trace the historical development of advanced nurse-specialists and their impact on the delivery of care.

What is the current state of the art of nursing research in psychosocial health care? Who are the leaders in this level of care? Evaluate the educational status in psychosocial nursing as compared to other psychosocial professionals.

Case Study 1: Sally
LOUISE L. LASTELICK

The beginning of a theoretical framework for me had to include a concept that is vital to the nursing profession — the concept of *high-level wellness* (a term devised by Dunn (1961) to make the person who uses it think of wellness in terms of degrees or levels). He defines high-level wellness as:

an integrated method of functioning which is oriented toward maximizing the potential of which the individual is capable. It requires that the individual maintain a continuum of balance and purposeful direction within the environment where he is functioning [1, pp. 4–5].

Along with being armed, as it were, with this important concept, I like to ask myself two basic questions while I am interviewing a patient: (1) What has made this person sick? (2) What will it take to help him get well? I may use several approaches to therapy, depending on the patient, although I do not use all of them at the same time. I may use two or more, and I am aware of which theory or theories that I will be using as I elicit the information I need to make an assessment of the patient. The assessment tool I use consists of questions that are derived from psychoanalytic theory, Rogers' client-centered therapy, Transactional Analysis, reality therapy, and Gestalt techniques.

From psychoanalytic theory I identify the psychosexual stages of development, the tasks that should be accomplished at each stage, and the unfinished tasks that may be a part of the presenting problem. Identification of the defense mechanisms is another part of assessment, and if the mechanisms are used in a given situation, this will be noted.

Rogers' client-centered theory is unique in that it grew directly out of a clinical practice that began over 40 years ago [2, 3, 4]. From Rogers I draw the concept that each individual is a unique person with a unique problem and is worthy of being treated with dignity and respect. Rogers expresses this as having unconditional positive regard for a client. When a client experiences this positive regard, he is congruent in the relationship; he keeps a positive self-regard, which increases with the positive regard shown him. This nondirective, client-centered therapy focuses on the client's frame of reference and its meaning in his life [3].

Rogers says that by allowing the client to freely express himself the therapist can gain a better understanding of what is going on inside the individual, how he is feeling. By reworking and reflecting on what has been said, the therapist is able to convey to the client that he is understanding and experiencing the client's problem. If feelings of anger or other negative feelings are experienced, the therapist feels free to convey these to the client and explore the significance of them. The client will then feel the "genuineness" of the therapist [4].

Another concept from Rogers is the valuing process and how it affects the behavior of the individual. Rogers [4, p. 21] notes that the infant learns his values through experience and exploration and selects what is pleasing to him. As he develops he introjects the values of others because he finds that these bring him love and acceptance and these two things are necessary for life. But the organism is constantly changing and values must change, and the values introjected throughout childhood must be reevaluated at adulthood because they may not fit. The fully functioning individual is open to his experiences and exhibits no defensiveness. His self-structure changes with every experience and is congruent with the assimilation of each new experience.

In accord with Glasser [5] I believe that every individual seeking psychiatric treatment suffers from one basic inadequacy: the inability to fulfill his basic needs. This takes different forms, depending on each individual's problem. In their unsuccessful efforts to fulfill their needs, all patients deny, to some extent, the reality of the world around them. Therapy will be successful when patients give up this denial and recognize that reality not only exists but that they must fulfill their needs within its framework. Glasser's therapy, which leads all patients toward reality, is thus accurately called "reality therapy." Glasser notes that need fulfillment requires involvement with at least one other person who cares about us and for whom we care. This other person must be in contact with reality. Helping patients to feel important to themselves and to others is the basis of reality therapy; this therapy places the responsibility for getting well directly upon the patient and does not allow a shifting of responsibility to past experiences or past events.

Utilizing Transactional Analysis (TA) theory I identify the ego states of Parent, Adult, and Child in the patient. I also carefully identify my own ego status and my feelings about what the client is saying. In my tool I make an effort to identify the life script of the patient. Then I can introduce a counterscript or help him become aware that he is living a script. Although the client is probably unaware that he is living a script, he is aware that nothing seems to go right no matter how hard he tries. Setting himself up to fail, he fails every time [6].

One technique that I draw from Gestalt therapy is that of enactment, the dramatization within the therapy scene of some problem in the client's life. An example is the two-chair technique, having the client move from chair to chair, enacting a discussion between himself and another or presenting two ideas that are extremes of a situation. Enactment can very effectively bring certain behavior into focus. In my own work with patients, then, the use of an eclectic approach has enabled me to assist the patient to become aware of his feelings, become more self-actualizing, accept responsibility for his actions, identify his script, and become aware of how his behavior is affecting his life. I believe that the goal of therapy is reached when the patient experiences his feelings, identifies them, places them in proper relationship in his environment, experiences growth and openness in his relationships, and thereby increases his self-worth.

Assessment Tool
CHIEF COMPLAINT
Present illness:
Previous similar episodes:
Relationship between present illness and past history:

Who do you feel is responsible for your being in the condition
   you are today?
What happens to people like you?

FAMILY HISTORY
Has anyone in your family experienced these same kinds of
   feelings that brought you here today?
Will you share that with me?
Tell me about your relationship with your mother.
What did you want most from your mother as a child that you
   never received?
What do you want from her now?
What is your relationship with your father?
What was your favorite fairy tale?
What was your favorite nursery rhyme?
Who read it to you?
Do you have any brothers and sisters? List their birthdays.
What was it like for you being the (oldest) (youngest) (middle)
   child?
How did your parents act when things got tough?
Do you think I could handle your parents?
Were your parents very powerful?
Was your birth difficult for your mother?
What did she tell you about it?
What did other family members tell you about it?

EDUCATION
What was school like for you?
Who was responsible for your (success) (failure) at school?
How long did you go to school?
What was college like for you?
How would you describe your feelings about school?
Did you win a scholarship?

OCCUPATIONAL HISTORY
Present position:
Length of employment:
Previous employment:
Your feelings about leaving:
Reason for leaving:

MARRIAGE AND FAMILY LIFE
Age at marriage:
Reason for marriage:

How does being married make you feel?
Children? Ages? Sex?
What does being a parent mean to you?
Do you and your children enjoy each other?

HABITS
Do you smoke? How much?
Do you drink? How much?
Do you take any medications? What kind?
Why did the doctor prescribe that for you?
Have you ever abused drugs?

SIGNIFICANCE OF RELIGIOUS FACTORS
Do you attend church?
What meaning does religion have in your life?
What church do you attend?
What church do your parents attend?
Are your religious feelings similar to or different from your
    parents?

SOCIALIZATION AND RECREATION
What do you like to do for fun?
Do you have any hobbies?
Are you creative?
Do you like social gatherings with people whose ideas are
    different from yours?

RESPONSE TO THE AGING PROCESS
What is growing older like for you?
How long are you going to live?
How did you pick that age?
What will they put on your tombstone?
What would you put on your tombstone?
Have you experienced any feelings regarding the present
    economy?
Do you find it difficult to live on a budget?
Have you ever attempted suicide?
How far ahead do you begin to worry about things?
How long do you worry about things after they are over?

PAST HISTORY
Have you had any operations? Describe.
Have you had any illness? Catastrophic illness?
Have you had any emotional problems?

LEGAL FACTORS
Have you ever been arrested?
Can you describe the incident?
Do you have any charges pending against you at this time?
Are you in the process of getting a divorce?
Are you separated?

Data Base: Patient Profile
Sally, a 30-year-old Mexican female, voluntarily admitted herself to the in-patient unit of the Mental Health Clinic in a large metropolitan city on May 23, 1978. She is thin and frail in appearance, looks younger than her 30 years, and dresses neatly with well-coordinated clothes and neatly styled hair. She sits rigidly in the chair and clasps her hands tightly together except when she is smoking. Her nails are manicured and her total appearance is attractive. Her mood is depressed, her affect sad and fearful. She admits that she is afraid of people but is not afraid of me because I am wearing a name pin. She says that means I am here to help. She did agree to sit in a small room and have her interview taped.

CHIEF COMPLAINT
"My nerves got bad . . . broke down. I have been seeing people where they are not supposed to be, in trees and other places. I thought I would have a heart attack, I was so scared. I couldn't breathe. I am afraid of people and think that someone is trying to drive me crazy."

CURRENT MEDICATIONS
The patient is currently taking the following medications: Mellaril, 25 mg. and Thorazine, 100 mg. Chloral hydrate was added July 25, 1978, and Haldol and Artane on July 26 to replace the Mellaril and Thorazine.

PAST MEDICAL HISTORY
One year ago she had a hysterectomy for cervical cancer. A series of Pap smears had consistently come back positive. She states, "I still get depressed, I cry real easily. I guess I have never really accepted it. The doctors throw it into your mind that you have to have surgery. I wanted more children. Doctors throw it into your mind that you might not have had that one, and that is supposed to make up for the fact that you are so young and your whole body, your whole life style has to change. You change and go on because you got to go on. Unfortunately,

Mexican men don't accept hysterectomies. They think it makes you different, takes something away from you. It doesn't, but they haven't been educated to that."

FAMILY HISTORY

She is the fourth of six children. She has two older sisters, one older brother, and two younger brothers, all of whom are living and well. Their grandmother lives with her. Her parents have been married almost 40 years. She describes her relationship with her mother as "close" and can share her innermost thoughts and confide in her, but she cannot do this with her father. She sees him as the head of the family, making all the decisions; she feels that her mother agrees and is never allowed to state an opinion different from her father's. She describes her mother as "sweet, quiet, seeing good in everyone." Recently she and her father had an argument about her 10-year-old daughter joining the church. She did not visit for a month and told her father that she would never visit if it wasn't for her mother. She sees her father as always right in everything and that makes her mad; she would like to be right sometime, too.

Her grandmother has cancer and has had radium needles implanted; she will have a hysterectomy in a few weeks. This has upset Sally very much as she says, "Cancer means death to me. I can't imagine living without my grandmother."

PAST LEGAL FACTORS

She states that in May of 1974, while returning from a party for her oldest brother she stopped at a club she goes to frequently for a drink. She had a drink, did not stay long, and left alone. The next thing she knew, she was waking up in jail and was told that her car was found wrecked in the parking lot of a Sears store. There was some marijuana found in the car, but she denied ever smoking or possessing marijuana. The strangest thing about it to her was the fact that she was arrested for driving while intoxicated, but nothing was said about the marijuana. She remembers feeling drugged when she awakened and thought that someone "slipped her a Mickey" while she was at the bar. She cannot believe she was driving at the time of the accident because although the car was badly damaged, her hair was not even "messed up" and she had no bruises. When she tried to find out about the accident she was told not to worry about it. She was given a year's probation and told not to worry about it.

SOCIAL HISTORY

She has lived all her life in the city and attended schools there. She made very good grades and would have won a scholarship, but four months before graduation she became pregnant. Her father said she could have the baby and keep it but could not go to school pregnant and unmarried. She did not want her husband to feel forced to marry her, but she went through with it so she could graduate. He was irresponsible and would not work, and she had to go to work so they would have an income. She feels that she let her parents down when she became pregnant, because she had had a bright future with several available scholarships that she could not use after she married. Her older sisters finished college, and she feels that she let herself as well as her family down by her irresponsible behavior.

She divorced her first husband after a short time. She married her present husband two years ago. She feels that marriage is too confining, that she always has to do what her husband wants to do, never getting to do what she wants to do. She would like to have an open marriage. When he left her in May when she first started having problems, she felt that he could stay gone when she got O.K. "If someone is not there when you need them, why should you take them back when you get straight?"

She is now sharing a house with her grandmother and her daughter. She calls it a "raggedy little house," but the tone of her voice and the look on her face tells of her love for her grandmother and the house.

OCCUPATIONAL HISTORY

She has been employed at a department store for ten years. She feels that her employment was a "token gesture" and that she has not been promoted as rapidly as other employees. She has trained others for the positions they held but was not allowed to get the positions for herself. She admitted that the people she trained had college degrees, but she thinks if she was smart enough to train someone for a job, she should be smart enough to have the job herself. It was getting on her nerves that she was unable to get a position because she didn't have a degree.

SIGNIFICANCE OF RELIGIOUS FACTORS

She was raised in a religious home. Church was an important factor in their lives; they not only attended Sunday school and church but every other function during the week. If someone was sick and couldn't attend they were restricted for the rest of the week. Sally's mother expressed her religious belief in this way: "I feel an inward peace. I don't want to hurt anybody or be hurt or do anything to hurt anybody. I want to treat everyone right regardless of whether they are white or black or whatever. I can truthfully say that you are walking with God, you don't have to be sitting in a church."

Problem List
Active problems as of July 26, 1978, were:

Unresolved feelings about grandmother's cancer and impending
    death
Unresolved feelings about femininity and sexual identity
Hallucinations
Paranoid ideas: fear of people
Problems with authority figures
Irresponsible behavior
Identity and self-image
Separation from husband and possible divorce
Pressure on the job
Strong dependency needs

There was one inactive problem:

Premarital pregnancy

Problem List (S.O.A.P.) *
**PROBLEM 1. UNRESOLVED FEELINGS ABOUT GRANDMOTHER'S
CANCER AND IMPENDING DEATH**
  S: "My grandmother has cancer and will have surgery in three
     weeks. Cancer means death to me. I can't imagine living with-
     out my grandmother."
  O: Acutely anxious, ready to cry.
  A: Patient's feelings about her own cancer were not completely
     resolved and are now identified with her grandmother's.
  P: To explore her feelings about her cancer and help her to
     resolve them. Then talk about her grandmother's condition.
  E: This was done. She said that she knows hers was in an early
     stage, only in the cervix, and she fears that her grandmother's
     is farther advanced. She can never remember her grandmother
     being sick, except for one time when she had minor surgery

---

*S = subjective data; O = objective data; A = assessment; P = plan; E = evaluation.
See Chapter 1 for more details about S.O.A.P.

and her father did the cooking and washing. At that time she knew that her grandmother would be coming home soon. This she feels is different.

PROBLEM 2. UNRESOLVED FEELINGS ABOUT FEMININITY AND SEXUAL IDENTITY

S: "Mexican men, the ones I know, think hysterectomies make you different, take something away from you. It doesn't but they haven't been educated to that. My present husband treats me different, sexually and every other way."

O: Seems to be feeling hurt and bitter. Voice changed. Husband and other men have reinforced her feelings of being different after her hysterectomy. She appears to be having not only feelings of sexual inadequacy, but loss of sexual identity as well.

P: Help her to explore these feelings, realize them for what they are, admit them to herself, and plan her future life.

PROBLEM 3. HALLUCINATIONS

S: "I see people in trees. There are no faces, only shapes, and they are wearing hats, cowboy hats and golf hats. My father wears golf hats, and my husband wears cowboy hats. I see flashing lights in the bushes around my house."

O: Appears frightened by these hallucinations.

A: Hallucinations seem to be about feeling watched by her husband and father.

P: Explore with her the significance of the hats.

E: This was done. She said it might be guilt engendered by the feeling that her father and husband were watching everything that she did and would not approve of some of the things she did do.

PROBLEM 4. PARANOID IDEAS: FEAR OF PEOPLE

S: "I am afraid of people I don't know. I would be afraid of you, but you are wearing a name pin and you are here to help. I have always been outgoing with people and this disturbs me, being afraid of people."

O: Looks afraid, voice is quivering.

A: Her fears have changed her from a friendly, outgoing person to a person who is afraid of everybody. This change is disturbing her.

P: Gain her confidence. Explore the feelings of being afraid and help her to realize that the fears are not real. Help her to get out of her Child ego state into her Adult. Teach her to trust people.

PROBLEM 5. PROBLEM WITH AUTHORITY FIGURES

S: "My father was angry because my daughter has not joined the church. I don't think she is ready, but my father thinks not making her join the church makes me a bad mother. She goes every Sunday, but I don't think she understands what joining the church means.

O: Her voice changes and she looks hurt and angry.

A: She is hurt because her father thinks she is not a good mother because her daughter has not joined the church.

P: Discuss what her daughter thinks about it. What does she want for her daughter? Use Gestalt techniques to relieve anger.

E: This was discussed. She wants her daughter to be able to tell the priest why she wants to join and what it is all about. She also cannot see the connection between her daughter Mary joining the church and her being a good mother, and this has made her angry. She used the two-chair Gestalt technique and worked out a lot of anger.

PROBLEM 6. IRRESPONSIBLE BEHAVIOR

S: "I reached for help and did not receive what I wanted or I would not be here (clinic) today."

O: Seems to be angry and very upset over this.

A: She has placed the responsibility for her being here on somebody else.

P: Tell her that she is responsible for her condition. Ask her why she did not ask for a therapist if that could have helped.

E: This was discussed. She cannot see her own part in her recovery at this time. Will explore it later.

PROBLEM 7. IDENTITY AND SELF-IMAGE

S: "I worked for 10 years. My employment in 1966 was a 'token' gesture. I was not allowed to advance as rapidly as others. I often trained others for their positions and I thought that if I could train others for their positions I could handle the job."

O: She is bitter and angry; changes pitch of voice.

A: Feels discriminated against but is not able to convey this to her employers. It seems to have made her very angry that she was hired to fill a quota of Mexican employees. Lack of self-esteem is noted.

P: (1) Make her feel good about herself by pointing out that she must have had the qualifications or she would not have been hired.

(2) Explore with her why she feels so badly about it.

E: This was done. She admitted that those who advanced had college degrees, and she felt inferior because she could have had a degree if she had gone on to college. When she became pregnant, she had had to change her plans.

PROBLEM 8. SEPARATION FROM HUSBAND AND POSSIBLE DIVORCE

S: "My husband keeps bugging me to resume our marriage. When I work this out, I will do it on my own. He has not helped me; he thought I was very, very confused. If someone is not there when you need them, why should you take them back when you get straight?"

O: There was some anger and bitterness in her voice at first, then happiness that she could be on her own.

A: She does not feel that her husband was supportive of her problems when she had them, so she doesn't want him back when she gets well.

P: Explore with her what meaning it will have for her to live alone.

E: This was done. She said that she had some bills (a car note) that had to be paid and that it would help her financially if they were together. However, she enjoyed being able to do what she wanted, because all her life she had done everything other people wanted her to do. She wanted to have the feeling of being able "to do her own thing."

PROBLEM 9. PRESSURE ON THE JOB

S: "I feel so much pressure at my present job. It doesn't take much sense to mix drinks, but I really don't like to be around drinking people. We never drank in my father's home. My boss is so hung up because he owns the place, and he doesn't know how to talk to people."

O: Looks nervous talking about it, wringing her hands.

A: She is uncomfortable on the job and does not like to be around drinking people.

P: Explore further with her the pressure and not liking to be around drinking people. My idea is that it is a reaction formed against her stern and strict rearing. Check it out later.

PROBLEM 10. STRONG DEPENDENCY NEEDS

S: "I thought when I married I would be taken care of, but I have worked all my life. It would be nice to stay at home sometime. I like to stay with my grandmother, she babies me, fixes what Mary and I like to eat. She is so strong, she has brought me through this."

O: Looks happy when talking about grandmother.

A: Her dependency needs were not met through her marriage but are now being met through her grandmother.

P: Explore with her what is important in being taken care of. Help her in her struggle for independence. Support her feelings.

PROBLEM 11. PREMARITAL PREGNANCY

S: "I really feel like I let my parents down when I got pregnant. I was the fourth child and last girl; the others did fine, and I had to do that. I was four months pregnant before I told my father about it. I thought he would kill me, but I was surprised at how understanding he was. But I realize now that this incident has affected my whole life."

O: Feels and looks upset while talking about it, even though this was years ago.

A: Although this problem is resolved, some thoughts about it are still troubling her.

P: Use some Gestalt techniques to bring her feelings and her father's into awareness.

E: This was done. She received great benefit from hearing the love and hurt of her father when she spoke for him. She seemed relieved of some of the old feelings.

Progress Notes

JULY 26, 1978

Initial interview consisted of establishing a rapport and collecting data for formulation of Problem List. We discussed her hysterectomy in some detail and the meaning it had in her life. We also discussed all the other problems and planned to continue the discussion every Monday and Thursday as long as she will be in the hospital. She was cooperative during the interview, although anxious and depressed.

JULY 30, 1978

After discussing all the identified problems with her again, she admitted that her grandmother's condition was the factor that precipitated her trip to the hospital. We discussed this in great detail, and she admitted that her hysterectomy had caused some drastic changes in her life, something that she had never admitted to anyone before. She also admitted that she and her husband were mismatched from the start; they didn't even like the same things and he definitely treated her differently after the hysterectomy.

She admitted that she didn't like being forced to do things that she didn't want to do; forcing her to attend church as a child made her not want to go now. She said her father had been a big influence in her coming to the clinic because he realized that she needed more help than he could give. She admitted that she thinks of everything she does in terms of what her parents would think of it, and this has influenced her life to a great extent.

AUGUST 3, 1978

She is feeling much better today. She went for a ride yesterday and did not see anything in the trees, was not even afraid to look. She wonders if she really did see things or imagined it. Taking a new approach, we role-played two important incidents in her life: the argument with her father over her daughter's joining the church, and the old incident of telling him she was pregnant. His love and concern over the old incident were brought into awareness, but she has taken a strong stand on and will stand by her feelings in the recent one. I can see a real growth in insight and ego strength.

AUGUST 7, 1978

Her mood is elated and her affect happy. She is discussing plans for discharge. She has worked out all her problems except for her marriage and she is talking with her husband about that. She does not want to return to her former job and plans to go out for an interview and see if she can find a job she will like. She is also planning to go to college a little at a time, probably at night. She really wants her degree, to make up for all the things she feels she has missed in her life without it. Her relationships are all smoothing out and she feels good about herself. She plans to return in one month to see the doctor, and I will see her once a week for two more weeks.

Discharge Notes

Sally, age 30, was admitted to the In-patient Clinic of the Mental Health Clinic on May 23, 1978, with a diagnosis of stress reaction with paranoia and hallucinations. After treatment with medication, she began to show some improvement. She also had individual therapy twice weekly starting June 1, 1978 in an effort to reach a solution to some of the problems that were bothering her at that time. On July 26, medications Haldol and Artane were added to her regimen. She has shown remarkable improvement and was discharged on August 7. Her progress will be followed by a student and she will return to the Medication Clinic in one month.

Crisis resolved.

REFERENCES

1. Dunn, H. L. *High-Level Wellness*. Arlington, Virginia: R. W. Beatty, 1961.
2. Rogers, C. R. *Counseling and Psychotherapy*. Boston: Houghton Mifflin, 1942.
3. Rogers, C. R. *Client-Centered Therapy*. Boston: Houghton Mifflin, 1951.
4. Rogers, C. R. *Person to Person: The Problem of Being Human*. Lafayette, Ind.: Real People Press, 1967.
5. Glasser, W. *Reality Therapy*. New York: Harper & Row, 1965.
6. Berne, E. *What Do You Say After You Say Hello?* New York: Bantam Books, 1973.

SELECTED READINGS

Brill, A. A. *Basic Principles of Psychoanalysis*. Garden City, N.Y.: Double-day & Co., 1949.

Perls, F., Hufferline, R. W., and Goodman, P. *Gestalt Therapy*. New York: Dell Publishing, 1951.

Case Study 2: Mari

PATRICIA A. CAIN

In rendering individual therapy to clients, I draw from several theories and modalities. Basically, however, I believe that people who present themselves for counseling or therapy are in some degree of crisis at that particular time of their life. They are facing problems they cannot readily solve by using the coping mechanisms that have worked for them before [1]. My overall goal for doing therapy then would be to help individuals reestablish order or equilibrium in their lives.

Easily incorporated with the crisis model are the reality principles set forth by William Glasser [2, 3, 4, 5]. The objectives of this therapy are to support and strengthen the individual as he is guided toward responsibility and acceptance of reality. The methodology of this therapy includes honesty, concern, confrontation, personal authenticity of the therapist, and presence of an optimistic rather than a cynical outlook.

Both reality and crisis therapy necessitate a deep involvement with the client. I believe an individual has the right to select and choose his own values. My role, as a therapist, will be to try to help and guide him in making responsible decisions for his own life. Both therapies discourage preoccupation with the past and attempt to pull interpretation from the present. The history is important only as it helps the therapist to work with present problems. I believe in encouraging the client to practice new patterns of healthy behavior that will fulfill his needs within the confines of the reality of daily living.

With the crisis and reality modalities I interrelate the principles of client-centered therapy as demonstrated by Carl Rogers [6, 7, 8]. I believe in a more direct approach than he advocates but adhere to his method of providing a setting in which clients will feel safe from threat and be able to examine their true feelings without fear of rejection. The therapist must believe in the strength of clients and their ability to cope, each individual accepting the responsibility for his or her own actions and behavior. This theory, also advocated by Glasser, is based on a basic faith and belief in the individual.

From the theory of Transactional Analysis I am able to identify an individual's ego state to better clarify his behavior myself. I identify games to show them how relationships with others are affected. I use "strokes" to show I approve of and accept the individual. I also find it helpful to use the contract or commitment technique to actively involve the client in identifying therapeutic goals [9, 10, 11].

From Jourard [12] I get the concept of self-disclosure. I feel that sharing myself with clients, although not allowing them to become the therapist, will show a genuine and caring empathetic understanding of their conflicts. Reality therapy also advocates this principle.

Gestalt therapy methods are used to demonstrate specific points. This modality emphasizes the here and now and works well with the methods of reality therapy and Transactional Analysis. The techniques are used to effect change and move the person toward more adequate functioning. This therapy is strongly allied to an emphasis on positive directions and goals of living by using techniques directly and immediately designed to produce them. The Gestalt general approach and theory require the clients to specify the changes that are desired, assist them to increase the awareness of self-defeat, and aid them toward experimentation and change [13].

In all these therapies, the therapist exhibits genuineness and places value on the client. All stress a change from a negative to a positive attitude, Glasser in particular stressing a positive behavior change. I use fragments of each to move the client toward

self-awareness and self-acceptance by placing the responsibility
for behavior change on the individual.

Assessment Tool

IDENTIFYING PROBLEM

Why did you come today?
What is it in your life that distresses you?
When did it happen?
What does this problem mean to you?
What effect might this have on your future?
What is it that you expect in the way of help?

COPING MECHANISMS

Has this situation ever happened before?
What did you do about it then? Did it work?
Have you tried the same solution this time?
If not, why not?
What do you usually do to handle stress, tension, anxiety,
        depression, and so on?
What do you feel would reduce these symptoms?
How do you see the problem being solved?
How could you feel better?
Are there alternative methods to explore?

LEVEL OF STRESS

Who are you having the most trouble with now?
Are you worthwhile?
Have you ever thought of suicide or homocide?
When? In what ways?
Do you still feel this way?
Make suicide (no suicide) contract if necessary.

SOCIAL AND SITUATIONAL SUPPORTS

Are you loved?
Who is your best friend?
Whom can you turn to (close people in your life)? Why?
Whom do you trust?
How are you responsible?

PAST HISTORY IN RELATION TO PRESENT

Events leading up to this visit.
General health.
Previous hospitalizations.
Current medications.

Allergies.
Number of pregnancies and living children.
Military service.

ASSESSMENT OF CLIENT

How is the problem affecting client's normal daily functions?
Is he or she able to work, study, go to school, care for family,
  and so on?
Relationship with others?
What is client's self-esteem?
Appearance?
Behavior, mood, affect?

APPROACH

Client-centered, reality-oriented.
List assets: as client sees them, as therapist sees them.
Explore client's self-worth.
Find what client enjoys doing, past and present.
Recognize feelings and help bring them out into the open.
Help reduce tension.
Explore coping mechanisms and alternatives.
Begin to reopen client's social world.

GOALS OF THERAPY

Reinforce coping mechanisms.
Reinforce learning that has taken place during therapy.
Make realistic future plans.
Provide anxiety relief.
Return to at least pretherapy level of functioning or better.

CONTRACT OR REFERRAL PLAN

Make contract with client on specific goals to work toward.
No suicide contract if necessary.

PROGRESS NOTES

To be written following each interview.
Problems discussed according to S.O.A.P.

Data Base
SUMMARY OF PERTINENT DATA

Mari, the client, is a 26-year-old single black female four and
one-half months pregnant with her second child. She has been
employed as a secretary for the past year. She resides in an apartment with her six-year-old son, Terry, for whom she provides

total support. Mari has been self-supporting most of her life, having been raised in numerous foster homes. Her mother has been a patient at a state mental hospital since the client was small; she describes her father by saying, "He told me he hated me." Mari, who has no close friends, and no family supports, has presented herself to the health clinic frequently during the past few weeks with numerous emotional and somatic complaints. She has been referred for crisis counseling at this time because of her inability to make a decision about placing her unwanted baby.

IDENTIFYING PROBLEM
Why did you come here today? How do you think I can help you? "The other nurse in the health center says you can help me decide what to do with this baby. I'm not going to keep it if it's born and lives and I don't know what to do with it or who to give it to."

Tell me more about what is distressing you. "I was raped by my boyfriend and now I'm pregnant with a baby I don't want. It's a dirty pregnancy and I'm dirty because of it. I hate him for doing this to me and I don't want to keep it."

When did this happen? "About June while I was on the pill. I told him I didn't want to have anything to do with him but he went ahead and raped me in front of my little boy."

What does this problem mean to you? "It has really screwed up my life. I sure don't want to be pregnant and fat, plus I need to work to support Terry and pay my bills. I hate this baby — it's not mine, it's his and he can have it."

What effect does this have on your future? "Everything right now. I'll have to lay off work and get someone to take care of Terry. I don't have anybody to take care of me except me. I don't want to have to go on welfare."

What is it that you expect in the way of help? "Help me solve the problem and make arrangements for me to take this baby off my hands. I don't want it and I need someone to listen to me and help me do something about this thing I am carrying."

COPING MECHANISMS
Has this situation ever happened before? "No, I've been pregnant before, but I wasn't raped and I wanted the baby."

What do you usually do to handle problems in your life, stress and tension, for example? "I usually get mad and cuss people out or tell them to leave me alone. I really don't trust people as they all disappoint me and let me down when I need them. I try and mind my own business and expect others to do the same and leave me alone."

What do you feel would reduce these symptoms? "For me not to be pregnant, for the baby to be born now and die. Yes, I want it to die. I'll be so happy when it's all over."

How do you see the problem being solved? "For me to find someone to take this baby or for it to die. Then I wouldn't have to be sorry about it anymore. I don't think March will ever get here; in fact, I know it will be over before then."

How could you feel better? "By not being pregnant, now or ever again."

LEVEL OF STRESS
Who are you having the most trouble with now and what does this mean to you? "The father of this baby, my ex-boyfriend. If he doesn't leave me alone I will call the law on him. I am through with him and when I say I am through with somebody I really mean I am through. I really tried to love him but he hurt me, and now I am really through with him and nobody can change my mind about that. All people that I have ever tried to get close to or love have hurt me. That's my trouble, I am too good to people and they always hurt me."

Have you ever thought of suicide? Homicide? "No, he's not worth it, and I don't want to go to jail. I can get the law to make him leave me alone and he knows it. I'm not afraid of him, and he better know better than to try and mess with me any more."

SOCIAL AND SITUATIONAL SUPPORTS
Are you loved? "Yes, by my little boy. I am not close to my father, as he told me that he hated me and didn't want me. I grew up in foster homes where I was used for housework and babysitting. No one ever really cared for me other than for the work they could get me to do. I'm not really close to anyone."

Who is your best friend? "I have several girlfriends that I can call on the phone and talk to but nobody real close. I had a close friend from home that I could share things with, but I am mad at her now for moving to Florida and leaving me here. I miss talking to her but she let me down when she moved away."

Who can you turn to (close people in your life)? "Nobody except my girlfriend in Florida and she is too far away. I can sometimes talk with my babysitter — we are fairly close — but she has her own family problems. My father and I have never been close."

Who do you trust? "Nobody really. Maybe I can trust you. All the people at my job talk trash to me and I won't put up with that. All men are bad and people let you down."

How are you responsible? "I pay my own bills and try to get better jobs for myself. Terry has too many clothes and toys but I like to buy things for him and have him look nice. I try and be a good mother to Terry, but I know he is a spoiled brat. I had him so that I wouldn't be alone any more and could have someone to take care of."

PAST HISTORY IN RELATION TO PRESENT
What were events leading up to this visit? "I had an abortion done [by her private doctor] in February. I was on the pill and had just finished taking the month's series when I was raped. We had been going together for about two months and had been having sexual relations, but I refused him this time, and he became very angry and raped me in front of my son. I didn't believe I was pregnant, and by the time I went to Planned Parenthood they said I was too far along to have another abortion, and my blood was too bad for it to be done. I tried to take an overdose of aspirin but it just made me sick. I also was going to get rid of it with a coat hanger but I couldn't make that work."

General health. Good. Normal, nonpregnant weight is 120 pounds. She has constant constipation for which she takes various patent laxatives and an occasional enema. Complains of extreme fatigue at this time.

Previous illnesses. No history of any illnesses or medical problems other than pregnancy six years ago.

Current medications. Prenatal vitamins and iron.

Allergies. None.

Pregnancies. Has had one pregnancy; child is now six years old. She was anemic during this pregnancy and had abnormal bleeding postpartum. She had an abortion in February with an apparent normal recovery. Current pregnancy was conceived in June, 1978 with a due date of March, 1979.

ASSESSMENT OF CLIENT
How is the problem affecting client's normal daily functions?
According to clinic records, Mari has come to the clinic on two previous occasions before being referred for crisis intervention. Each time she came because she was emotionally disturbed and hyperventilating. Several times recently, she states, she has stayed home because she was too tired to go to work or has gone home early from her job because of extreme fatigue. She is able to care for her child and her minimal daily care needs. She states that she is rarely hungry and eats little but exhibits a steady weight gain. She reports she eats a lot of what she calls junk food and snacks; these she does not consider meals.

Is she able to work and care for her family? She is having job problems. She would like the therapist to believe she has exceptional job capabilities, yet she relates past job experiences involving constant problems with peers who accuse her of having a chip on her shoulder. She vehemently discounts the possibility that her general attitude while at work could in any way relate to her problems with supervisors or co-workers. At present she is still holding down her job in the secretarial pool, although she has had two interdepartmental transfers since she was employed over a year ago.

Relationships with others. Mari does not relate with her co-workers in any way other than with casual daily routine conversations; she states that they think she is snobbish and distant. She seems afraid to make any permanent relationships, as she says that she always gets hurt if she gets too close to anyone. I feel she is a very lonely girl who is looking for love and acceptance; in seeking it she sets herself up for personal pain and degradation. She withdraws from people and manages to repress many of her feelings in this way. She feels people have a bad opinion of her because she is unmarried and pregnant.

Self-esteem. There is evidence that she is not caring for herself physically during this pregnancy. She is not concerned about keeping her doctor's appointments, refuses to regularly take her prenatal vitamins, does not watch her rapid weight gain, nor does she use caution and common sense about straining or getting overly fatigued. She exhibits little or no insight into the physiological processes of pregnancy and deals mainly in fantasy where her health and general welfare are concerned. She asks for approval and yet questions compliments received, which demonstrates her basic insecurity and lowered self-esteem.

Appearance. Mari is an extremely attractive, well-dressed girl who is usually smiling and laughing. Her posture is erect, and she walks as if she is confident and self-assured. She has a very clear complexion, large brown eyes, and an attractive hair style. She is not wearing maternity clothes at this time.

Behavior, mood, affect. She displays a most inappropriate affect in that she verbalizes many concerns and problems while laughing or smiling constantly. She does not appear depressed in therapy sessions, yet tells of being extremely tired and listless. Her actions, behavior, and facial expression in no way picture her many problems. She seems to be trying to deny the existence of the pregnancy by expressing the fantasy that the baby will be born early and dead.

Problem List
On October 23, 1978, Mari's active problems were:

Inability to make future plans
Unresolved anger at parents, boyfriend, and peers
Incomplete acceptance of pregnancy
Poor self-esteem

First and third problems were resolved as of November 14.

List of Assets
HOW THERAPIST SEES CLIENT
The client's assets, or good points, as seen by the therapist, include the points that she is:

Attractive
Neat in appearance
Uses cosmetics well and to her advantage
Always smiling
Good conversationalist

Intelligent
Financially responsible
Highly motivated toward financial independence

HOW CLIENT SEES HERSELF
The client, on the other hand, sees herself a little differently.
She feels that she is:

Excellent secretary
Average in appearance
Independent (a loner)
Loving mother
Good cook
Ambitious to better herself and make more money
Making herself financially independent for herself and her son.
Fighter for her beliefs
Strong-willed when she feels she has been wronged.

Plan
PROBLEM 1. INABILITY TO MAKE FUTURE PLANS
 S: "I know a schoolteacher who wants a baby. I may let her
have it. I will give this baby to its daddy. I want to give it
away but don't know what to do with it. I'm sure it will be
born soon and die."
 O: Talks of many things; thoughts, ideas, alternatives are flighty
but she is unable to satisfactorily settle on a suitable solution.
Eyes are bright and speech is rapid; she smiles while conversing, avoids direct eye contact.
 A: Obviously concerned with outcome of pregnancy but unable
to settle on an acceptable plan for the baby. Seems to be
dealing in fantasy plans and unable to settle on realistic and
acceptable goals for her or her baby's future. Expresses many
ambivalent feelings.
 P: (1) Explore alternatives for placement of baby, such as private agencies, public welfare agencies, or have her private
doctor handle the placement.
  (2) Encourage honest confrontation by patient with her doctor to discover his attitude regarding her plans. Will he
help her, discourage her, and so on?
  (3) Explore her feelings about keeping or giving up the baby.
Aim for her total acceptance of her decision.
  (4) Explore and discuss realistic alternative or plans.
  (5) Accept her realistic plans and encourage her to accept
responsibility for future decision-making.

(6) Discuss realistic labor and delivery plans with her.

(7) Discuss future financial planning: antepartum confinement, and postpartum.

(8) Explore her plans for a job after delivery.

(9) Discuss realistic plans for her confinement period: living arrangements, child care for Terry, financial arrangements.

(10) Encourage her in appropriate decisions and explore consequences of irrational behavior.

(11) Aim for returning her life to its precrisis level.

PROBLEM 2. UNRESOLVED ANGER

S: "He [boyfriend] raped me. He's no good and trash — I hate him. It's his baby and not mine. I'm through with him. My father told me he hated me. Nobody cared for me when I was little. I wish I could be a little girl again. All the men at work talk trash to me, and I don't have to take it."

O: While describing her problems she is laughing and smiling. Even when telling about being raped, she is fairly serious for only a short time before again starting to laugh and smile. Appears composed and calm, does not fidget or appear embarrassed or nervous. Eyes flash at times when relating an experience that seems to anger her.

A: Client has had a lifetime of hiding her true feelings. Her anger seems to be primarily focused toward the men in her life, yet it always returns to hurt her. She rationalizes and denies many feelings about herself and how she appears to others. She denies responsibility for these feelings by playing the "yes-but" game.

P: (1) Explore feelings of anger and how it feels to be angry at so many people, e.g., boyfriend, parents, co-workers, peers.

(2) Help her resolve her anger by getting her to realize she can overcome this by knowing herself and rising above her past problems, in this case by profiting from her mistakes (reality testing).

(3) Emphasize the reality of the present situation and relationships while making acceptable plans for the future.

(4) Discuss and explore what she is today as a responsible person and let the past serve as a maturing factor in her life.

(5) Explore with her the relationship between angry feelings and her behavior toward peers.

(6) Explore how she appears to her job peers and whether she feels she threatens their job security.

(7) Give much reassurance that she is OK.

(8) Empathize and show understanding of her problem.

(9) Aim for reduction of angry feelings.

PROBLEM 3. INCOMPLETE ACCEPTANCE OF PREGNANCY

S: "I know the baby will be born dead when it's born or it will die; I just know it will. My girlfriend had one that came early and died, and this one will too. It's a dirty thing and not my baby. I'm just doing him a favor by carrying it for him. Why am I so very tired all the time?"

O: Physical signs of 4½-month pregnancy visually observable. Feet and ankles are only slightly edematous. Has gained approximately eight pounds during the past month. Is not wearing maternity clothes as yet.

A: She has many fantasy wishes about the pregnancy and seems to be trying to deny the reality of her condition. She is unable to see that she had any part in getting pregnant and pushes the condition upon the boyfriend (denial and transference). Fantasizes that one day she will suddenly awaken and it will all be gone. Denies that pregnancy could and does affect her general health and well-being.

P: (1) Encourage her in reality thinking and acceptance of situation.

(2) Reemphasize the fact that an early termination of the pregnancy is possible but not very probable, despite her wish for such an event.

(3) Emphasize how her feelings of denial of the pregnancy are a detriment to her general health and well-being.

(4) Confront her with her denial of her physical condition and explore her feelings concerning acceptance of the reality of the situation.

(5) Emphasize the real physical facts of pregnancy.

(6) Clarify and answer questions about her condition that might arise, e.g., why is there a rapid weight gain, why the edema of feet and ankles, why the blood pressure could be elevated, what is importance of vitamins and rest, what precautions should be taken?

(7) Reassure her that body changes are expected with pregnancy.

(8) Emphasize her acceptance of responsibility for own care.

(9) Point out to her how she manages to evade responsibility with games of "what if," "maybe when" and "yes but" (this also fantasy).

PROBLEM 4. POOR SELF-ESTEEM

S: "I'm really not pretty, do you think? I don't need vitamins or iron now. I'll be OK as soon as I get rid of this thing. My father told he he hated me and placed me in foster homes to be raised. I was kept by some nice people but only for the money they got and for me to help clean and care for their children."

O: She looked sad when speaking of her childhood. She brightened considerably when given a compliment but immediately questioned and then discounted the praise.

A: She is unable to realize that her behavior demonstrated how little she thought about herself. She gave evidence of dislike for self and disbelief of her own self-worth by putting herself in a position to get pregnant. She seems to set herself up to get hurt or punished. Punishment of self is a way of life for her so she can prove she is not worthy of good things or feeling loved. She had anemia and hemorrhage problems with her last pregnancy, but she is ignoring the possibilities that they could occur with this pregnancy also. This denial of physical needs is also a type of punishment for herself.

P: (1) Explore her self-worth. Make an asset list from the client's and the therapist's frame of reference. Elicit her feelings on how she sees herself.

(2) Give much support and encouragement that she is worthy of care and love.

(3) Explain pregnancy facts as they come up and emphasize and back up her doctor's plan for her health and general physical well-being.

(4) Encourage her to have honest confrontations with her doctor as to her feelings about giving the baby up for adoption and other problems she might have with this pregnancy.

(5) Encourage her to seek her doctor's counsel, which she deserves as his private-paying patient.

(6) Explore how she might appear to others in her job and discuss her feelings toward developing better peer relationships to make her feel more accepted in her job.

(7) Encourage her to take responsibility for her own care.

Progress Notes as of October 23, 1978

PROBLEM 1. INABILITY TO MAKE FUTURE PLANS

S: "I don't know what to do with this baby. Maybe I'll give it to its daddy. He's told me I better not give it away. OK, it's his and he can have it. I'll just go leave it on his doorstep and if he doesn't treat it right, I can go get it and give it to somebody else. I really do have problems, don't I? What would you do if you were me?"

O: She is talking very fast but distinctly. She is sitting calmly and usually looks at the therapist, although occasionally she will look at the floor, but still smiling.

A: She does seem to care where the baby is placed and often expresses concern that it won't have to grow up as she did; but then she decides that she is not interested in what happens to it because it really isn't hers. There is much evidence of ambivalent feelings, indecisiveness, and fantasy planning. She came with a specific question about placement of the baby through an agency, but then became vocal in discounting them by saying she doesn't trust them.

P: (1) Continue with same plan, with emphasis on her being able to make a decision about the baby and then being able to live comfortably with her decision.

(2) Encourage her in appropriate decisions and explore consequences of irrational behavior.

(3) Explore feelings if a decision is made.

E: The patient was in crisis because of her indecision about her future plans, both for herself and the child she is carrying. She exhibited anger at her situation, ambivalence toward her condition, and a general flightiness in her thought content. The specific goal for this therapy session evolved from her answer to the question: "Why are you here?" She stated she needed to know where to go and how to go about giving up her baby. I felt she deserved an answer and explorations of specific agencies at this time; I planned to explore with her her true feelings about actually giving up the baby on another session day. She was asked primarily what specific agencies she wanted to know about and what she would expect them to do. She then changed direction by stating she didn't trust agencies because of her experiences as a child and again began fantasizing what she would do to punish her boyfriend.

There was no problem in establishing communication with Mari. When asked how she could see her problem being solved, she answered that she trusted her doctor and wanted to ask him to make arrangements for her but that he never would take her seriously. Since the doctor had delivered her first baby and performed her previous abortion, we explored the reality of her statement. I feel she is afraid to talk with the doctor and manages to set the stage herself for their light conversations. We explored how she could convey her seriousness to the physician, and she agreed that on her next visit she would try and approach him about this subject. She feels this is her best choice and would solve this immediate worry by getting his cooperation and approval. She agrees to discuss this with him.

PROBLEM 2. UNRESOLVED ANGER

S.O.A.P. same as stated under *Plan.*

E: As this was our first session, this problem was identified only today and plans made for future work.

PROBLEM 3. INCOMPLETE ACCEPTANCE OF PREGNANCY

S.O.A.P. same as stated under *Plan.*

E: In dealing with this problem, I refused to get caught up in her fantasy belief that the baby would die or be born dead. I emphasized that what she desired — early termination of the pregnancy — was possible but not too probable, and that we would deal with her problems and questions on a day-to-day reality level. We explored the reasons why she thought she was so tired. It was difficult for her to see that the fatigue related in any way to her pregnancy. She seems to have very little insight into the physiology of pregnancy, so health teaching was initiated to explore what she did know and answer her questions about her body during this period. I confronted her with the reality of the pregnancy by always referring to the here and now of her condition and refusing to get caught up in her responsibility-evading games. This emphasis was to continue throughout the time we spent together.

PROBLEM 4. POOR SELF-ESTEEM

S.O.A.P. same as stated under *Plans.*

E: I let Mari know soon after our first meeting that I thought she was a very attractive girl with a dynamic personality. I let her know that I felt she was OK and hoped we could work out a satisfactory solution to her problems together, but that the decisions would be hers and not mine. We discussed her assets from what I could observe from our first encounter, and I asked her to be thinking of positive things about herself to share with me the next time we met. She was given encouragement to get and use her doctor's counsel, which she deserves as his private-paying patient. We explored her feelings as to why she did not feel worthy of bothering her doctor, whom she described as much too busy to talk with her. She was encouraged to take the responsibility of seeking care for herself.

Progress Notes as of October 30, 1978
PROBLEM 1. INABILITY TO MAKE FUTURE PLANS

S: "I saw the physician last week and he says that he will make arrangements for the adoption of the baby for me. I think he already has a family in mind and I feel better that he is going to help me. I may move in with my babysitter to save money. I will borrow money from the credit union to help pay my bills while I can't work."

O: She is smiling as usual but acting more composed than on the previous visit and is able to maintain eye contact for longer periods today. Has not visited the health clinic for somatic complaints during the past week.

A: She seems to be living more in reality today in making the decision about placement of her baby. She was able to relate to her doctor on an adult level, which shows a beginning in making stable plans. She is comfortable with her decision at this time. Her flighty speech has disappeared, which shows evidence of stability in her thoughts. Reality planning is evidenced in her verbalization of housing and financial plans.

P: (1) Continue discussing future plans and her ability to live with them.
(2) Give positive support for adult decisions made.
(3) Continue with previous plans as needed.
(4) Listen for change of feelings toward placement of baby and plan for intervention as needed.
(5) Terminate soon.

E: Mari seems more composed today. Her feelings toward the adoption of her baby seem sincere in that she states she only wanted one child and has plans to ask the physician to do a tubal ligation at the time of delivery. We explored how she would feel if the ligation was refused her, and she felt she had other resources to use if the doctor refused. She feels confident that her doctor will help her in this way. She is making positive plans toward giving up her apartment and securing less expensive housing to save money. She has also made tentative plans for her confinement period. I was able to sincerely praise her for her decision-making and for her ability to relate to her doctor. By being supportive of her decisions, I feel I have shown that I accept her as a worthwhile individual. I feel we have a trusting and therapeutic relationship in which she can get approval and information when she needs it.

PROBLEM 2. UNRESOLVED ANGER

S: "I hate him. I don't like my job as my boss wants to talk trash to me. I don't have to put up with people telling me what to do. I do my job and don't have to associate with trash like I work with. I was stabbed in the back by my supervisor as he knows I am smarter than he is."

O: Her eyes are flashing in anger, yet she is smiling and laughing when talking about her problems. Her voice is strong yet whining in tone. She appears agitated at times. Her voice tone softens when she tells how unfair workers are to her. She laughs and smiles when expressing anger or hurt.

A: Her affect is inappropriate to situation. There is evidence from past job experiences that someone at some time during her employment tried to do her in and take her job because she wouldn't play around. She feels co-workers are jealous of her, which causes her job problems. She exhibits much rationalization and denial of how her behavior appears to others. She seems to set herself up to accept hurt from men. She wants love and a close relationship with a man but expects too much from men and sets herself up to be hurt. She makes many excuses for her behavior.

P: (1) Allow her angry feelings to come out.
   (2) Encourage her to express her feelings of hurt, anger, and frustration.
   (3) Explore with her how changing her behavior could keep her from being hurt in the future.
   (4) Accept reality of anger and show her that she is only hurting herself.
   (5) Accept and understand her anger.
   (6) Continue with plans on page 206.

E: Mari was very agitated today when speaking of her job. We explored her past jobs, and I confronted her with my feelings of how she appeared in a job situation. I stated that I would feel very threatened by her superior attitude and unfriendliness if I worked with her. This statement was most unacceptable to her, and she rejected it as not true. We explored her feelings about her job and what a good work relationship would be, but she could not or would not believe that she had precipitated any adverse feelings among her co-workers. Her perception of her peers is that they are all jealous of her and her ability to fight for her rights. I feel Mari is using repression and denial to cope with her angry feelings at this time. She is making progress in her adjustment to her future plans now, and unless this problem becomes too great for her to cope with, I will plan to terminate her soon.

PROBLEM 3. INCOMPLETE ACCEPTANCE OF PREGNANCY

S: "How do you like my new maternity dress? I'm really gaining weight and am still so tired. My weight gain must be fluid as I never eat. I still don't see how I got this way [pregnant] as I was on the pill."

O: She looks more comfortable in maternity clothes this week. She is very attractively dressed, with her hair in a new style. Facial makeup is very appropriate and attractive. Her feet and ankles show 2-plus edema. She is smiling as usual and her voice is quiet and calm.

A: She seems to be more realistically accepting her pregnancy now; she is making future plans relative to her condition and not living in fantasy. She is still unable to see her body changes in relation to the pregnancy, which could be a basic lack of physiological knowledge. She is using denial in accepting any active responsibility for her state of pregnancy.

P: (1) Continue with same plans as on page 207.
   (2) Show acceptance of her as a worthwhile person.
   (3) Compliment her and give support for her progress.
   (4) Support her realistic and appropriate decisions.
   (5) Confront her with fantasy versus reality.
   (6) Terminate soon.

E: We discussed the reality of her condition, and she was complimented and upheld in the decisions she made relative to her pregnancy. Compliments were given for her appearance and her acceptance of the responsibility of making realistic plans for herself. Support was given for her reality planning and orientation to the present. She did not seem to be playing her what-if and yes-but games this week. Her questions about the physical changes in her body, her elevated blood pressure and anemia, vitamin-taking and its importance, and diet problems were all answered in simple terms. I feel that more questions related to the physical changes in her body will arise throughout her pregnancy. These can be effectively answered as they occur, and she is adapting well to her condition at this time. This no longer appears to be a crisis problem and plans are being made for termination in the near future.

PROBLEM 4. POOR SELF-ESTEEM

S: "The doctor says I have low blood and gave me a prescription for iron. I don't think I need it as I'm already taking vitamins.

I never eat any more as I'm not hungry. My weight gain must be just fluid. I have so many problems; I know you have never had any problems."

O: She is smiling as usual. She has gained five pounds since last week. Her eyes appear slightly puffy, and her feet and ankles show 2-plus edema. She was observed eating potato chips and a large peanut candy bar earlier in the day.

A: She has little insight into the possibility of complications with the pregnancy if she fails to take care of herself. She will not assume responsibility for understanding the complications of pregnancy and how they could harm her or the baby. There is no understanding of how dietary habits are related to edema and weight gain.

P: (1) Explore feelings of punishment for self.
   (2) Continue to explore feelings of her own self-worth. Reevaluate asset list.
   (3) Continue with reality orientation in regard to physical condition and caring for herself.
   (4) Plan for termination in the near future.

E: Asset list is compiled by the client and compared with the therapist's. She agreed that she did think she was worthy of good things but rarely got them. At this time she is still unable to see the relationship between her feelings and her behavior. I confronted her with the reality of her weight gain and explored her eating habits with her; I then correlated the two in relation to pregnancy complications. She uses denial to reject what she is unable to accept on a conscious level at this time. She appears to be coping and adjusting much better at this time and plans are being made to terminate soon.

Progress Notes as of November 7, 1978
PROBLEM 1. INABILITY TO MAKE FUTURE PLANS

S: "I am so tired today. I guess it's because I moved all weekend and then have had the flu. I will call a cab when I have to go to the hospital. It's a long way to the hospital."

O: She is still smiling but looks tired and does not have the usual bounce to her walk. She is attractively groomed. Maintains fairly constant eye contact. Speech is somewhat slower than usual.

A: She is obviously tired from moving and having had the flu. Apparently adjusting well to the move and is content with her decisions. She has made, carried out, and adjusted well to these plans for her immediate future. I feel she has resolved her indecision and is now functioning well in this area.

P: (1) Continue with positive support.

(2) Terminate.

E: Mari is coping well at this time. As she is leaving her job for our clinic appointments, I feel she is using this time to escape from work. I do not feel this is best for her employment relations nor is it good for the institution. I put this feeling to her, but she did not feel that her job was in jeopardy. Nevertheless, we did discuss termination. She was left with the option to return ad lib so she would not feel that I was leaving or rejecting her as so many others had done previously.

PROBLEM 2. UNRESOLVED ANGER

S: "My supervisors know that I have an appointment in the health clinic every Thursday, and they had just better let me go. If they don't, I'll just leave anyhow. I haven't seen him [boyfriend] in three weeks. A couple of friends are trying to get us back together, but it will never work. He knows better than to bother me any more."

O: She is laughing and smiling and appears happy today.

A: Her laughter is a defense mechanism, used to deny her anger. To avoid being hurt by people, she withdraws from them. She avoids painful situations by staying away from them, and she avoids painful people by getting them out of her life.

P: (1) Evaluate progress.

(2) Terminate.

E: We explored her feelings in regard to termination, and it is fairly acceptable to her. It was explained that her peers and supervisors could think she was using her health and pregnancy as an excuse to avoid work. She was reluctant to accept this but was relieved when informed that I would be available to her if she needed help at any time, and that she would be welcome. We explored her feelings about men and how she had managed to let herself be hurt in every relationship with a man. She feels she has been too giving in her relationships and feels too that a sexual relationship without a closeness to the partner is only the first step toward hurting herself. We explored ways she felt she could have a mature relationship with a man without leaving herself open for hurt and rejection. She replied that she wanted nothing to do with a male at this time, which is a mechanism she uses to avoid getting hurt. I feel she rejects men first when she feels she is losing control of a situation and might get hurt.

Her way to cope is to withdraw from the person and the situation.

PROBLEM 3. INCOMPLETE ACCEPTANCE OF PREGNANCY
S: "I am so tired — I guess it's because I moved and had the flu. I missed two days' work because I was just so tired."
O: She is smiling but looks tired and rather pale. Her eyes appear sluggish, as if she does not feel well.
A: Is still unable to make a realistic assessment of her fatigue in relation to her pregnancy.
P: (1) Give her assurance that she is OK.
   (2) Assure her of my interest and genuine concern.
   (3) Be available to answer any questions concerning her pregnancy.
   (4) Terminate.
E: Mari is able to correlate her fatigue with her having the flu but seems unable to relate it to her pregnancy. There is other positive evidence that she is resigning herself to carrying this pregnancy to term, e.g., she is making plans in relation to her confinement during labor and delivery. There will be questions concerning the pregnancy that will arise but these can be handled as they arise. Much reassurance is given to her that she is doing OK, and I have urged her to ask her doctor about things she is worried or concerned about or to seek answers rather than worry about things.

PROBLEM 4. POOR SELF-ESTEEM
S: "I need to keep coming to see you. I have lots and lots of problems. You are easy to talk to and I have nobody else to relate to who can help me with my many problems."
O: She is smiling while speaking of her sadness at losing our weekly relationship.
A: She needs to feel dependent on someone as she has been forced to depend on herself most of her life. She is evidently afraid of losing a secure relationship and is afraid to depend on others as she always gets hurt. She expresses a need to continue with our relationship but is accepting it as she always has accepted rejection, not with anger this time but with resignation.
P: (1) Give continued reassurance that she is OK.
   (2) Check out with her the reality of her being OK.
   (3) Reassess assets from patient's and therapist's frame of reference as the relationship progresses.
   (4) Be available to her as needed but not on regular basis.

E: She was vocal about ending the relationship. I explained to her my purposes as a therapist and a helping person, and she was reassured that I would still be available to her if she needed me. I feel she needed the reassurance that I was not ending the relationship completely and that I would be available on an as-needed basis; all we were terminating was a regular weekly schedule. This she seemed able to accept and seemed pleased with herself that she was able to do this. At present I feel she is coping fairly well in this area.

Discharge Summary, November 14, 1978
PROBLEM 1. INABILITY TO MAKE FUTURE PLANS
It is with this problem that the most work has been done, as this was the statement of her crisis. We have accomplished the goals as stated, and I feel she is functioning well on an adult level and living well with the decisions she has made. This visit was aimed at reviewing her decisions and accomplishments and reevaluating her comfort with her decisions. I feel we have established a working therapeutic relationship based on confidence and mutual respect. She has developed an adult relationship with her doctor and has been able to arrange with him the placement of her baby; these arrangements are satisfactory to all concerned (the doctor, adoptive parents, and herself). She seems confident of her ability and her right to secure help when needed. She seems happy and satisfied with her decisions for the present and future. She vocalizes no problems at this time though laughingly says she will be sure and think up some so she can return. This shows her basic insecurity and lack of other situational supports, which she needs. Therapy gives her a sense of belonging and of being a worthwhile, deserving person. I reemphasized how well I thought she was doing and congratulated her on making such viable and appropriate decisions for her life.

PROBLEM 2. UNRESOLVED ANGER
Mari has many repressed angry feelings that she copes with by denial and letting herself be hurt. She continues to reject what I see as her relationship with peers on the job but is apparently able to live with this at this time. She recently related to me that she has been offered the job of head of the steno pool, so she is evidently improving in her relationships in this area. I feel she needs a lot of work in the area of an acceptable relationship with a man or men in general. At present she is coping by withdrawing from all male relationships and has totally severed the relationship with her boyfriend, the father of the baby. I feel it

would take long-time individual and group therapy to work out
her angry feelings in an acceptable and therapeutic way for her.
This intervention is not appropriate to her crisis situation at this
time.

PROBLEM 3. INCOMPLETE ACCEPTANCE OF PREGNANCY
I feel she has resolved this problem and has gained some insight
into the physiological processes of pregnancy. Part of our therapeutic relationship was based on my ability to accept her as a
worthwhile person and to support her in her realistic and appropriate decisions for herself. Work in this area has been concentrated on the day-to-day physical changes resulting from her
pregnancy. Questions from her have been answered honestly and
simply, while the necessity of her being responsible for caring
for herself has been emphasized. In making concrete future plans
for herself, her six-year-old son, and for the baby she is carrying,
she has grown to accept the pregnancy as a real event in her life.
She has gone on from there to make concrete plans concerning
what is best for her future.

PROBLEM 4. POOR SELF-ESTEEM
Mari is keeping her doctor's appointments now, although she is
still reluctant to call him between appointments if she is feeling
bad or has some questions on her mind. She requires regular
assurance by peers that she is OK. She is taking care of herself
fairly well and drops in at the school health clinic often, as if to
reassure herself that our relationship is not totally broken. I gave
her my home telephone number as an additional support for
her, and she has not taken advantage of this privilege. I felt that
she needed the assurance of a continuing relationship with an
understanding person who could give her the support she needs
during this period in her life. She has gained some self-confidence
by sharing good points about herself (e.g., she is a good mother,
a good worker, a good cook), and I feel that it is appropriate to
compliment her on her assets while pointing out positive actions
I have observed. I feel long-term therapy and group interaction
would be beneficial to her in helping her to feel more secure
with herself and in her relationships with others.

She has worked out a good relationship with her doctor, and
I feel they are communicating with each other on an adult and
understanding level. She seems able to express her feelings and
desires to him. She feels too, that they have worked out the
details of the placement of her baby and financial arrangements
to the satisfaction of each.

She has gained help for herself by receiving compliments for work performed well on her job and is flattered that her supervisor has offered her the position of head of the steno pool. She is now considering taking the position but only with an increase in salary. This offer has helped her self-image, and I feel has made her more comfortable with her job.

REFERENCES

1. Aguilera, D. C., and Messick, J. M. *Crisis Intervention, Theory and Methodology.* St. Louis: C. V. Mosby, 1974.
2. Glasser, W. *Mental Health or Mental Illness.* New York: Harper & Row, 1960.
3. Glasser, W. *Reality Therapy: A New Approach to Psychiatry.* New York: Harper & Row, 1965.
4. Glasser, W. *Schools Without Failure.* New York: Harper & Row, 1969.
5. Glasser, W. *The Identity Society.* New York: Harper & Row, 1972.
6. Rogers, C. *Client-Centered Therapy.* Boston: Houghton Mifflin, 1951.
7. Rogers, C. *Becoming a Person.* Austin, Texas: The University of Texas, Hogg Foundation for Mental Hygiene, 1956.
8. Rogers, C. *Carl Rogers on Encounter Groups.* New York: Harper & Row, 1970.
9. Berne, E. *Games People Play.* New York: Grove Press, 1964.
10. Berne, E. *Principles of Group Treatment.* New York: Grove Press, 1964.
11. Berne, E. *What Do You Say After You Say Hello?* New York: Grove Press, 1973.
12. Jourard, S. M. *The Transparent Self.* New York: Van Nostrand-Reinhold Co., 1971.
13. Fagan, J., and Shepherd, I. L. *Gestalt Therapy Now.* Palo Alto, Calif.: Science and Behavior Books, 1970.

SELECTED READINGS

Abrams, G. M. Setting limits. *Archives of General Psychiatry* 19:113−119, 1968.
Bach, G. R., and Wyden, P. *The Intimate Enemy.* New York: Avon Books, 1970.
Eaton, M., and Peterson, M. *Psychiatry.* New York: Medical Examination Publishing Co., 1969.
Enelow, A. J., and Swisher, S. N. *Interviewing and Patient Care.* New York: Oxford University Press, 1972.
Fawcett, J., et al. Suicide. *Archives of General Psychiatry* 21:129−137, 1969.
Harmatz, M. G. Verbal conditioning and change on personality measures. *Journal of Personality and Social Psychology* 5:175−185, 1967.
Hurst, J. W. The art and science of presenting a patient's problems. *Archives of Internal Medicine* 128:463−465, 1971.
James, M., and Jongeward, D. *Born to Win: Transactional Analysis and Gestalt Experiments.* Reading, Mass.: Addison-Wesley, 1971.

Larson, D., and Easter, P. A group treatment program for masochistic
　　patients. *Hospital and Community Psychiatry* 25:525–528, 1974.

May, R. *Love and Will.* New York: Dell, 1969.

Powell, J. *Why Am I Afraid To Tell You Who I Am?* Niles, Ill.: Argus
　　Communications, 1969.

Reid, F. T. Impact of leader style on the functioning of a decision-making
　　group. *Archives of General Psychiatry* 23:268–276, 1970.

Sager, C. J., and Kaplan, H. S. *Progress in Group and Family Therapy.*
　　New York: Brunner-Mazel Publishers, 1972.

Sargent, S. S. *Basic Teachings of the Great Psychologists.* New York:
　　Dolphia Books, 1965.

Satir, V. *Conjoint Family Therapy.* Palo Alto, Calif.: Science and Behavior
　　Books, 1972.

Some comments on self-assessment of psychiatric knowledge. (Editorial)
　　Archives of General Psychiatry 21:513–514, 1969.

Case Study 3: George
LINDA MATTHEWS

In my review of the many psychosocial models I have found it
very difficult to identify myself with only one model. However,
when I attempted to view my values objectively, I was able to
choose a model with which I most nearly agree in its entirety:
the existential model.

The existential model of man emphasizes the uniqueness of
the individual, his quest for values and meaning, and his need
for freedom of self-fulfillment and self-direction. In this way it
is highly similar to humanistic psychology, and in fact many
humanistic psychologists are also referred to as existentialists.
The existential model, however, represents a somewhat less
optimistic view of man and places more emphasis on the irrational trends in man's nature and the difficulties inherent in
self-fulfillment. The existentialists in their attempts to understand and deal with man's problems place considerably less faith
in modern science and more faith in the inner experiencing of
the individual.

The existential model is not a highly systematized school of
thought. It is unified by a central concern with the ultimate
challenge of human existence, namely, the need to establish a
sense of personal identity and to build meaningful links with
the world. Its basic concepts stem mainly from the writings of
such European philosophers as Martin Heidegger, Karl Jaspers,
Sören Kierkegaard, and Jean-Paul Sartre. Especially influential
in the development of existential thought in the United States
have been the theologian Paul Tillich and the psychologist
Rollo May.

From the existential viewpoint, man's basic motivation is to find the best possible way of life, to actualize his potentialities, and to fulfill himself as a human being. Thus a basic theme of existentialism is that the individual's existence is given, but what he makes of it — his essence — is up to him.

A second basic theme of the existentialists is the finding and choosing of satisfying values. For it is in his value choices that the individual shapes his essence. And the individual is viewed as having complete freedom in choosing his values and the kind of person he is to become.

An existential theme that adds an urgent and painful note to the human situation is that of nonbeing, of nothingness. In the idiom of the existential theories, nonbeing is the opposite of being and in ultimate form is death, the inescapable fate of all men [1].

The vocabulary of existential psychology has firmly entered into our language. *Existential crisis* is a common term now for the critical point in psychotherapy [2].

After applying my developed tool in the clinical area, I have evaluated it and feel that it is broad enough to be used with various types of therapy. More specifically, it can easily be applied to short-term psychotherapy or crisis intervention. The case now presented shows its use in crisis intervention.

Assessment Tool
Client's Complaint
Patient Profile

Medical history
    Past illnesses
    Present illnesses

Medications being taken at present

Psychological assessment

Socioeconomic and cultural factors
    Educational level
    Religious affiliation
    Income vs. expenses
    Transportation
    Valuable persons to individual
    Leisure activities

Ability to make decisions

Data Base

CLIENT'S COMPLAINT

September 17, 1978: "I have to talk to somebody or I'm going to harm myself."

PATIENT PROFILE

This client is an 18-year-old, single white male, a high-school student, who came to the out-patient clinic after calling for an appointment. He was referred by a physician after he took an overdose of sleeping pills that he got from his doctor by "lying and telling her I needed them." The first interview, which was by telephone on September 14, 1978, indicated that he was not an immediate suicidal risk. At that time a verbal contract was made that he would not harm himself until he was seen. During the first personal interview he laughed inappropriately at times and expressed suicidal feelings.

SOCIOECONOMIC AND CULTURAL FACTORS

Relationship to family members. He lives with his mother who has been divorced for several years. Client states that he sees his father very seldom and does not think his father is interested in him at all. His mother is described as "yelling all the time." He plans to live with her until he finishes school.

Ability to make decisions. He feels there is no use in making decisions. Says he can't get interested.

Leisure activities. He shows little interest when talking about activities. He has nothing to do but go to school and go home. No activities are done in school. Used to go with groups to play Frisbee.

Educational level. He has completed the 11th grade. He is now finishing the 12th grade as he failed some subjects last year.

Religious Affiliation. None.

Income. Unemployed.

Transportation. His mother brought him to the clinic. He is dependent upon her for his transportation.

Valuable persons to the individual. He has no one whom he considers a valuable person in his life.

MEDICAL HISTORY

Past Illnesses. He denies having any illnesses other than minor and common problems.

Present Illnesses. He states he has no known medical problems at present.

MEDICATIONS BEING TAKEN AT PRESENT
No medications are being taken now. He denies having any
medication of any type in his possession.

PSYCHOLOGICAL ASSESSMENT
He is neat and well-groomed in appearance. He is oriented to
time and place. He denies any auditory or visual hallucinations.
He has an adequate memory of events past and present. His
affect is one that changes from inappropriate or embarrassed
laughter to one of sadness, the latter particularly when he is
asked specifically about his former girlfriend. He admits to
thoughts of suicide but denies that it is urgently pending. He
states that he eats well, although he does have difficulty sleeping; some nights he sleeps only three or four hours.

List of Assets
When he was first seen on September 17, a list of his assets were
made: These were:

(1) He has excellent physical health.
(2) He has no history of other attempts at suicide.
(3) There has been no history of repeated threats or depression.
(4) No further suicidal plan has been formulated.
(5) He seems very interested in finding ways to help himself.

Problem List
George's active problems as of September 17, 1978, were:

(1) Suicidal feelings
(2) Unresolved grief from loss of girlfriend
(3) Insomnia
(4) Inadequate social skills
(5) Dependence upon relationship with girlfriend.

Problem 4 was resolved September 24, problem 3 on September
28, and problems 1, 2, and 5 by October 12, his last contact
with the therapist.

PROBLEM 1. SUICIDAL FEELINGS
This young man states he first felt he didn't want to live about
two weeks ago when the girl he was dating went out with someone else. He said when he found out about this, he went and got
some sleeping medication from his doctor and used them for an

overdose. He went driving after taking the overdose and was arrested for driving while drinking. He apparently had not taken a fatal dosage as he was released from the hospital later. He states he now feels he must talk to someone or he will harm himself again.

PROBLEM 2. UNRESOLVED GRIEF FROM LOSS OF GIRL FRIEND
He says that he wants to be able to forget his girl friend, but he can't. He continues to feel as though he will harm himself if he sees her with someone else. He says he can't help the feelings, and they don't go away. He asks very directly, "How can I forget her?"

PROBLEM 3. INSOMNIA
This client says he can't sleep because he thinks of his girl friend all the time. He relates that he stays awake until 3:00 A.M. sometimes and only gets three or four hours of sleep most of the time.

PROBLEM 4. INADEQUATE SOCIAL SKILLS
This is the first girl that he has been seriously interested in. He says if he tries to ask a girl out, she doesn't tell him anything, so he feels that she doesn't want to go out with him. Says he can't enjoy himself anyway and that he really can't get interested in going out.

**PROBLEM 5. DEPENDENCE UPON RELATIONSHIP
WITH FORMER GIRL FRIEND**
He has no close friends. He was able to talk to this girl; they were very close and he trusted her. He feels she was good to him and that she knew he was true to her. He feels that he can no longer trust her and feels she is a liar.

Initial Plans — September 17, 1978
PROBLEM 1. SUICIDAL FEELINGS
S: George states that he feels he will harm himself because he can't forget his girl friend. He says he took an overdose of sleeping pills two weeks ago because she was going out with another guy. He feels that he has nothing to live for.
O: He appears to be sad when talking about his girl friend.
A: He has a recent primary loss of social supports, and his dependency needs are not being met.
P: Determine other sources of social support.
   (1) Help him find possible forgotten sources.
   (2) Direct him to find new supports.

(3) Maintain contact with him. Obtain a verbal contract from him that he will not harm himself. Point out that this is his responsibility.

PROBLEM 2. UNRESOLVED GRIEF FROM LOSS OF GIRL FRIEND
S: He states that he wants to forget this girl friend.
O: He appears to be very interested in any direction or suggestions on how to say good-bye to this girl.
A: He shows willingness to learn how to cope with his loss.
P: Share and understand grief by:
   (1) reviewing relationship with lost object;
   (2) pointing out that he must accept the pain of loss;
   (3) encouraging him to express his sorrow and sense of loss.

PROBLEM 3. INSOMNIA
S: Client says he can't sleep for thinking about his girl friend.
O: He appears apprehensive but shows no signs of fatigue.
A: No long period of loss of sleep is evident.
P: Allow verbalization to relieve tension. Give support and direction so that he may have other alternatives if he wants them.

PROBLEM 4. INADEQUATE SOCIAL SKILLS
S: Client states that he can't talk in groups and is reluctant to talk to old acquaintances.
O: He appears uncertain or embarrassed when talking to me about this.
A: This young man is unable to use social skills to resocialize himself.
P: Give several alternatives for action:
   (1) use the therapist for practice in improving social skills;
   (2) point out to him that there are always possible consequences and encourage him to examine them to see if he is ready for them;
   (3) point out to him that he must take responsibility for accepting or rejecting the alternatives.

PROBLEM 5. DEPENDENCE UPON RELATIONSHIP WITH GIRL FRIEND
S: Client says he could talk to her and he trusted her.
O: He seems very eager to talk to me, and this seems to lessen his anxiety.
A: He needs a source to verbalize feelings to and to establish trust in.

P: Provide a source for contact and trust. Make a contract for him to call the therapist when he feels he needs to talk to someone. Point out that this is his responsibility.

Progress Notes
PROBLEM 4. INADEQUATE SOCIAL SKILLS (September 24, 1978)
S: Client says he is keeping busy and going out with school chums.

O: He seems to be making progress in reestablishing social contacts.

A: He is improving his use of social skills, new and old.

P: Encourage continuation of this behavior.

PROBLEM 3. INSOMNIA (September 28, 1978)
S: He says he is sleeping well and at least six or seven hours a night.

O: He seems relaxed while talking and is pleased that he is feeling better.

A: Restoration of normal sleeping patterns is evident.

P: Encourage him to report to the therapist any change.

Discharge Summary
My first contact with this client was by telephone as a call-in on September 14, 1978. His complaint at that time was, "I am going to harm myself if I don't get someone to talk to. My girl friend is going out with someone else and I can't forget her."
A verbal contract was made that he would not harm himself and that he would see me on September 17. During evaluation, this well-groomed, sometimes uncertain, young male seemed highly motivated to find some alternatives for himself. During therapy he was supported through the grief process of losing his girl friend with a subsequent lessening of his suicidal feelings.

My last contact with him was on October 12 after two prior appointments were broken. At this time I reviewed with him over the telephone all the points relating to his suicidal feelings. He confirmed that he hadn't had any of these feelings for more than two weeks. He went on to say that he doesn't feel a need for therapy any longer.

As this client did make progress in the three sessions we had, I see his prognosis as good. He was reminded that any time he felt he needed some help he could use the agency.

REFERENCES

1. Coleman, J. C. *Abnormal Psychology and Modern Life*. Glenview, Ill.: Scott, Foresman and Co., 1972.
2. May, R. *Existential Psychology*. New York: Random House, 1969.

SELECTED READINGS

Aguilera, D. C., and Messick, J. M. *Crisis Intervention*. St. Louis: C. V. Mosby, 1974.

Enelow, A. J., and Swisher, S. N. *Interviewing and Patient Care*. New York: Oxford University Press, 1972.

Mazur, W. *The Problem-Oriented System in the Psychiatric Hospital*. Garden Grove, Calif.: Trainex Press Corp., 1974.

Case Study 4: Jean

BILLIE J. ROBINSON

As a therapist, I believe that it is very important to collect all available data related to the difficulty for which the client seeks help. In this vein, I pay particular attention to how the person sees himself in relation to his definitions of his real self and his ideal self, and how he sees himself in relation to how he thinks his significant others see him. My entire therapy plan very much depends on what is contained in this data because it is my basic belief that a person becomes emotionally disturbed because of an interaction difficulty or ineffective communication between a person's self and significant others. Interaction difficulty results in gross misunderstandings about the self, others, the self's expected role, others' expected role, definitions of situations by self and significant others, expected contribution by self and significant others, and so on. In essence, this continuing state of misunderstanding, whose origin ultimately lies in a poor self-image *learned* from a significant other, is the basis for one acquiring an out-group membership status in a significant-others group.

It is this resulting, overwhelming feeling of alienation that either drives a person to a therapist to learn how to correct the interaction difficulty via the avenue of a meaningful encounter, or drives him to the adjustment of "craziness." The encounter therefore is designed to help the person feel comfortable enough to explore what the problem is and to devise his own ways and means of bringing about change. The encounter is also mutually defined by client and therapist as a safe, experimental setting in which the client can practice new methods of coping and can determine their effectiveness by trial and error.

Assessment Tool
  I. Presenting Complaint (subjectively stated):
 II. Data Base
     A. Profile
     B. Precipitating factors
     C. Primary-group relationships
        1. Mother-child (or husband-wife, etc.)
        2. Father-child (or significant other)
        3. Sibling-child (whoever is relevant)
     D. Normative behaviors
        1. Life style
        2. Value system
        3. Role definitions
     E. Reference group relationships
        1. Significant others (dyads, peers) and normative
           behaviors
           a. Life style
           b. Value system
           c. Role definitions
        2. Task group — colleagues
        3. Normative behaviors
           a. Life style
           b. Value system
           c. Role definitions
III. Medical history (as is relevant)
 IV. Mental status examinations (as is relevant)
  V. Assets list
     A. Client's frame of reference
     B. Therapist's frame of reference
 VI. Problem list
VII. S.O.A.P. of problems
VIII. Progress and evaluation (S.O.A.P. both of previously iden-
      tified problems and "emerging" problems)
 IX. Discharge summary

Presenting Complaint
"I'm here to get my head on straight. I tried to kill myself with
sleeping pills a week ago and it scared me . . . made me realize
how sick I was."

Data Base
PROFILE
Jean is a 23-year-old, single, Caucasian female surgical technician
who is currently employed by a local hospital.

The client's "mussed" hair and the absence of makeup reflect a lack of interest in her appearance. Her tense, somewhat stilted posture, tight jaw lines, and tearful, subdued vocalizations suggest an anxious and frightened young woman. Jean's intermittent weeping during the encounter, accompanied by verbal self-criticisms for not being able "to stop crying," suggests a desperate struggle for self-control.

Most verbalizations reflect a serious concern with feelings of alienation: "I just don't fit in anywhere — not in my family or in my work. Oh, I'm a good technician, but those nurses have known each other for years and they have their cliques. I'm a big disappointment to my parents — I was a difficult child to rear. I was always rebelling against my parents and still am! Isn't that stupid! I'm the one who is really suffering for it! I can't even keep a boy friend — boys 'use' me and it's my own fault.

"What can you expect when you pick them up; I do this because I'm lonely — even though I know I'm the one who's going to get hurt — I've just got to get my head on straight! I went to a health spa for a while to try and lose weight. It made me feel better for a while, but it didn't change anything with my boy friend . . . he still made fun of me. So, I just quit trying, I figured, what's the use!"

PRECIPITATING FACTORS
According to Jean, the fact that she was living with a boy "who didn't give a damn about me" began to make her feel very guilty and this became coupled with an urgent need to confess all to her parents. She stated that she had experienced these guilt feelings for about ten days prior to hospitalization. She finally phoned her parents and told them everything, which resulted in their coming to visit her in order to "get the boy out of the apartment." During the interim, she began to have second thoughts about wanting her parents to interfere and, upon their arrival, expressed these feelings, which resulted in their expressing much anger toward her. After an angry interchange, her parents returned home, telling her that they were "terribly disappointed in her but, should she decide to change her ways, she knew how to reach them." Jean stated that she was glad they had decided to leave and, wanting to forget the whole thing, suggested to her boyfriend that they go out on the town. Both she and her boy friend drank heavily during the evening, and after returning home, he began to tease her about her weight and told her that he didn't care anything about her. Jean stated

that she began to feel "really down to the point that I didn't care if I lived or died. So I calmly walked over to the medicine cabinet, took a bunch of sleeping pills, calmly walked into the living room and told my boy friend that I was going to kill myself, that I had taken the pills." She was really shocked to discover that all her boy friend did was just laugh, saying that he did not believe her "even after showing him the bottle!" Jean became frightened "because I knew I needed someone to help me and he wasn't going to." She then phoned an old girl-friend who came over, "fed me gallons of coffee, and walked me all night long." Upon inquiry, Jean stated that because of her medical status, she was both too embarrassed and humiliated to go to the emergency room, adding that she was willing to take her chances with the above-stated remedy.

Jean stated that the morning following the suicidal gesture found her feeling "like a damn fool and realizing how sick I really was" — which caused her to again phone her parents. She talked with her mother, told her of the suicidal gesture, and asked them (parents) to come help her to arrange for psychiatric treatment. According to the client, her mother contacted the family physician who recommended a local psychologist. She saw the psychologist on an out-patient basis twice. He recommended that she be hospitalized because of "severe depression." Jean volunteered that she is continuing to see this psychologist both in a group and on an individual basis three times a week. Jean expressed many positive feelings towards the psychologist: "because I trust him. He will tell my parents the truth, how sick I am . . ."

PRIMARY-GROUP RELATIONSHIPS

Mother-child relationship. From Jean's point of view, she and her mother have always been "at odds." When Jean was 3 years old, her mother became ill with tuberculosis, causing Jean to be placed with her maternal grandmother for one and a half years. During this separation period, her mother gave birth to Jean's only sibling, a brother, who also contracted TB; this lengthened the separation period. While Jean did become extremely close to her grandmother, she still recalls how much she resented her baby brother. In this vein she expressed the belief that her parents preferred her brother. She began relating times when, as a child, she had frequently conspired to get him into trouble with them. She added that most of her efforts in this regard had been unsuccessful — her parents always knew that she was behind the mischief. When her mother and baby brother returned home,

"I would climb up on the kitchen counter and wet my pants, and Mother would become furious and whip me."

Jean stated that when she began dating, both parents disapproved of her choice of suitors. "They felt that I deliberately picked out the crumbs to upset them, and now that I think of it, maybe I did." She stated that her mother once hurt her very deeply by telling her that "you'll never have the beaux I did," adding that her mother had been drinking at the time.

Upon inquiry, Jean stated that on only one very recent occasion had she experienced a closeness with her mother; this occurred following the maternal grandmother's death. "We both seemed to feel the same for the first time, but that quickly ended. The only thing my mother likes about me is the fact that I became a surgical technician. Her friends have told her that I'm a good one and I believe that she's proud of me for this." Upon inquiry, she said that the decision to become a surgical technician had been hers and was one of the very few that her parents went along with.

An interview with Jean's mother showed her to be an attractive, neatly dressed woman who appeared to be in her mid-fifties. Both appearance and behavior were appropriate to the situation. She frequently displayed concern for her daughter's welfare during our encounter. When asked why she felt that Jean needed hospitalization, she responded that she believed that Jean had been sick since she was a little girl; a pediatrician had once told her that he thought Jean was a pathological liar, but she had not taken the doctor seriously enough.

She also expressed the opinion that hospitalization was necessary in order to prevent her daughter from being "completely destroyed" by her boy friend. She volunteered that Jean had informed them of the living arrangement with this young man, adding that it had hurt and upset both her husband and her very much. "It was all we could do to keep our cool when we met that boy — it is so obvious that he doesn't care anything for Jean, that he is just using her . . . that's why we went back home . . . we were afraid to use force because of what it might do to Jean . . . we were afraid that it would drive her away completely . . . it's the most miserable feeling in the world!" The mother felt that Jean seemed to let boy-girl relationships "completely consume her" to the point that she "is unable to do anything else." She volunteered that both she and her husband had always had the feeling that Jean sought out the "low-life, gigolo types," and appeared at a complete loss to understand why.

Jean's mother frequently expressed the feeling that they as parents had tried to do right by both their children, adding that their child-rearing methods had worked well with Jean's 20-year-old brother but not with Jean. When asked about this she stated that she and her daughter had never really been close, that she sensed that Jean was always rebelling against her. She added that Jean never appeared to give much forethought to anything and cited as an example her going away to study. "Jean had wanted to be a technician all her life but had never given any thought whatsoever as to where to study. So I had to make the decision to send her to school, where she did fine until she got involved with a boy and got kicked out. Then we arranged for her to have an apartment near us and she finished in a junior college." In this vein, the mother stated that Jean's choice of girl friends had also left something to be desired. "While she was in training this past year, she ended up letting girls move into her apartment and we footed the bill! Jean's always been a difficult child — I just hope and pray that this hospital can straighten her out. I don't know what else to do!"

Father-child relationship. According to Jean, she got along somewhat better with her father than her mother. "It was really great to sit on his knee whan I was little, before my brother was born . . . but then he began to side with Mama . . . we're not close like I've heard other girls are with their dads. In fact, he and mother sound like a broken record — I'm a real disappointment to them, always have been."

During our interviews, Jean's father was pleasant-looking and neatly dressed, a man who gave the impression of being successful in business. He appeared younger than his wife (mid-forties) and also appeared content to let his wife do most of the talking. He expressed essentially the same feelings as his wife, giving the impression that he was the passive partner in this relationship.

He acknowledged that he could not recall a time when he and Jean had been close, stating that he was at his wit's end regarding his daughter's behavior, focusing particularly on her past relationships with "gigolos." He added that Jean had hurt them, but that she was still his daughter and he only hoped that she could get straightened out. "I wonder where we went wrong . . . we have always tried to see to it that the kids never wanted for anything . . . my wife and I started out on a shoestring and have built a pretty good business. It's kept us pretty busy, I'll admit, but we really tried not to neglect the kids . . . after all, we were really working for them so they wouldn't have to go through

what we did when we were growing up. But looks like it didn't
work out that way, did it, Mother . . .?"

Sibling-child relationship. According to Jean, her younger,
20-year-old brother is truly the "white sheep" of the family.
"He's really pretty nice; he's been marvelous to me since I've
been here. He's written me often and I believe that he really
does care for me." Jean added that this recent realization made
her feel really bad and very guilty for being so jealous of him
when they were small. The brother still resides in the family
home and works for her parents. "Mother and Dad have always
been proud of him . . . I just wish that it could have been that
way with me, too."

According to Jean's parents, Jean had always been jealous of
her brother and had frequently tried to conspire against him
for attention. They did volunteer that it had always been much
easier to get along with the boy than Jean. They said that as
children, Jean and her brother fought often but "do appear on
the surface to get along well at present." They added that their
son presently is very concerned for his sister and her welfare and
that, without any suggestion from them, he has corresponded
frequently with Jean during her hospitalization. The parents
expressed the belief, when asked about it, that Jean feels that
they prefer her brother to her although this was staunchly denied.

NORMATIVE BEHAVIORS
The client's primary group (her family) reflects loose-knit relationships among its membership. It gives an impression of one
"out-going" member and three "in-group" members.

Primary-group interaction suggests middle-class values: work
hard, acquire comfortable living standards, exhibit socially
acceptable morals and standards, go to church, meet "nice"
people, make good grades in school, be a lady.

Role definitions are as follows: *Mother* — strong, dominant,
controlling, co-breadwinner, chief disciplinarian; *Father* — passive, mother's silent partner, co-breadwinner; *Client* — black
sheep, copes in rebellious child role, programmed to self-destruct
in order to cope with mother, the bad child; *Sibling* — white
sheep, passive, another silent partner, the good child.

REFERENCE GROUP RELATIONSHIPS
Jean stated that she has only had one close girl friend (peer
dyad). "Mother doesn't approve of her and her mother doesn't
like me either — they think we're bad for one another." She

admitted that this relationship has continued on the sly for the last 10 years. Jean stated that "we were pretty mischievious while growing up but we never really did anything bad. She's like a sister to me; we have had a lot of the same kind of problems. Emotionally she's a stronger person than I am." Jean says that this friend had tried to run her boy friend off on several occasions because she was concerned for her "but I was stubborn and wouldn't listen to her!" Jean added that this girl friend had recently separated from her husband and had moved into an apartment close to Jean. She volunteered that the living arrangement had put a strain on their relationship, but that she had been the one who took care of her during the suicide attempt.

It appears that Jean and her girl friend (the dyad) have a very close relationship, to the extent of its being a closed unit. This relationship, however, appears to be built on negatives: rebellious behavior toward parental figures, similar adjustment problems. This relationship needs evaluation, in terms of "healthiness," to determine the extent of reciprocation of healthy versus sick needs, and so on.

The roles of both the client and her friend are defined as: nurturing, smothering mother; lonely, alienated child.

About her relationships with her colleagues, Jean stated, "I'm a good technician. My supervisor says I can have my old job back when I'm well, and she told Mother that she had arranged for a leave of absence. I'm always on time and try to do a good job, but I don't have any close friends there — they're just people to work with . . . they have their own offices. I'm wondering if my supervisor will tell anyone about my illness . . . I wonder if she'll keep it a secret. I couldn't stand them staring at me like I'm crazy or weird."

The client has adapted professional standards related to confidentiality, ethics, and so on. She values work-related interaction; she has stated that allegiance to medical standards had saved her from the drug scene.

She defines her role as "a good technician who is ashamed of present difficulty."

Medical History

The initial physical examination revealed that Jean is currently experiencing a bout of cystitis and is under medication. A vaginal smear revealed trichomoniasis infection that is now being treated.

Client regards herself as a social drinker. "I've only been intoxicated twice in my life." She is a nonsmoker. She has no food or drug allergies and no history of drug addiction.

Mental Status Examinations
Jean is an intelligent young woman who is oriented to the three spheres. Both her appearance and behavior reflect a moderately severe state of depression, the origins of which can be traced to early childhood. Psychological tests reveal an essentially immature personality with paranoid tendencies. In this vein, the primary finding was low self-esteem, suggesting a neurotic depression. Prognosis: "guarded"; she may succeed at a suicide attempt under severe stress. It is my understanding that these findings are commensurate with other test battery results from the psychologist's office.

Assets List
CLIENT'S FRAME OF REFERENCE
Jean feels that her good points are that she: (1) is a good technician, and (2) possesses artistic talents. These feelings were expressed at the beginning of this therapist's involvement with her.

THERAPIST'S FRAME OF REFERENCE
From the therapist's point of view she has many positive aspects about her. These are that she: (1) has the potential for becoming an attractive young lady with some input of self-interest — nice features and body build; (2) is talented in arts and crafts; (3) possesses some degree of insight into her difficulty; (4) is motivated toward change in spite of fighting herself in this area. She wants to learn how to form meaningful relationships with others. She wants to like herself and has verbalized this as a first step. She is asking for help to accomplish these goals and "to grow."

Problem List
Jean's active problems as of May 7, 1978, were:

(1) Attempted suicide
(2) Low self-esteem, which greatly interferes with daily life except when on duty as a technician
(3) Conflicting relationship with parents, both in past and present
(4) Intellectualization with lack of emotional content
(5) Inability to select and maintain adequate relationships

Another problem — the fear that she was pregnant — was resolved on May 24 when a pregnancy test and examination were negative.

(6) Inability to cope effectively with staff disciplinary action
— cropped up on June 11.

Data Base for Problem List as of May 7, 1978
PROBLEM 1. ATTEMPTED SUICIDE
S: "I tried to kill myself with sleeping pills a week ago and it scared me."
O: Swallowed undetermined number of sleeping pills.
A: Suicidal gesture apparently a result of an inability to cope with feelings of guilt and anger; both related to interconflict and intraconflict of value systems.
P: Therapist: establish "anti-suicide" contract; provide support system by first establishing rapport and then, subsequently, a meaningful relationship.
   Client: will honor contract; will honor request as to what can be done by her to change her destructive life-style; will be ready to discuss her "thoughts" next session.

PROBLEM 2. LOW SELF-ESTEEM
S: "I just don't fit in anywhere — not in my family or in my work."
O: Client has "mussed" hair and no makeup and posture is tense; she weeps intermittently.
A: Her general appearance and verbal behavior suggest both a lack of interest in and a valuing of herself.
P: Focus on her assets; discuss what she likes about herself. Therapist: focus on relationships with significant others; give client a choice as to what to work on first.
   Client: agrees to make the decision as to what to work on.

PROBLEM 3. CONFLICTING RELATIONSHIP WITH PARENTS
S: "I'm a big disappointment to my parents."
O: She is weeping and vocal tones are angry; she is expressing much concern over her immediate family relationships.
A: Patient sees herself as the black sheep in the family. She appears to have assumed the "rebellious child role." Her role contribution is not acceptable to herself or to others.
P: Therapist: focus on relationship with significant others; involve patient in Gestalt-type interchange (role playing) with significant others in order to teach her how to think, how to feel about self, and how she is affecting others.
   Client: will make decision to work on relationship with parents first; will engage in Gestalt-type role playing.

**PROBLEM 4. INTELLECTUALIZATION WITH
LACK OF EMOTIONAL CONTENT**

S: "I was always rebelling against my parents and still am. Boys use me — I do this because I'm lonely, even though I know I'm the one who's going to get hurt."

O: She is expressing an analysis of her difficulties.

A: The patient is protecting herself from experiencing feelings by intellectualization. She is apparently not internalizing or experiencing feelings with verbalized concepts.

P: Therapist: use feeling-type words during encounters; when appropriate, call attention to her intellectualization of content; use Gestalt interchange (role-playing) to elicit feeling experience (hopefully she will become comfortable with same in time!).

Client: will evaluate feelings related to Gestalt interchange.

**PROBLEM 5. INABILITY TO SELECT AND TO
MAINTAIN ADEQUATE RELATIONSHIPS**

S: "Boys use me and it's my own fault . . . what can you expect when you pick them up?"

O: She is weeping, expressing hurt and anger on an intellectual level.

A: She is exhibiting self-depreciating, destructive behavior with peers and intellectualizing the reasons why.

P: Therapist: explore with patient what she expects from a relationship.

Client: explore what's hurting her in opposite-sex relationships; explore what can be done to prevent or avoid pain in future relationships with the opposite sex.

Progress and Evaluation

**PROBLEM 3. CONFLICTING RELATIONSHIP WITH PARENTS —
May 10, 1978**

S: "If my parents cared anything about me, they would not have chased my boy friend off. They've never liked any of my friends."

O: She is weeping and expressing hostile feelings toward parents.

A: The patient is still quite depressed but is beginning to express some hostility. She is again assuming the role of rebellious child.

P: Put into effect plan for Problem 3. Focus on relationships with significant others through Gestalt interchange.

E: In role-play, she chose to seat her mother farthest away. She had great difficulty in getting into the character of Mother.

She depicted Father as a passive, silent partner in the relationship. An attempt was made to avoid Gestalt experience by either focusing on the past with all its hurts and injustices or by involving the therapist in an intellectualizing process of Transactional Analysis ego-states. I would have to say that it was only a fair first try. She only attempted to portray her mother to a degree. She is very angry but is afraid to express it on a gut level.

PROBLEM 3. CONFLICTING RELATIONSHIPS WITH PARENTS —
May 14, 1978

S: (Role-play response to Mother) "I wish you had given me more time and attention when I was little. I wish you hadn't forgot me when [younger brother] was born . . ."

O: There is a desperate quality to voice; she is expressing her feelings of neglect and jealousy over the birth of her baby brother.

A: The patient experienced some feeling regarding what it feels like to be reduced in status and out-group membership.

P: Continue with Gestalt interchange; have client evaluate how she is feeling when it is appropriate to do so.

E: This was a better session; she didn't intellectualize as much. I believe the Gestalt experience provided a feeling experience and insight for both therapist and patient regarding the patient's present difficulties. Following role-play, the patient said, "I guess I really need to be here, to grow up."

PROBLEM 2. LOW SELF-ESTEEM — May 21, 1978

S: "I've been so wrong about my parents; they do love me and care for me . . . had a fantastic weekend with them . . . do you think it would be a copout if I decided to move back home with them? I do have doubts . . . I'm afraid I'll just be running away again and I don't want to do that anymore."

O: Her vocal tones are happy and excited; her appearance and behavior reflect good feelings related to progress with her problem. She is expressing doubts in her ability to make the "right" decision.

A: The patient is exhibiting a reaction-formation in her present attitude toward parents. The exhibited mood and speech are reminiscent of an adolescent who either is way up or way down. She appears to have already made a decision about a move and is either seeking validation or an opportunity to explore pros and cons and hence "think through" her decision aloud.

P: Focus on assets — implying your confidence in her ability to make the decision. Give the patient an opportunity to discuss the pros and cons related to the decision. Reinforce, with appropriate, complimentary response, her efforts to make the decision.

E: Jean decided to remain in her apartment and attempt to "pick up the pieces" at this time. She appeared pleased with her own ability to make an independent decision and to have made it in the direction of an independent move toward growth and maturity. The therapist was pleased with the outcome.

PROBLEM 5. INABILITY TO SELECT AND MAINTAIN ADEQUATE RELATIONSHIPS; AND FEAR THAT SHE IS PREGNANT — May 24, 1978

S: "I've already worked through this with the psychologist, but I want you to know that I was late starting my period the other day and thought I was pregnant. I had decided to have an abortion, but the pregnancy test came back yesterday and thank God I'm not!"

O: Her low, subdued tones reflect a mixture of both anxiety and relief.

A: She is expressing a need to review this episode with the therapist. She wants to finish working on feelings associated with this experience.

P: Permit the patient an opportunity to discuss and feel the experience. Appropriately reflect with her with feeling words. Focus on and explore with the patient the relationship existing between her risking pregnancy and self-punitive behavior.

E: The patient expressed much relief over what was described as a narrow escape and commented on how this episode had "reinforced" her to avoid future relationships of this nature. Also, she expressed anger at the behavior exhibited by the psychologist, who gave the patient the impression that "I can't behave like a virgin." In the therapist's opinion, this last remark was what this session was all about — she apparently wanted me to reinforce her belief that she is capable of avoiding a similar circumstance. In this vein, the therapist suggested that only she was in a position to make this decision and to keep it, adding that Jean had exhibited recently an ability to make independent decisions and could do so again.

PROBLEM 6. INABILITY TO COPE EFFECTIVELY WITH STAFF DISCIPLINARY ACTION — May 28, 1978

S: "I'm furious with the psychologist! He canceled my weekend pass with my parents! He said that my mother called him and told him that I was worse than ever when I was home last weekend and that she didn't want me to come home. He told me not to say anything to them, that they would not admit it and all that would happen would be that all of us would be mad at him. Well, I could see this reverse psychology! I called mother and she said that she never said such a thing! All she said was that she didn't want me to drive home by myself and asked the psychologist if my girl friend could drive me. As far as I'm concerned he is no longer my doctor, he's put on extinction!"

O: This was said in a very angry, hostile voice.

A: The patient is coping with anger in her rebellious child role. She is choosing to withdraw and pout rather than confront the psychologist with her angry feelings. She is so fearful of losing any ground gained in the parental relationship that she is unable to permit any hostile feelings toward her mother on a conscious level.

P: Permit this angry ventilation. Focus on her assumption of adult role and how to handle anger on that level: confront rather than pout. Explore the pros and cons of the extinction of any relationship with the psychologist from the viewpoint of what is gained versus what is lost by her behavior. Verbalize therapist acceptance of angry feelings . . . let her know it's an OK feeling.

E: The patient verbalized her anger but was unable to assume an adult role in order to consider a confrontation. Rather she took a firm stand to avoid and have nothing to do with the psychologist. She expressed fear of being given electroshock treatments or being put in the locked ward if she were to say anything to him about telling her mother what he had said.

Upon the request that she give this decision more thought between now and our next session, she said that she would "for your sake" but she did not expect to change her mind. When it was suggested that the decision was for her sake, not the therapist's, she repeated that the psychologist was "extinct." There was not much progress in this session from the therapist's point of view.

PROBLEM 5. INABILITY TO SELECT AND MAINTAIN ADEQUATE RELATIONSHIPS

PROBLEM 6. INABILITY TO COPE EFFECTIVELY WITH STAFF DISCIPLINARY ACTION — May 31, 1978

S: "Things are no different with the psychologist. I talked with him about it and he did say that he thought the whole thing

was a mistake, that he had confused me with another patient
. . . well, he can go and make his mistakes with someone
else . . . I don't want anything else to do with him!"

"Harvey [another therapist] is just wonderful . . . he held
me in his arms the other day and let me cry . . . he said he
was going to arrange to see me more often . . . that I need
more attention. I just want a close relationship, like I have
with Harvey and you [weeping]."

O: There is a shrill, almost hysterical quality to her voice and
she is weeping through most of the encounter.

A: Although she says that she wants a meaningful relationship
without sexual overtones with the young, handsome psychologist at this agency, the previously related content plus a
dream she had in which there was a love affair between the
patient and the psychologist, cause this therapist to focus on
unconscious motivation in this direction. These expressed
ambivalent feelings appear to suggest a need for a continued
reality base of what this relationship *can* and *cannot* offer
the patient.

The patient is still choosing not to work on a resolution of
the difficulty existing between herself and the psychologist.
I am beginning to get the impression that she is manipulating
people in the hope of gaining allies.

P: Focus on (1) what she is expecting in her relationship with
the psychologist; (2) the reality of what can be expected in a
therapist-client relationship. (3) how the relationship with a
female versus a male therapist may be expected to differ,
particularly with regard to embracing; and (4) her need to
form meaningful relationships without sexual connotation.
Try to avoid her manipulative tactics related to carrying
messages for her when she is in a position to deliver them
herself. In this vein remind patient that she is in a position
to talk to the psychologist without the therapist's help.

Encourage the patient to continue to examine the extinction behavior being exhibited toward the psychologist, particularly from the standpoint of nothing being gained and
the ultimate futility of it; attempt to have patient define her
"role," i.e., adult versus child, in this regard.

E: I was manipulated into talking with the psychologist on the
patient's behalf. When I replayed the taped session, I began
to feel like a real "patsy." When this came up later in the
week during supervision, I was really angry with myself for
being so stupid! I guess it was those sad eyes and sobs that
got to me . . . really have to fight that maternal instinct. . .

hopefully, won't happen again . . . she's so darn good at manipulating!

The patient is still resisting the therapist's attempts to resolve her conflict with the psychologist, hence growth in this realm is being stunted. This was not too productive a session, except from the standpoint that there was less intellectual and more expression of feeling related to her need for meaningful relationships.

PROBLEM 2. LOW SELF-ESTEEM — July 7, 1978

S: "I'm really down today. The psychologist told me that my latest test results indicate that I've only grown from the infant stage to four years of age. He says that I'll need to be here for another month. I wasn't even angry with him, only very hurt. I'm so disappointed [weeping] . . . I thought I was ready to go home!"

O: She is weeping, head dropped, body slumped; she is crying in the therapist's arms.

A: The patient is very depressed over her failure to attain anticipated growth and maturity. She is unable to permit herself to recognize her anger with the test findings and/or the psychologist.

P: Provide a nurturing climate; let her know that it's OK to be dependent when she is feeling like she is now. Focus on an opportunity to help her express anger at the situation, utilize feeling words and appropriate reflection for this purpose. Explore with her her knowledge of the maturation process and how she relates it to herself; point out the fact that growth is hard work, takes time, and is characterized by steps forward and backward and spurts. Focus on her contribution to growth, i.e., she has the responsibility for working to effect the desired outcome.

E: This was a good session from the standpoint that more feeling than usual was exhibited throughout the encounter. The patient frequently attempted to resort to familiar patterns of intellectualization, in this case of what is needed at age four, rather than focusing on picking up the pieces and moving on from there. She finds it extremely difficult to deal with reality-based content; she is fighting to hang on to past perceived injustices. When the therapist would focus on the present situation and what she can do about it, the patient would respond with irritated tones, "The psychologist wants me to talk about my past." When it was suggested that she seemed angry with the therapist, the patient would flatly deny it. "Oh, no! You remind me of my mother and I don't want to be angry with her." I am really beginning to feel that this patient is involved with too many therapists, which is not beneficial to her in the long run — it's a watered-down treatment regimen.

PROBLEM 6. INABILITY TO COPE EFFECTIVELY WITH STAFF DISCIPLINARY ACTION — June 11, 1978

S: "I'm going home. I was discharged this morning. I was promised that I'd never have to be in 'lockup' and they locked me up when I got back from a really good session Friday afternoon. I was taken completely by surprise! The evening nurses said that they had orders from a doctor, who I don't even know, to put me in the lockup unit. When I asked why, all they could say was that the head nurse had told the doctors that I was trying to 'nurse' patients on this unit, and that he had then said to put me in lockup. She [head nurse] never said a *word* to me about this! I begged the nurses to call my doctor, and they said that they too felt it was a mistake but they had their orders and would not call him. I even begged them to please call my doctor and they refused. I have never been so frightened in all my life! It's just terrible . . . I felt like a trapped animal! I confronted the head nurse this morning about why she had said that I was nursing the patients. I told her that if she felt this way then she should have told me, that I was sorry but I'm a kind-hearted person! The other nurses told me that it was a mistake, that all she wanted to do was to move me to another cottage, but the doctor wrote the order for lockup! All the head nurse would say was 'uh-uh,' etc. She wouldn't even discuss it! So, I'm leaving . . . there's no way I could stay now . . . I'm so paranoid . . . I feel that if I said the least thing they would lock me up again. My doctor was mad as hell! He said that they should have called him! He said that he could understand me wanting to go home. He said that although he felt that I wasn't ready to leave, he could see why I couldn't stay! He said that they will continue therapy with me on an out-patient basis. I'm still going to see my therapist also. Things are fine between us and I still want to see you. But that's it! Mother's real mad too. I had my girl friend call her. She was in the office when the doctor promised I'd never have to be locked up! She should be here any minute to take me home! So that's it!"

O: The patient verbalized in angry, irritated, hostile, shrill tones.

A: She is unable to cope with difficulty on an adult level; like a child, she's picking up her marbles and going home. She is exhibiting paranoid feelings toward hospital personnel. Her tone seems to be saying, "See, I told you so . . . there's hardly anyone you can trust . . . as soon as you let the guard down, they'll stab you in the back." She is failing to exhibit any latitude of acceptance toward the staff. She refuses to deal with the "human error" aspect of the situation and is being very rigid and adolescent in this respect.

P: Encourage her to explore which role she is utilizing to cope with this circumstance, i.e., adult or child.
Therapist: focus on reality of circumstances; reinforce her need to continue therapy on an out-patient basis (if it's necessary). Let her know that the anger is acceptable, but try to get her to explore whether or not it's being handled in a constructive manner . . . who is it really hurting in the long run?
Client: Client agreed to explore only to the point that she felt that she still did need therapy and would continue on an out-patient basis.

E: This was a stormy session. It was interrupted by the lunch hour, which gave the therapist an opportunity to acquire more data. New data suggested that there may have been some mistake regarding disposition of patient, i.e., was she to go to the cottage or lockup. Feedback from personnel, however, suggested that the patient had been growing increasingly hostile on the unit and that some degree of discipline was in order. The staff expressed the feeling that the patient's psychologist was out of line in making a promise that really couldn't be kept, adding that this was not an unusual thing for him to do, that it had happened with other patients. This therapist concurs about this "promise." It had indeed become an immovable obstacle when attempting to work with the patient to resolve the difficulty with staff. This is not a happy ending by any standard. In summary, there was only very minimal growth for the patient during hospitalization, which can be attributed to any one or all of the following factors:
(1) Client had successfully involved (manipulated) too many helpers in her treatment, resulting in an extreme lack of consistency in approach.
(2) There was poor communication between her therapists. They should have met for round-table discussions on a regular basis, but interest in this was minimal or non-existent among most.

(3) Patient had the staff in a compromising position from the beginning, which permitted her to continue the same kinds of behavior in the hospital that had gotten her in trouble in the first place. Some of this compromise existed in form of "rescuers": mother, doctor, and so on. Staff was thus really not in a position to control her. A set of ground rules was needed for *all* interested parties.

(4) Client's high degree of manipulative skills, coupled with her youth, worked against her.

Discharge Summary

Jean, a 23-year-old single Caucasian female, was admitted to this hospital on May 7, 1978, several days after a suicide attempt, with a diagnosis of depression with suicidal tendencies. The local clinical psychologist who referred her to this hospital agency continued a regimen of regularly scheduled individual and group therapy sessions with her throughout the hospitalization period from May 7 to June 11.

A detriment to good treatment outcome was the almost non-existent communication between the patient's therapists. This resulted both in an inconsistent treatment regimen and increased opportunities for the patient's manipulative behavior. Regularly scheduled round-table discussions would have been beneficial, both from the standpoint of providing opportunities to validate observed behaviors (hence, "keeping pace" with the patient) and for formulating a common set of ground rules for her. That the patient was admitted under what might be referred to as a compromising situation — she had a therapist, and managed to acquire many more and some "rescuers" — really placed the hospital staff in a position of not being able to exert appropriate control from the beginning. A set of ground rules was needed for *all* interested parties!

This therapist feels that Jean made only minimal progress during her hospitalization. Her hospital history of frequent acting out behaviors and her angry hospital exit are the bases for this impression. Hopefully, a reduction in the number of therapists, coupled with a regular and consistent treatment regimen on an out-patient basis, will prove to be beneficial.

11 Formal Preparation of Traditional Psychiatric Team Members

MARY JO TRAPP BULBROOK

Trying to identify the educational preparation needed by varying health providers has been an interesting and complicated task. Depending on which source you read or who you talk to, you will come up with conflicting views on standards, criteria for training and education, as well as interpretations of the various roles of the providers! The psychiatrist, for example, views himself and interprets the roles of the other health team members. He forms opinions or prejudices and conceptualizations of who he is, what he does, who others in his profession are, what they do, who other professionals are, and what they do. Multiply that one person's view times the number in his profession, add the same process for the other health team professionals, add the opinion of the recipients of the services (who have varying levels of comprehension), and you have a huge communication problem!

The lack of understanding and the contention that goes on between professionals in different fields, as well as between professionals in the same field is amazing. As a result, the consumer scratches his head, trying to make sense out of who to go to to get what is needed. It is almost an impossible task, and it is up to us as professionals to begin to solve this problem.

What will be given in this chapter will not be a definition of all the specifics for each profession, but rather a basic identification of the role of each profession. Licensing regulations dealing with education and preparation differ not only for each profession but usually in each state. And the criteria is changing so fast that what is printed today may already be outdated.

From my experience as a recipient and provider of health care, it is not always the label — A (the psychiatrist, usually the most educated) or B (the nurse) or C (the psychologist) — that determines the psychosocial care that is wanted and needed in health care. Sometimes it is someone without any "paper" credentials (e.g., a friend who has the authentic credential of love and the willingness to give of self as needed without any strings attached) who can give the mental health intervention needed. So I encourage you to begin to develop more genuine criteria for each profession and provide answers to these questions: Who are we? What do we do? Is that what the consumer needs? Are interventions based on outcomes?

The current psychiatric team has grown to include mental health and auxiliary team members. Psychosocial intervention has also come to include pastoral counselors, teachers, occupational, recreational, dance, art, and music therapists, guidance counselors, and so on. Within each category varying degrees of expertise are gained through educational and supervised clinical training. For our purposes here I will focus on the primary psychiatric team members. This in no way minimizes the contribution of the other professions, though. One can never know who will be the key to help unlock the door of pain. The profession isn't the key, the person is.

Since this book focuses on the education of therapists, I am primarily concerned with the health team members as psychotherapists. Who can do psychotherapy and what is psychotherapy are probably the most complex questions facing the psychosocial mental health team, including those holding violently opposed positions. My personal goal is to describe how nurses can make their contribution to psychosocial intervention, which includes the use of psychotherapy. In addition, the process nurses go through and the theories they use are not really different from that gone through and those used by others who work in the fields of medicine, psychology, psychiatry, or social work, although this fact does complicate the problems identified previously.

Knowledge is knowledge. But, it has little value until it is used by someone. Each profession must man its own house and clearly identify who its members are, how its members work, and how they provide dialogue on understanding the interrelationship between therapist and client. *Oneupmanship is destructive.*

THE PSYCHIATRIST
The psychiatrist is a physician who specializes in treating mental conditions. His education consists of three or four years of

premedical studies in a liberal arts college and four years in the medical college, leading to an M.D. degree. He then has one year of an approved psychiatric residency and two years experience in the practice of psychiatry. These are the criteria for membership in the American Psychiatric Association.

Psychiatry is the medical specialty which deals with the diagnosis and treatment of mental disorder. As a physician, the psychiatrist possesses special skills in comprehensive evaluation, including the organic causes of mental illness and the psychiatric complications of organic disease, the management of psychiatric emergencies, the competent use of psychoactive medications, and the use of other physical treatments for mental illness. His role includes that of consultant to primary health care practitioners and to other medical specialists, as well as that of diagnostician, therapist, administrator, researcher, supervisor, and member of the mental health care team [1].

THE PSYCHOANALYST

Psychoanalyst training varies from country to country. In the United States, medical training has been required for a number of years. The additional training is not carried out in a college but one of the 17 psychoanalytic institutes in this country. Training includes a thorough personal analysis, courses in psychoanalytic theory and technique, performance of a stipulated amount of psychoanalytic treatment under close supervision, and the successful completion of an examination.

THE CLINICAL PSYCHOLOGIST

To become a member of the American Psychological Association, Division of Clinical Psychology, the candidate must have: four years in a liberal arts college with a psychology major, usually leading to a B.A. degree; Ph.D. from an APA-approved program of clinical psychology; and one year at an approved clinical center for psychological internship.

The clinical psychologist aids in the handling of the psychiatric patient through interview and observation. The expertise of this psychologist is in the assessment of psychological functions and the application of psychological principles to the resolution of mental disorder, but it also does include an emphasis on research knowledge and skills. Assessment is made through diagnostic workup which includes psychological testing. In some states the clinical psychologist can perform psychotherapy.

THE PSYCHIATRIC SOCIAL WORKER

The psychiatric social worker is a graduate of a recognized professional school of social work. This professional provides a variety of social and human services aimed at fostering growth in individuals, families, and groups. He or she has two years of graduate work leading to a Master's degree in social work with a major in psychiatry. In addition, there is a field work placement in social case work, social group work, and community work.

The psychiatric social worker deals with a wide range of social problems and the personal problems of individuals or families. The focus is on solutions that will help the member adjust to his or her culture. Functions include: working with social environment; providing housing, employment, or financial support; providing care and help with feelings; and coordinating agencies and individual's social history.

THE PSYCHIATRIC NURSE

The nursing profession is currently attempting to sort through the many variations in expertise and skill and levels of competency manifested by those persons who are now included under the term *psychiatric nurse.* My own operational definitions follow.

A psychiatric aide (attendant, technician, or nursing assistant) is a person who performs activities within the scope and function of nursing practice and who is supervised by a registered nurse (R.N.). The person's education is usually limited to the in-service type and it varies in length and content. There is a movement to place such preparation in an educational setting such as a vocational, technical high school program or a junior college.

A licensed vocational practical nurse (LVP), has a longer formal and relatively standardized education, usually one year of both academic preparation and practice in nursing. Such education is obtained in a vocational school of nursing in a hospital. There is currently a trend to move vocational nursing programs to a junior college. LVPs are found primarily in institutions and function under the supervision of an R.N.

The registered nurse is licensed in her state to practice nursing. She has graduated with a diploma, associate's degree, or bachelor's degree from an approved nursing program that has included academic background and clinical experience in a variety of settings. The educational period can be from two to five years. At the end of her education, the nurse qualifies to sit for state board examinations to become registered.

Any of the above persons can be labeled incorrectly as a psychiatric nurse if he or she works in a psychiatric setting. Each can perform with varying levels of expertise, based on their knowledge, experience, and level of preparation.

However, the American Nurses' association has the *official* definition of the types of practitioners of psychiatric and mental health nursing practice. Included below from the *Statement on Psychiatric and Mental Health Nursing Practice* (1976)* is the definition of the psychiatric and mental health nurse and psychiatric and mental health nursing specialist.

Psychiatric and Mental Health Nurse

A psychiatric and mental health nurse is a licensed, professional nurse who has demonstrated expertise in psychiatric and mental health nursing practice through a formal review process. The recommended educational preparation for this role is a baccalaureate degree in nursing. The demonstrated level of performance of the psychiatric and mental health nurse exceeds that which is acquired in basic nursing education, or which is expected of the beginner in the field. Thus, professional nurses who practice in a psychiatric and mental health setting are identified by the profession as psychiatric and mental health nurses *only* when they demonstrate the profession's standards of knowledge, experience, and quality of care through formal review processes. Throughout the career of the psychiatric and mental health nurse, continued clinical competence is insured by supervised clinical practice, continuing education, and revalidation of clinical competence through formal review processes.

One mechanism for formal review of professional achievement is certification in psychiatric and mental health nursing through the Division on Psychiatric and Mental Health Nursing of the American Nurses' Association. The basis for such certification is an assessment of knowledge by examination and documentation by colleagues of the nurse's demonstrated expertise in clinical practice. To be eligible for certification as a psychiatric and mental health nurse, the individual must have two years of practice as a registered nurse in this field and be currently engaged in clinical practice.

The contributions of the psychiatric and mental health nurse to the mental health field can be evaluated through the responses of clients to nursing care within the framework of the Standards of Psychiatric and Mental Health Nursing Practice. Major strengths stem from the nurse's ability to observe and distinguish a broad range of problems of a physical and social-psychological nature and to intervene in such problems in order to regain and/or maintain optimum health. The nurse proceeds by a systematic approach which includes: the assessment of the client's status, the plan of nursing action, implementation of the plan, and evaluation. Throughout the nursing process the client is involved as an active participant and is provided opportunities for learning experiences.

*From the American Nurses' Association, Division on Psychiatric and Mental Health Nursing. Reprinted by permission.

To be effective at this level of performance, the psychiatric and mental health nurse must demonstrate a knowledge of theories concerning personality development and behavior patterns, an understanding of sociopsychological principles, an ability to communicate to clients what she/he understands their messages to mean, and a willingness to try to correct misunderstandings and assist them toward health. In addition, the nurse needs a knowledge of theory to understand family and group dynamics. The nurse needs knowledge about the contributions of other disciplines to psychiatric care, and about the dynamics of interpersonal relationships, in order to participate effectively within the health care system. To plan and implement effective nursing care, the nurse must also acquire knowledge of the theories and methods of treatment of mental illness, the expected effects of such treatments upon client behavior, and their relationship to nursing care.

Psychiatric and Mental Health Nursing Specialist

The specialist in psychiatric and mental health nursing is distinguished by: graduate education; supervised clinical experience; and depth and amount of knowledge, competence, and skill in the practice of psychiatric and mental health nursing.

The minimum level of preparation for the specialist level nurse is a master's degree in psychiatric and mental health nursing. Academically supervised clinical practice and study in the theoretical bases for therapeutic intervention characterize the core of these educational programs. Psychiatric and mental health nursing has derived its theoretical rationale for practice from the social, biological, and behavioral sciences as well as from medical theories of psychotherapy and has induced other components of theory by abstracting concepts and principles from observation and examination of clinical and nonclinical interpersonal data. Emphasis is placed on the synthesis, application, and validation of theories and concepts related to mental health problems of individuals, groups, families and communities.

Recently, doctoral education in psychiatric and mental health nursing has become available to a substantial number of nurses. These programs generally follow one of two traditions in graduate education at the doctoral level: 1) research and theory development in the science of psychiatric and mental health nursing; or 2) advanced development of the nurse-therapist role with the research component directed toward the investigation of specific clinical problems. The first type of program, the traditional research oriented focus, generally leads to a Ph.D. degree, whereas the second usually leads to a D.N.S. degree. Doctorally prepared nurses from these types of programs contribute to the advancement of knowledge in the field of psychiatric and mental health nursing through research and scholarship.

The clinical practice of the specialist is distinguished by the acquisition of an increased depth of knowledge and a more refined ability to apply such knowledge to the solution of problems in the mental health fields. As a consequence of collecting relevant and detailed data about clients and applying theoretical insights to such data, the specialist is able to predict behavior of clients and to identify probable nursing care problems. The specialist's knowledge and experience, coupled with involvement on the part of client(s) in developing a plan of action, allows the nurse and client(s) opportunities to devise creative approaches to the solution of problems. Intervention at the specialist level demands expertise in the psychotherapeutic methodologies associated with a variety of client systems (individual, group, family, and community). Systematic evaluation of the outcome of intervention is performed utilizing the Standards of Psychiatric and Mental Health Nursing Practice. The revision of future plans for intervention is based on the outcome of evaluation.

Some of those nurses who have specialized in psychiatric and mental health nursing at the graduate level assume the role of a clinical specialist within the mental health delivery system. Selected clinical nurse-specialists have entered the independent practice of psychotherapy. Other nurses who specialize in psychiatric and mental health nursing choose to perform in indirect roles, i.e., education, administration, or research. Specialization assumes continuation of clinical expertise through practice, regardless of a selected role within the mental health delivery system.

Formal review of the clinical practice of the specialist has evolved within the American Nurses' Association. The nurse who seeks recognition for professional achievement as a specialist must evidence a high degree of proficiency in interpersonal skills, in the use of the nursing process, and in psychiatric, psychological, and milieu therapies. The specialist is expected to show evidence of leadership qualities by assuming responsibility for the advancement of nursing theory and practice.

Although any specialist nurse may elect to be certified, it is expected that the nurse who is self-employed in the practice of psychotherapy will obtain formal credentials certifying her/his ability to perform as a competent nurse psychotherapist."

The standards of the psychiatric mental health nursing practice as published in *The American Nurse* (July, 1974), the official publication of the American Nurses' Association, are an attempt to provide criteria for determining excellence in psychiatric nursing practice. These standards (*Standards of Psychiatric-Mental Health Nursing Practice* [1973]), which give specific ways to identify such excellence, are found in their entirety in the Appendix. The revised 1976 *Code for Nurses with Interpretive Statements*, drawn up and revised by the Congress for Nursing Practice of the American Nurses' Association, is found in the Appendix.

REFERENCE

1. The President's Commission on Mental Health. *Task Force Panel Reports.* Washington, D.C.: U.S. Government Printing Office, 1978.

Appendix

*STANDARDS OF PSYCHIATRIC-MENTAL
HEALTH NURSING PRACTICE**
This statement sets forth Standards of Nursing Practice developed by the Executive Committee and the Standards Committee of the American Nurses' Association Division on Psychiatric-Mental Health Nursing Practice.

Psychiatric Nursing is a specialized area of nursing practice employing theories of human behavior as its scientific aspect and purposeful use of self as its art. It is directed toward both preventive and corrective impacts upon mental illness and is concerned with the promotion of optimal mental health for society, the community and those individuals and families who live within it. The dependent area of Psychiatric Nursing Practice is implementation of physicians' orders. The independent areas are assessment of nursing needs and development and implementation of nursing care plans, including initiation, development and termination of therapeutic relationships between nurses and patients. Psychiatric Nursing is practiced largely in collaboration and coordination with those in a variety of other disciplines who are working concomitantly with the patient. Thus, a high degree of interdependence with colleagues from other professions is inherent.

The Practice of Psychiatric Nursing is characterized by those aspects of clinical nursing care that involve interpersonal relationships with individuals and groups as well as a variety of other activities. These activities include: providing a therapeutic milieu, concerned largely with the sociopsychologic aspects of patients' environments; working with patients concerning the here-and-now living problems they confront; accepting and using the surrogate parent role; teaching with specific reference to emotional health as evidenced by various behavioral patterns; assuming the role of social agent concerned with improvement and promotion of recreational, occupational and social competence; providing leadership and clinical assistance to other nursing personnel. Joint planning or cooperative and collaborative efforts with other professionals are an essential part of providing nursing service. Most psychiatric settings employ an interdisciplinary team approach which requires highly coordinated and frequently interdependent planning.

Direct nursing care functions may involve individual psychotherapy, group psychotherapy, family therapy and sociotherapy. Psychiatric Nurses engaged in these therapies may employ a variety of approaches, particularly in the rapidly emerging area of sociotherapy and community mental health. With the national trend toward community mental health, Psychiatric Nurses are more and more involved in providing services aimed toward prevention of mental illness and reinforcement of healthy adaptions in addition to corrective and rehabilitative services.

The indirect nursing care roles of the Psychiatric Nurse are those of administrator with emphasis on leadership functions; as well as clinical teaching; director of staff development and training in a clinical facility; consultant or resource person, and researcher. In some of these indirect care roles, nurses will also be involved in providing direct nursing care services to improve their own clinical skills and to serve as role models. All of these roles require coordinative and collaborative efforts with other disciplines.

The purpose of Standards of Psychiatric Nursing Practice is to fulfill the profession's obligation to provide and improve this practice. They provide a means for determining the quality of nursing which a client receives regardless of whether such services are provided solely by a professional nurse or by professional nurse and non-professional assistants.

The Standards are stated according to a systematic approach to nursing practice: the assessment of the client's status, the plan of nursing actions, the implementation of the plan, and the evaluation. These specific divisions are not intended to imply that practice consists of a series of discrete steps, taken in strict sequence, beginning with assessment and ending with evaluation. The processes described are used concurrently and recurrently. Assessment, for example, frequently continues during implementation; similarly, evaluation dictates reassessment and replanning.

These Standards of Psychiatric Nursing Practice apply to nursing practice in any setting. Nursing practice in all settings must possess the characteristics identified by these Standards if patients are to receive a high quality of nursing care. Each Standard is followed by a rationale and assessment factors. Assessment factors are to be used in determining achievement of the standard.

Standard I
Data are collected through pertinent clinical observations based on knowledge of the arts and sciences, with particular emphasis upon psychosocial and biophysical sciences.

Standard II
Clients are involved in the assessment, planning, implementation and evaluation of their nursing care program to the fullest extent of their capabilities.

Standard III
The problem-solving approach is utilized in developing nursing care plans.

Standard IV
Individuals, families, and community groups are assisted to achieve satisfying and productive patterns of living through health teaching.

Standard V
The activities of daily living are utilized in a goal directed way in work with clients.

Standard VI
Knowledge of somatic therapies and related clinical skills are utilized in working with clients.

Standard VII
The environment is structured to establish and maintain a therapeutic milieu.

Standard VIII
Nursing participates with interdisciplinary teams in assessing, planning, implementing and evaluating programs and other mental health activities.

Standard IX
Psychotherapeutic interventions are used to assist clients to achieve their maximum development.

Standard X
The practice of individual, group or family psychotherapy requires appropriate preparation and recognition of accountability for the practice.

Standard XI
Nurses participate with other members of the community in planning and implementing mental health services that include the broad continuum of promotion of mental health, prevention of mental illness, treatment and rehabilitation.

Standard XII
Learning experiences are provided for other nursing care personnel through leadership, supervision and teaching.

Standard XIII
Responsibility is assumed for continuing educational and professional development and contributions are made to the professional growth of others.

Standard XIV
Contributions to nursing and the mental health field are made through innovations in theory and practice and participation in research.

AMERICAN NURSES' ASSOCIATION: RECOGNITION OF PROFESSIONAL ACHIEVEMENT AND EXCELLENCE IN PRACTICE
On July 1, 1976 the American Nurses' Association Division on Practice initiated a new process to achieve certification and diplomatic status in a new American College of Nursing Practice for certified nurses that was established by a task force.

The rationale for the new process was to provide a means of recognizing professional achievement and excellence in nursing practice.

The current approved 1978–79 criteria for certification for competence follows:

The Certification Process
Certification is based on assessment of knowledge, demonstration of current clinical practice, and endorsement by colleagues. It is tangible acknowledgment of achievement in a specific area of nursing practice.

It is a voluntary program designed to recognize those nurses whose clinical emphasis is on providing direct patient care.

Candidates must demonstrate currency in practice beyond the requirements for licensure, thereby elevating standards of professional practice in order to insure high quality of nursing care for all.

Following are some of the advantages of certification for the registered nurse:

Certification serves, through provision of national credentials, to expedite employment. A certified registered nurse will discover new opportunities for vertical and horizontal mobility.

Certification recognizes performance that clearly reflects the application of current knowledge, consideration of alternatives and strategies in nursing actions, and the derivation of new insights based on clinical data. A certified registered nurse will be identified as having achieved clinical expertise in a specific area of nursing practice.

Certification reinforces conscious use of theory in the planning and implementing of nursing care. Certified registered nurses will experience greater incentive to expand their knowledge to enhance clinical practice.

Certification

The entire certification process takes several months to complete. The Certification Board of each Division of Nursing Practice makes the final decision to certify, based on complete review of the candidate's performance. The sequence through which applicants will be evaluated includes:

Application
Determination of Eligibility
Testing: Assessment of Knowledge
Endorsement by Colleagues and Evidence of Clinical Performance
Evaluation of Evidence
Certification

Upon successful completion of the process, each candidate will receive a certificate and will be listed according to the area of practice in the ANA Directory of Certified Nurses.

Eligibility

To be eligible for certification the candidate must submit an application which includes evidence of:

a. A current license to practice professional nursing in the United States.
b. Experience as a registered nurse in the area in which certification is sought.

After eligibility is established, the candidate is required to achieve a satisfactory level on a national examination and submit evidence of practice. This evidence may include descriptions of setting, context, and nature of practice experience; descriptions of a number of individual cases or other clinical data; reports of innovations or behavior illustrating the applicant's significant contributions to patient care; illustrations of continuing growth as a practitioner; and references.

Recertification
Certification will be granted for a period of five years, at the end of which time the individual has the option of submitting evidence and credentials for renewal.

The procedure for reevaluation will be a continually updated process developed by each division on nursing practice.

REVISION OF CODE FOR NURSES WITH INTERPRETIVE STATEMENTS, MAY 17, 1975 BY CONGRESS FOR NURSING PRACTICE AMERICAN NURSES' ASSOCIATION [ANA] *

Preamble
The Code for Nurses is based upon belief about the nature of individuals, nursing, health, and society. Recipients and providers of nursing services are viewed as individuals and groups who possess basic rights and responsibilities, and whose values and circumstances command respect at all times. Nursing encompasses the promotion and restoration of health, the prevention of illness, and the alleviation of suffering. The statements of the Code and their interpretation provide guidance for conduct and relationships in carrying out nursing responsibilities consistent with the ethical obligations of the profession and quality in nursing care.

Introduction
The development of a code of ethics is an essential characteristic of a profession and provides one means for the exercise of pro-

fessional self-regulation. A code indicates a profession's acceptance of the responsibility and trust with which it has been invested by society. Upon entering the profession of nursing, each person inherits a measure of the responsibility and trust that has accrued to nursing over the years and the corresponding obligation to adhere to the profession's code of conduct and relationships for ethical practice.

The Code for Nurses, adopted by the ANA in 1950 and periodically revised, serves to inform both the nurse and society of the profession's expectations and requirements in ethical matters. The Code and the Interpretive Statements together provide a framework for the nurse to make ethical decisions and discharge responsibilities to the public, to other members of the health team, and to the profession. While it is impossible to anticipate in a code every type of situation that may be encountered in professional practice, the direction and suggestions provided here are widely applicable.

The requirements of the Code may often exceed, but are never less than those of the law. While violations of the law may subject the nurse to civil or criminal liability and the constituent associations may reprimand, censure, suspend or expel ANA members from the Association for violations of the Code, the possible loss of the respect and confidence of society and one's colleagues are serious sanctions which may result from violation of the Code. Each nurse has a personal obligation to uphold and adhere to the Code and to insure that nursing colleagues do likewise. Guidance and assistance in implementing the Code in local situations may be obtained from the American Nurses' Association or its state constituents.

CODE FOR NURSES

1. The nurse provides service with respect for human dignity and the uniqueness of the client unrestricted by considerations of social or economic status, personal attributes, or the nature of health problems.
2. The nurse safeguards the client's right to privacy by judiciously protecting information of a confidential nature.
3. The nurse acts to safeguard the client and the public when health care and safety are affected by the incompetent, unethical, or illegal practice of any person.
4. The nurse assumes responsibility and accountability for individual nursing judgments and actions.

5. The nurse maintains competence in nursing.
6. The nurse exercises informed judgment and uses individual competence and qualifications as criteria in seeking consultation, accepting responsibilities, and delegating nursing activities to others.
7. The nurse participates in activities that contribute to the ongoing development of the profession's body of knowledge.
8. The nurse participates in the profession's efforts to implement and improve standards of nursing.
9. The nurse participates in the profession's efforts to establish and maintain conditions of employment conducive to high quality nursing care.
10. The nurse participates in the profession's effort to protect the public from misinformation and misrepresentation and maintain the integrity of nursing.

GROUP THERAPY DEFINITIONS*

Group guidance. This provides the individual with accurate information that will help him make more appropriate decisions and plans affecting his life. It is oriented toward the *prevention* of problems and is recommended for everyone. It can be done with relatively large groups of people. The content of group guidance includes educational-vocational and personal social information not otherwise taught in academic courses.

Group counseling. This type of counseling makes a direct attempt to modify attitudes and behaviors by emphasizing affective involvement in small intimate groups. It is oriented toward both the prevention of problems and their remediation. It is prevention-oriented in the sense that the client is capable of functioning in society but may be experiencing difficulty in life. He uses counseling to help resolve these problems and prevent serious personality disorders. It is remedial for those individuals who have already begun a pattern of self-defeating behavior but who are capable of reversing this pattern without counseling intervention. However, with the counseling, the individual is likely to recover more quickly and with fewer emotional scars.

Group Psychotherapy. Group psychotherapy, which is remedial in orientation, is characterized by supportive and reconstructive depth analysis, focuses on the unconscious, and

*Written by Judith Keith.

emphasizes neuroses or other severe emotional problems. It is usually long-term and employs small intimate groups to help individuals who are unable to reverse their pattern of self-defeating behavior without therapeutic intervention.

Group dynamics. This term refers to individuals interacting in small groups. The word *dynamics* implies adjustive changes occurring in the group structure as a whole as they are produced by changes in any one part of the group.

T-group. A T-group is an unstructured group that allows the participants, usually eight to ten in number, to study group processes by being involved in them. Learning takes place through the group's struggle to create a meaningful structure for itself out of a largely unstructured situation. The T-group was first used by Kurt Lewin and the National Training Laboratories in the late nineteen-forties.

Psychodrama. Psychodrama involves role-playing by a person of his own past, present, or future situation. The individual acts out his own problem; the group counselor is the director; a "stage" is used; and the group is the audience. The creation and development of psychodrama is largely the work of J. L. Moreno, who defines psychodrama as the science that explores psychological meanings through dramatic methods.

PROPOSED BASIC HELP CURRICULUM FOR PSYCHOSOCIAL INTERVENTION FOCUS
Process
For the beginning therapist three particular psychiatric theories are recommended for understanding and dealing with process. The three, behavior modification, transactional analysis, and person-to-person theory, are based on different philosophical concepts but each provides, at a beginning level, specific, easily understood terminology needed to analyze process. Such a selection is not meant to minimize the contributions of the other theories. It is simply that these three theories provide concepts easily transferable to other clinical and nonclinical settings and kinds of BASIC HELP that may be needed. Thus, for example, medical-surgical interventions or the fields pediatrics, obstetrics, and so on could benefit. (The reader is referred back to the text for the details of each theory.)

Process needs to be analyzed in several ways. It includes exchanges between teacher/student, student/student, student therapist/client, supervisor/supervisee, clients/clients, student/

staff, or staff/staff. An analysis of all or each of these relationships is needed at varying times in a student's period of educational activity.

The emphasis is *educational, not therapeutic.* A built-in mechanism must be present to protect the student personally and professionally from the prospect of the two becoming inseparable. There is a thin line between educationally therapeutically needing to tolerate pain and therapeutically needing to tolerate pain. In the former, the teacher allows a time for painful growth; in the latter, the teacher oversteps the line. Each school needs to develop a way to identify the thin line and a policy to deal with it. Then and only then will we maximize the learning therapeutic process.

Content
I. Growth and Development — Birth to Death
   A. Normal
      Growth
      Developmental tasks
      Personality traits
      Health care
   B. Crisis intervention during normal growth and development
II. Concepts of Health/Illness Care Delivery Systems
   A. Role relationships between professionals/profession interdependent/dependent
   B. Role relationship between agencies
   C. Audit of patient care
   D. Recording of patient-centered care
   E. Administration/service interrelationships; POMR — Comprehensive BASIC Assessment System
   F. System innovations
      1. Open, client-centered health care system model by Leininger
      2. BASIC HELP System by Bulbrook
   G. Health/illness (adaptation — nonadaptive behavior; homeostasis — disequilibrium/stress)
   H. Prevention (primary, secondary, tertiary)
III. Investigation of Impact of Value-Producing Mechanisms — Transcultural Implications
   A. Heritage
   B. Family
      1. Nuclear
      2. Extended
   C. Work occupations

D. School
E. Recreation
F. Religion
G. Culture
H. Government
I. Health
IV. Psychotherapeutic Theories
   A. Psychoanalytic
   B. Interpersonal
   C. Adlerian
   D. Behavior modification
   E. Crisis intervention
   F. Gestalt therapy
   G. Client-centered therapy
   H. Carkhuff model
   I. Existentialism
   J. Transactional analysis
   K. Person-to-person theory
   L. Reality therapy
V. Therapeutic Interventions
   A. Chemotherapy
   B. Physical techniques
   C. Psychosocial technique
      1. Individual psychotherapy
      2. Group psychotherapy
      3. Family psychotherapy
      4. Marriage psychotherapy
      5. Child psychotherapy
      6. Milieu therapy
      7. Psychodrama
      8. Encounter movement
      9. Body integration
      10. Dance therapy
      11. Art therapy
      12. Recreational therapy
      13. Occupational therapy
      14. Community mental health
      15. Others
VI. BASIC Growth
   A. Reparative Needs
      1. Physical history and examination
      2. Physiological health enrichment
      3. Adaptation to alterations in body functioning
      4. Normal sexuality

      5. Sexual deviations
      6. Conversion hysteria
      7. Hypochondria
      8. Dying
      9. Organically caused neurotic/psychotic conditions
    10. Psychosomatic illness
 B. Affective
      1. Psychological testing
      2. Normal affective responses appropriate to setting
      3. Depression
      4. Anxiety
      5. Mania
      6. Hostility
      7. Negativism
      8. Grief
      9. Paranoia
 C. Social
      1. Sometric testing
      2. Divorce
      3. Social relationships: peers, family, community
      4. Drug abuse
      5. Alcoholism
      6. Suicide
      7. Groups
      8. Communities
      9. Loneliness
    10. Role identification
    11. Institutions
    12. Battered child
    13. Antisocial behavior
    14. Disturbances in mate selection (idealizing partner, romanticism, learning to live without partner, interracial marriage, marriage in different cultures or religions)
    15. Being single
    16. Poverty
 D. Intellectual
      1. IQ testing
      2. Learning needs at various levels
      3. Retardation
      4. Thinking disorders
      5. Obsessive compulsions
      6. Hallucinations
      7. Illusions
      8. Misperceptions

E. Communicative
  1. Verbal/nonverbal exchanges
  2. Separation anxiety
  3. Autism
  4. Death
  5. Extrasensory perception and related phenomena
VII. Kinds of Intervention (agency orientation)
  A. Mental Health — Wellness
    1. Well baby clinics
    2. Drop-in clinics
    3. Churches
    4. Schools
    5. Family (parenting)
    6. Community mental health
  B. Psychiatric Illness
    1. Inpatient
    2. Outpatient
    3. Hospitalization, acute
    4. Long-term hospitalization
    5. Day treatment
    6. Night treatment
    7. Community mental health
    8. Emergency care
    9. Partial hospitalization
  C. Intermediate
    1. Halfway house
    2. Foster care
    3. Community health
    4. Rehabilitation
    5. Community mental health
VIII. Therapeutic Use of Self (as applied to learning needs vs. therapy needs)
  A. Identify self concept
  B. Explore ego states, basic life position
  C. Transactional communications with peers, teacher, other professionals
  D. Body image
  E. Threats to self
  F. Identifying learning needs
  G. Role identification
  H. Interviewing skills
  I. Philosophy of life
  J. Role of change agent
  K. Philosophy of profession (i.e., nursing)

Index

Activities, in transactional analysis, 129–130
Activity group therapy, psychoanalytic, 87–88
Actualizing tendency, 103–104
Adler, Alfred, 80, 113–115
Adlerian therapy
  assessment tool for, 117
  content of, 113–115
  group, 115–117
Adult ego state, 11, 127–128, 132, 184
Aguilera, D., 137, 138
Aikido, 35
American Journal of Psychotherapy, 127
American Nurse, The, 253
American Nurses' Association, 251, 253
American Psychiatric Association, 249
American Psychological Association, 249
Anal stage of personality development, 83
Anatol (ego-analyst), 78
Angular transaction, 128
Anticathexis, defined, 82
Auscultation, technique of, in physical examinations, 72
Awareness, levels of, 80–81

Bandler, Richard, *The Structure of Magic* (with J. Grinder), 13
Beers, Clifford, *A Mind That Found Itself,* 51
Behavior modification
  assessment tool for, 99–100

content of, 95–98
group counseling in, 98–99
Being-in-the-world, 111–112
Berne, Eric, 10
  Games People Play, 130, 131
  and transactional analysis, 127–132
Brücke, Ernst Wilhelm von, 78
Buddhism, Zen, 25, 34

Cain, Patricia A., 196
Caplan, G., 137
Caring, 39–42
Carkhuff model
  assessment tool for, 120
  content of, 117–120
Carkhuff, Robert R., 117–120
Carlson, J., 114–115
Cathexis, defined, 82
Chicago, University of, 17
Child ego state, 11, 127–128, 132, 184
Cincinnati Children's Hospital, 3, 4
Client-centered therapy, 183, 197
  content of, 100–105
  group, 107–109
  and Rogers' theory of counseling, 105
  tool for, 109–110
Cognitive processes, 93–94
Colorado, University of, 24, 25
Complementary transactions, 128
Comprehensive BASIC Assessment System and Tool, 65–72, 77

Concern, levels of, for patients, 28
Concreteness, 118–119
Conformist, defined, 112
Confrontation, 119
Consciousness, 80–81
Consumers, view of psychotherapy by, 51–64
Contingency, defined, 97
Coon, Beverly W., 51
"Creative coping," 15
Crisis intervention, 137–138, 196–197, 221
  assessment tool for, 138–139
Crossed transactions, 128
CUE to active psychotherapy, 39–42

Defense mechanisms, 183
  kinds of, 84
Denial of reality, 84
Dinkmeyer, D., 114–115
Displacement, defined, 84
Dreams, 85–86
Dreikurs, R., 116
Dunn, H. L., 182
Duplex transaction, 128
Dynamisms, defined, 93

Eclecticism, 117–118
Ego, 81
  function of, 82–83, 84–85
Ego states, 11, 127–128, 132, 184
Electroshock treatment, 28
Empathy, 39, 40–42, 118
Enactment, 184
Erikson, Erik, 78, 80, 84
Esalen Institute, 34
Excitement, importance of, 18
Existential crisis, 221
Existentialism, 6, 12–13
Existential therapy, 220–221
  assessment tool for, 112–113
  content of, 111–112

Faculty, recommendations for, 46, 47–48
Fagan, J., ed., *Gestalt Therapy Now* (with I. L. Shepherd, ed.), 124

Figure-ground formation, 122
Free association, 86
  defined, 85
Freud, Sigmund, psychoanalytic theory of, 77–87
Fromm, Erich, 80

Game analysis, in transactional analysis, 129, 130–131
Generalizations, 16
Genital stage of personality development, 84
Genuineness, 119
Gestalt Institute of Dallas, 35
Gestalt therapy, 5, 8, 34–35, 183, 184, 197
  assessment tool for, 125–127
  content of, 120–124
  rationale for group, 124–125
Glasser, William, 10, 197
  reality therapy of, 89, 91, 183–184, 196
Grinder, John, *The Structure of Magic* (with R. Bandler), 13
Group therapy
  Adlerian, 115–117
  behavior modification, 98–99
  client-centered, 107–109
  Gestalt, 124–125
  psychoanalytic, for children, 87–88
  transactional analysis, 133–134

HARA (Dallas), 34–35
High-level wellness, 182
Horney, Karen, 80

Id, 81, 82, 83
  impulses from, 84–85
Immediacy, 119
Individualist, defined, 112
Inspection, technique of, in physical examination, 71
Instincts
  aim of, 81
  death, 82
  object of, 81–82
  self-preservation, 82
  sexual, 82
  source of, 81
Integration, in Gestalt therapy, 124

Interpersonal model
  assessment tool for, 94—95
  content of, 93—94
Interpretation
  defined, 85
  dream, 85—86
Intimacy, in transactional analysis,
  129, 130
Intrapsychic aspect of therapy, 32
Introjection, 84

Jacobson, G., 137
Jaspers, Karl, 220
Johnson, Brenda, *A New Age of
  Healing,* 13
Jourard, S. M., 197
Jung, Carl G., 85

Kierkegaard, Sören, 220

Lama Govinda, 35
Lastelick, Louise L., 43, 182
Latency stage of personality
  development, 84
Leininger, M., 10
Levitsky, A., 124
Libido, 82
Life positions, basic, in trans-
  actional analysis, 130—131
Love, defined, 41—42
Low, Dr. Abraham, 63

Maddi, S. R., 111
Marriage Encounter movement,
  38, 39
Maslow, Abraham, 103—104, 111,
  122
Matthews, Linda, 45, 220
Maupin, Edward, 34
May, Rollo, 220
Messick, J., 137, 138
Montessori, Maria, 4
Morley, W. E., 137, 138

National Institute of Mental Health,
  3, 182
Negative reinforcement, 97
Neurosis, five layers of, 121
Nurse-physician colleagueship,
  6—10
Nurse, psychiatric and mental
  health, definition of, 250—252

Nurse, psychosocial, review of
  undergraduate students' comments on becoming, 48—49
Nurse therapist, graduate student
  narratives on becoming,
  43—48
Nursing specialist, psychiatric and
  mental health, definition of,
  252—253

Options, 54
Oral stage of personality develop-
  ment, 83
Organism, defined, 101

Palpation, technique of, in physi-
  cal examination, 71
Parataxic mode of experience, 93
Parent ego state, 127—128, 132,
  184
Pastimes, in transactional analy-
  sis, 129
Percussion, technique of, in
  physical examination, 71—72
Perls, Fritz, 10, 34
  and Gestalt therapy, 120—125
Personality development
  Freud's psychosexual stages of,
    83—84, 183
  Sullivan's six stages of, 94
Personifications, defined, 93
Phallic stage of personality
  development, 83
Phenomenal field, defined, 101
Philosophy, of therapy and teach-
  ing, 10—13
Physical examination
  equipment for, 72
  general principles of, 71
  techniques of, 71—72
Physician-nurse colleagueship,
  6—10
Pleasure principle, defined, 82
Positive regard, 118
  need for, 104
Positive reinforcement, 97
Powell, John, 10
  *Why Am I Afraid to Tell You
    Who I Am,* 9
Problem-Oriented Medical
  Records (POMR) system,
  65—66

Projection, defined, 84
Prototaxic mode of experience, 93
Psychiatrist, educational requirements of, 248–249
Psychoanalyst, training of, 249
Psychoanalytic therapy, 25, 183
   assessment tool for, 88–89
   for children, group, 87–88
   content of, 77–85
   techniques used in, 85–87
Psychodrama, 123
Psychologist, clinical, training and role of, 249
Psychosomatic medicine, 23–24
Psychotherapy, views of, by clients, 51–64. *See also* Therapy
PTP (person-to-person) therapy, 9, 10
Punishment, 97
   and guilt, 83

Rapaport (ego-analyst), 78
Rationalization, defined, 84
Reaction formation, defined, 84
Reality therapy, 183, 184, 196–197
   assessment tool for, 92–93
   content of, 89–92
Recognition hunger and strokes, in transactional analysis, 128–129
Reinforcement
   continuous, 97
   intermittent, 97–98
   negative, 97
   positive, 97
   in transactional analysis, 128–129
Relationships, clarification of, as aspect of therapy, 32–33
Repression, 85
   defined, 84
Repression proper, defined, 82
Resistance, defined, 86
Responses, behavioral, 97
Rituals, in transactional analysis, 129
Robertson, Mary Nell, 57–58
Robinson, Billie J., 227
ROCGET (reality-oriented

Christian Gestalt existential therapy), 8–9, 10
Rogers, Carl, 10, 122
   client-centered therapy of, 100–105, 107–109, 124, 183, 197
   his theory of counseling, 105–107

San Francisco Zen Center, 34
Sartre, Jean-Paul, 10, 220
Satir, Virginia, 5, 10, 34–35
Script analysis, in transactional analysis, 131–132
Self, Rogers' concept of, 101–102, 108
Self-actualization, 108
Self-disclosure, concept of, 197
Self-image, poor, 37, 39, 42
Selfishness, healthy, 55
Shepherd, I. L., ed., *Gestalt Therapy Now* (with J. Fagan, ed.), 124
Shunryu Suzuki Roshi, 34
Shutz, William, 34
Slavson, S. R., 87
Social masks, 37, 39, 42
Social worker, psychiatric, education and role of, 250
Sounds, noting of, in physical examination, 72
Southwestern Medical School, 22
Spitz, Dr. Rene, 26
Stevenson, Robert Louis, 55
Stimuli
   aversive, 97
   -delta, 97
   discriminative, 97
   environmental, 97
Strickler, M., 137
Strokes, recognition hunger and, in transactional analysis, 128–129
Sublimation, defined, 84
Suicide lethality scale, 69
Sullivan, Harry Stack, 10, 80
   Conceptions of Modern Psychiatry, 41
   personality theory of, 93–94
Superego, 81, 83, 84
Suzuki, D. T., *Zen and Psycho-analysis*, 25
Syntaxic mode of experience, 93

T'ai Chi, 35

Teaching, philosophy of therapy and, 10—13
Texas Women's University, 149
Therapist, professional factors in becoming, 6
Therapy. *See also* Adlerian therapy; Behavior modification; Carkhuff model; Client-centered therapy; Crisis intervention; Existential therapy; Gestalt therapy; Interpersonal model; Psychoanalytic therapy; Reality therapy; Transactional analysis
  clarification of relationships aspect of, 32—33
  goals of, 33, 37—38
  intrapsychic aspect of, 32
  and teaching, philosophy of, 10—13
  transference aspect of, 32
Tillich, Paul, 220
Time-structuring in transactional analysis, 129—130
Transactional analysis (TA), 183, 184, 197
  assessment tool for, 134—136
  content of, 127—128
  game analysis and basic life positions in, 130—131
  goal of, 132
  group therapy, rationale for, 133—134

proper, 128
  and recognition hunger and strokes, 128—129
  and script analysis, 131—132
  and time-structuring, 129—130
  and transactional trading stamps, 131
Transference
  aspect of therapy, 32
  defined, 85, 86
  discussion of, 86—87

Ulterior transactions, 128, 130
Understanding, 39, 40—42

Veterans Administration (VA) hospitals, 7, 26, 31, 149, 153
Vienna Society of Psychiatry and Neurology, 77

Watts, Alan, 25, 35
Weed, L. L., Problem-Oriented Medical Records system of, 65—66
Withdrawal, in transactional analysis, 129
Working-through phase of therapy, 33

Yoga, 35

Zen Buddhism, 25, 34
Zen Monastery (Tasajara, California), 34